Italian-English Parallel Text

Short Stories in Italian for Beginners

Beginner to Intermediate

Leonardo Mancini

© 2021 Leonardo Mancini.
All rights reserved.

INTRODUCTION

You're about to embark on a trip to one of the most beautiful and romantic countries in the world, *un viaggio in Italia*! These short stories have been written and designed for learners of Italian from beginner to intermediate level to both entertain and provide a sense of achievement. If there's a word or grammar structure you are not familiar with, you'll find the English translation just below, which makes reading this book an enjoyable and stress-free experience.

This book includes:

- Eight fun, easy-to-read short stories in a variety of genres set in Italy that will give you hours of enjoyment while you acquire a wide range of new vocabulary.

- Authentic Italian expressions and cultural knowledge that will prove very useful for students interested in Italian culture.

- Italian-English parallel text that will help you feel safe throughout your reading experience, so you learn new vocabulary and grammatical structures naturally, in a stress-free way while focusing on content and having fun.

At the end of the book you'll find the text in Italian without the English translation so you can read it when you feel confident enough.

The eight short stories in this book:

Vacanze a Rimini
Vacation in Rimini

Il quindicesimo compleanno della mia migliore amica
My best friend's fifteenth birthday party

La famiglia cresce
The family grows

Trovare l'amore a Cefalù?
Finding love in Cefalù?

Alberto o Giacomo?
Alberto or Giacomo?

Intervista a Pietro Abrami
Pietro Abrami Interview

Ricordi di mia nonna
Memories of my grandmother

Un intervista di lavoro
A job interview

Vacanze a Rimini
Vacation in Rimini

Il mio nome è Lorenzo Costa e ho vent'anni. Sono nato a Firenze, ma vivo a Roma da più di dieci anni.

My name is Lorenzo Costa and I am twenty years old. I was born in Florence, but I have lived in Rome for more than ten years.

Studio ingegneria all'università e mi piace molto praticare sport come il calcio e la pallavolo, e nei fine settimana mi piace passare ore a giocare ai videogiochi con i miei amici.

I study engineering at university and I really like to play sports like soccer and volleyball, and on the weekends I like to spend hours playing video games with my friends.

La mia vita è un po' noiosa perché passo molto tempo a studiare, ma l'estate scorsa è stata molto divertente.

My life is a bit boring because I spend a lot of time studying, but last summer it was a lot of fun.

A febbraio sono andato in vacanza con alcuni amici a Rimini. Rimini è una città molto turistica sulla costa adriatica con bellissime spiagge, un'ottima opzione per trascorrere una bella estate in un luogo affascinante.

In February I went on vacation with some friends to Rimini. Rimini is a very touristic city on the Adriatic coast with beautiful beaches, a great option to spend a nice summer in a fascinating place.

A Rimini ci sono molti centri commerciali, bar, discoteche e luoghi di intrattenimento per tutti i gusti. I miei amici ed io abbiamo affittato un appartamento un appartamento vicino al lungomare per una settimana.

In Rimini there are many shopping centers, bars, discos and entertainment venues for all tastes. My friends and I rented an apartment near the waterfront for a week.

È un piacere trascorrere del tempo con i tuoi amici in una città così bella e con una vista spettacolare sul mare. I tramonti sono molto belli!

It is a pleasure to spend time with your friends in such a beautiful city and with a spectacular view of the sea. The sunsets are very beautiful!

Siamo un interessante gruppo di amici. Claudia ha ventun anni e anche lei è di Roma. Studia ingegneria con me e nel tempo libero ama cucinare.

We are an interesting group of friends. Claudia is twenty-one years old and also from Rome. She studies engineering with me and in her free time she loves to cook.

Ho provato i piatti di Claudia e sono buonissimi, Claudia è un'ottima cuoca e una ragazza molto simpatica, ma è un po' timida e introversa.

I have tried Claudia's dishes and they are delicious, Claudia is a very good cook and a very nice girl, but she is a bit shy and introverted.

Samuele è di Milano, ha vent'anni e studia medicina, ma la sua passione sono le auto sportive. È molto socievole, ama le feste e conoscere nuove persone.

Samuele is from Milan, he is twenty years old and studies medicine, but his passion is sports cars. He is very sociable, he loves parties and meeting new people.

Infine c'è Alfredo, è uno studente di interior design ed è molto interessato alla moda e alle ultime tendenze.

Finally there is Alfredo, he is an interior design student and he's very interested in fashion and the latest trends.

Io ei miei amici ci conosciamo da un paio d'anni e, nonostante abbiamo interessi molto diversi, andiamo molto d'accordo, quindi vivere con loro per una settimana è stato molto bello.

My friends and I have known each other for a couple of years and, despite having very different interests, we get along very well so living with them for a week was very nice.

Il primo giorno della nostra vacanza è stato molto buono. La mattina ci siamo alzati molto presto per sfruttare al massimo la giornata. Siamo andati in spiaggia, siamo andati in mare e abbiamo nuotato per ore, poi io e Samuele abbiamo giocato a pallavolo mentre Claudia e Alfredo prendevano il sole.

The first day of our vacation was very good. In the morning we got up very early to make the most of the day. We went to the beach, went into the sea and swam for hours, then Samuele and I played volleyball while Claudia and Alfredo sunbathed.

A mezzogiorno faceva molto caldo e siamo tornati al nostro appartamento. Con un piccolo aiuto da parte nostra, Claudia ha preparato dell'ottimo pesce e patatine per il pranzo e poi abbiamo fatto un pisolino fino alle sei del pomeriggio.

By noon it was very hot and we returned to our flat. With a little help from us, Claudia prepared some excellent fish and chips for lunch and afterwards we took a nap until six in the afternoon.

La prima sera della nostra vacanza abbiamo deciso di andare in un bar vicino, ma Claudia non voleva andare. Claudia ha detto che era molto stanca e assonnata.

The first night of our vacation we decided to go to a nearby bar, but Claudia didn't want to go. Claudia said that she was very tired and sleepy.

Samuele, Alfredo e io abbiamo passato una serata molto divertente, abbiamo bevuto molta birra e parlato fino a tardi, ma ci siamo sentiti un po' male perché Claudia era sola nell'appartamento mentre ci siamo divertiti molto.

Samuele, Alfredo and I had a very fun night, we drank a lot of beer and talked until very late, but we felt a little bad because Claudia was alone in the flat while we had a great time.

Come ho già detto, Claudia non è molto socievole e non ama molto uscire, probabilmente la sua stanchezza era solo una scusa per restare a casa.

As I have said before, Claudia is not very sociable and does not like to go out a lot, probably her fatigue was just an excuse to stay at home.

Il secondo giorno di vacanza siamo andati anche al mare. La sera, con molta fatica, siamo riusciti a convincere Claudia ad accompagnarci a una festa elettronica sulla spiaggia. Eravamo tutti molto contenti che Claudia fosse con noi questa volta!

The second day of vacation we went to the beach too. In the evening, with a lot of effort we managed to convince Claudia to go with us to an electronic party on the beach. We were all very happy that Claudia was with us this time!

Claudia non sa molto di moda e stile, quindi Alfredo l'ha aiutata a scegliere cosa indossare e come truccarsi. Dopo questa trasformazione, Claudia sembrava bellissima, sembrava davvero una star di Hollywood.

Claudia doesn't know much about fashion and style so Alfredo helped her choose what to wear and how to put on makeup. After this transformation, Claudia looked beautiful, she really looked like a Hollywood star.

Quando siamo andati alla festa c'era molta gente, era piena di giovani e meno giovani. Tutti erano venuti perché un DJ molto famoso era stato invitato a suonare alla festa.

When we went to the party there were a lot of people, it was full of young people and not so young. Everyone had come because a very famous DJ had been invited to play at the party.

La musica era molto buona e l'atmosfera era rilassata. Sentivamo tutti che venire alla festa era stata un'ottima decisione. I ragazzi e io abbiamo deciso di andare a ballare, ma Claudia non voleva.

The music was very good and the atmosphere was relaxed. We all felt that coming to the party had been a very good decision. The boys and I decided to go dancing, but Claudia didn't want to.

Claudia è così timida! Non le piace ballare e lei rimase seduta a bere qualcosa mentre noi siamo andati a ballare.

Claudia is so shy! She doesn't like to dance and she sat and had a drink as we went to dance.

Dopo poco più di un'ora ci siamo stancati di ballare e siamo tornati dove avevamo lasciato Claudia, ma non siamo riusciti a trovarla. Dov'era la nostra amica? Eravamo molto spaventati e temevamo il peggio.

After a little over an hour we got tired of dancing and went back to the place where we had left Claudia, but we couldn't find her. Where was our friend? We were very scared and feared the worst.

L'abbiamo chiamata molte volte ma non ha risposto al telefono. Avevamo molta paura che le fosse successo qualcosa. Abbiamo cercato Claudia tra la folla e chiesto a molte persone se avevano visto una come lei, ma nessuno ci ha dato informazioni utili e non siamo riusciti a trovarla.

We called her many times but she would not answer the phone. We were very afraid that something had happened to her. We searched the crowd for Claudia and asked many people if they had seen someone like her, but no one gave us useful information and we couldn't find her.

Dopo un paio d'ore la festa finì e la gente iniziò a tornare a casa. C'era già pochissima gente e poi l'abbiamo vista: Claudia era con un ragazzo, lo baciava! È stato un grande sollievo e allo stesso tempo una grande sorpresa vedere la nostra timida amica così affettuosa con uno sconosciuto.

After a couple of hours the party ended and people began to go home. There were already very few people and then we saw her: Claudia was with a boy, kissing him! It was a great relief and at the same time a great surprise to see our shy friend so affectionate with a stranger.

Dopo averci visto, Claudia si è scusata per non aver risposto al telefono perché la musica della festa era così alta che non l'ha sentita. L'unica cosa che contava per noi era avere la nostra amica sana e salva.

Upon seeing us, Claudia apologized for not answering her phone because the music from the party was so loud that she did not hear it. The only thing that mattered to us was having our friend safe and sound.

Più tardi, Claudia e il suo nuovo amico si sono scambiati i numeri di telefono e si sono salutati con un bacio. Mentre tornavamo al nostro appartamento, Claudia ci ha raccontato del suo nuovo amico Louis.

Later, Claudia and her new friend exchanged their phone numbers and said goodbye with a kiss. As we walked back to our flat, Claudia told us about her new friend Louis.

Quella sera, quando l'abbiamo lasciata per andare a ballare, Louis è venuto a salutare Claudia e ha iniziato a parlarle. Nonostante la timidezza di Claudia, a poco a poco sono diventati amici e più che amici.

That night, when we left her to go dancing, Louis came over to greet Claudia and started talking to her. Despite Claudia's shyness, little by little they became friends and more than friends.

Louis è un ragazzo alto e molto attraente, ha ventiquattro anni ed è francese, ma è in vacanza in Italia, è anche un bravissimo poeta che ha vinto concorsi di poesia nel suo paese.

Louis is a tall and very attractive boy, he is twenty-four years old and he is French, but he's on vacation in Italy, he is also a very good poet who has won poetry competitions in his country.

Il giorno successivo abbiamo deciso di andare a San Marino che è poco distante da Rimini. San Marino è un paese indipendente completamente circondato dall'Italia, è uno dei paesi più piccoli del mondo. Quella mattina abbiamo preso un autobus e in circa un'ora siamo arrivati.

The following day we decided to go to San Marino which is not far from Rimini. San Marino is an independent country completely surrounded by Italy, it is one of the world's smallest countries. That morning we took a bus and in about an hour we got there.

La Città di San Marino è piena di antichi edifici, ristoranti e negozi per i turisti, oltre a diversi musei, e offre splendide viste sulle città e sulla campagna circostanti.

The City of San Marino is full of ancient buildings, restaurants, and shops for tourists, as well as several museums, and it has beautiful views of the surrounding towns and countryside.

Ci sono pochissime auto a San Marino e le strade sembrano molto medievali, come se il tempo non fosse passato qui. Una delle cose che ci è piaciuta di più sono state le mura della città che puoi scalare e percorrerla in alcuni punti.

There are very few cars in San Marino, and the streets look very medieval, as if time hasn't passed here. One of the things that we loved the most was the city walls which you can climb and walk along it at some places.

Abbiamo trascorso oltre due ore esplorando San Marino e girovagando per i suoi affascinanti vicoli. Ci siamo fermati a bere un caffè quando improvvisamente Samuele si è accorto che Claudia non era con noi. Claudia si era persa di nuovo?

We spent over two hours exploring San Marino and wandering around its charming narrow streets. We stopped to drink some coffee when suddenly Samuele realized that Claudia was not with us. Was Claudia lost again?

Non di nuovo! L'abbiamo cercata ma non era da nessuna parte. Poi l'abbiamo cercata in un piccolo giardino e finalmente l'abbiamo trovata, era sotto un albero con Louis. Spiegò che Louis era venuto a cercarla per uscire quella sera a un bar a Rimini.

Not again! We looked for her but she was nowhere. Then we looked for her in a small garden and we finally found her, she was under a tree with Louis. She explained that Louis had come looking for her to go out that night to a bar in Rimini.

Chi l'avrebbe mai detto? La nostra timida amica ha trovato il suo primo amore estivo in questa vacanza e ha trascorso il resto dei giorni con lui.

Who would have thought? Our shy friend found her first summer love on this vacation and spent the rest of the days with him.

Alla fine della settimana Louis doveva partire per Parigi e noi per Roma, così Claudia e Louis si salutarono, promettendo che l'anno prossimo si sarebbero incontrati di nuovo qui.

At the end of the week Louis had to leave for Paris and we for London, so Claudia and Louis said goodbye, promising that next year they would meet here again.

Non so se Louis e Claudia manterranno la loro promessa di rivedersi a Rimini il prossimo anno. Chi lo sa? Sarà più di un amore estivo?

I don't know if Louis and Claudia will fulfill their promise to see each other again in Rimini next year. Who knows? Will this be more than a summer love?

Non lo so, ma Samuele, Alfredo e io andremo probabilmente da qualche altra parte la prossima vacanza. Ci sono così tanti posti interessanti da scoprire!

I don't know, but Samuele, Alfredo and I will probably go somewhere else the next vacation. There are so many interesting places to discover!

Il quindicesimo compleanno della mia migliore amica
My best friend's fifteenth birthday

Mi chiamo Martina, ho quindici anni e vivo a Milano. Vivo con mio padre, mia madre e mio fratellino di dieci anni.
My name is Martina, I am fifteen years old and I live in Milan. I live with my father, my mother and my ten year old little brother.

Abbiamo anche un piccolo cane di nome Cesare e due canarini in gabbia. Mi piace sentirli cantare la mattina!
We also have a small dog named Pepo and two canaries in a cage. I love hearing them sing in the morning!

I miei genitori sono venuti dal Messico quando erano bambini piccoli e la nostra famiglia mantiene ancora vive molte delle tradizioni del nostro background messicano.
My parents came from Mexico when they were little children and our family still keeps alive many of the traditions from our Mexican background.

Come ho detto all'inizio, ho quindici anni, questa è un'età molto importante nella cultura messicana.

As I said at the beginning, I am fifteen years old, this is a very important age in Mexican culture.

In Messico, quando una ragazza compie quindici anni, si celebra una grande festa. Questa festa di compleanno si chiama "quinceañera" che in spagnolo significa "ragazza di quindici anni".

In Mexico, when a girl turns fifteen, a great party is celebrated. This birthday party is called "quinceañera" which in Spanish means "fifteen-year-old girl".

La festa inizia con l'arrivo della quinceañera, che indossa un abito realizzato appositamente per l'occasione, di solito un disegno ispirato agli abiti usati nelle danze antiche europee.

The party begins with the arrival of the quinceañera, who wears a dress made especially for the occasion, usually a design inspired by the dresses used in old European dances.

L'idea è che in questo giorno speciale ogni ragazza dovrebbe avere la fantasia di sembrare e sentirsi una bellissima principessa.

The idea is that on this special day every girl should have the fantasy of looking and feeling like a beautiful princess.

I festeggiamenti iniziano con l'ingresso della ragazza accompagnata dalla musica e dagli applausi degli invitati.
The festivities begin with the entrance of the girl accompanied by music and the applause of the guests.

Poi inizia il valzer, in cui la ragazza balla prima con il padre e poi con parenti e amici. Naturalmente c'è anche un grande banchetto in cui si fanno brindisi in onore della "quinceañera".
Then the waltz begins, in which the girl dances first with her father and then with relatives and friends. Of course there is also a great banquet in which toasts are made in honor of the "quinceañera".

La "quinceañera" è senza dubbio una festa indimenticabile per ogni ragazza.
The "quinceañera" is undoubtedly an unforgettable celebration for every girl.

Qualche mese fa ho avuto la mia quinceañera, tuttavia non voglio parlarvi della mia festa, ma della quinceañera della mia migliore amica Beatrice che è stata lo scorso fine settimana.

A few months ago I had my quinceañera, however I don't want to tell you about my party, but my best friend Beatrice's quinceañera which was last weekend.

Io e Beatrice siamo compagni di classe e stiamo sempre insieme, andiamo molto d'accordo.

Beatrice and I are classmates and we are always together, we get along very well.

Volevo avere un bell'aspetto per la quinceañera della mia amica, quindi il giorno prima ero andata al centro commerciale a comprare un vestito nuovo da indossare alla festa.

I wanted to look great for my friend's quinceañera, so the day before I had gone to the mall to buy a new dress to wear to the party.

Quel giorno mi sono alzata molto presto per andare a comprare un vestito e degli accessori. Ero accompagnata da mia madre, lei va sempre a fare spese con me. C'erano così tanti bei vestiti di tutti i colori, era molto difficile sceglierne uno.

That day I got up very early to go shopping for a dress and accessories. I was accompanied by my mother, she always goes shopping with me. There were so many beautiful dresses of all colors, it was very difficult to choose one.

Alla fine, dopo aver passato ore nel camerino, la mia scelta è stata un vestito rosso. Il rosso è il mio colore preferito e il design del vestito era molto moderno ed elegante. Tuttavia, c'era un piccolo problema: l'abito era molto, molto stretto.

Finally, after spending hours in the fitting room, my choice was a red dress. Red is my favorite color and the design of the dress was very modern and elegant. However, there was a slight problem: the dress was very, very tight.

Mia madre mi ha consigliato di scegliere un vestito un po' più comodo in modo che potessi godermi di più la festa, ma ho pensato che fosse un'occasione speciale e che valesse la pena essere un po' a disagio per avere un bell'aspetto.

My mom advised me to choose a slightly more comfortable dress so that I could enjoy the party more, but I thought this was a special occasion and it was worth being a bit uncomfortable to look this good.

Più tardi, sono andata al negozio di scarpe e ho comprato dei tacchi rossi che stavano perfettamente con il mio vestito. Alla fine sono andata in gioielleria e ho comprato un paio di orecchini e una collana d'argento. Era tutto molto bello!

Later, I went to the shoe store and bought red heels that went perfectly with my dress. Finally I went to the jewelry store and bought a pair of earrings and a silver necklace. It was all very beautiful!

Il giorno dopo, poco prima della quinceañera della mia amica, sono andata al salone di bellezza. Là mi hanno truccato, mi hanno dipinto le unghie e mi hanno pettinato i capelli. Quando ho finito mi sono guardata allo specchio e penso di non essere mai stata così bella prima.

The next day, just before my friend's quinceañera, I went to the beauty salon. There they did my make up, painted my nails and combed my hair. When I finished I looked at myself in the mirror and I think I had never looked so beautiful before.

Quando Beatrice fece il suo ingresso nella sua quinceañera, tutti furono colpiti da quanto fosse carina. Indossava un abito di pizzo rosa, sembrava una vera principessa.
When Beatrice made her entrance to her quinceañera, everyone was impressed by how pretty she looked. She was wearing a pink lace dress, she looked like a real princess.

Tutto è andato alla perfezione e abbiamo iniziato a cenare. Il cibo era delizioso! C'erano salmone alla griglia e aragosta ripiena. Amo il pesce e i frutti di mare, quindi ho mangiato molto. Dopo cena era ora di ballare.
Everything went perfect and we started to have dinner. The food was delicious! There was grilled salmon and stuffed lobster. I love fish and shellfish, so I ate a lot. After dinner it was time to dance.

Mi sentivo molto bene con il mio vestito rosso, ma siccome avevo mangiato tanto e il vestito era molto stretto, ora mi sentivo molto a disagio.

I felt very good in my red dress, but since I had eaten so much and the dress was very tight, now I felt very uncomfortable.

Non riuscivo quasi a respirare, ma non mi importava perché Daniele, il ragazzo più bello della scuola, mi aveva invitato a ballare. Dan è molto alto, intelligente e un ottimo giocatore di tennis. È il ragazzo perfetto!

I could hardly breathe, but that didn't matter to me because Daniele, the most handsome boy in school, had invited me to dance. Daniele is very tall, intelligent and a very good tennis player. He is the perfect boy!

La verità è che riuscivo a malapena a muovermi, ma ero così entusiasta di ballare con il ragazzo che mi piaceva che ho fatto del mio meglio per sembrare naturale.

The truth is, I could barely move, but I was so excited to dance with the boy I liked that I did my best to look natural.

Era orribile perché Daniele voleva ballare e io sembravo una mummia nonostante i miei sforzi per ballare normalmente.

It was horrible because Daniele wanted to dance and I looked like a mummy despite my efforts to dance normally.

Poi è successa la cosa peggiore che poteva accadere: la cerniera del mio vestito si è rotta. Una scena dell'orrore!

Then the worst thing that could have happened happened: the zipper of my dress broke. A horror scene!

Ho dovuto smettere di ballare e sono andata a sedermi rossa come un pomodoro. Poi ho salutato velocemente Daniele e Beatrice e ho lasciato la festa in taxi.

I had to stop dancing and went to sit red as a tomato. Then I quickly said goodbye to Dan and Beatrice and left the party in a taxi.

Sono uscita molto imbarazzata con il mio vestito rosso strappato. La quinceañera di Beatrice è finita per essere un'esperienza orribile per me, quando sono tornata a casa ho chiuso la porta della mia camera da letto e ho pianto molto.

I left very embarrassed with my torn red dress. Beatrice's quinceañera ended up being a horrible experience for me, when I got home I closed my bedroom door and cried a lot.

Anche il giorno dopo mi sentivo molto male, ma poi ho parlato di quello che mi era successo con mia madre e mi sono sentito un po' meglio.
The next day I also felt very bad, but then I talked about what had happened to me with my mother and I felt a little better.

Questo è successo lo scorso fine settimana, da allora sono stata a casa sperando che tutti abbiano dimenticato quello che è successo. È così imbarazzante! Non credo di essere mai stata così imbarazzata prima.
This happened last weekend, since then I have been at home hoping that everyone has forgotten what happened. It's so embarrasing! I don't think I've ever been so embarrassed before.

Ma almeno tutto questo mi ha aiutato a imparare due cose: primo, ascoltare il consiglio di mia madre e, secondo, non comprare mai più un vestito troppo stretto, per quanto bello.

But at least all of this has helped me learn two things: first, listen to my mother's advice, and second, never buy a dress that is too tight again, no matter how beautiful.

La famiglia cresce
The family grows

Mi chiamo Francesco, ho trent'anni e vivo con mia moglie Julia, ventinovenne, a Napoli, in Italia.
My name is Ralph, I am thirty years old and I live with my twenty-nine-year-old wife Julia in Napoli, Australia.

Sono italiano, ma mia moglie è francese, è venuta a Napoli con la sua famiglia quando aveva quattordici anni.
I am Australian, but my wife is British, she came to Napoli with her family when she was fourteen years old.

Nonostante abbia vissuto in Italia per molti anni, ha ancora un po' di accento francese, che mi piace molto.
Despite having lived in Australia for many years, she still has a bit of a British accent, which I really like.

Julia e io ci siamo conosciuti alla festa di compleanno di un amico comune tre anni fa. Fu amore a prima vista! Dal primo momento in cui abbiamo parlato non abbiamo smesso di vederci.

Julia and I met at a mutual friend's birthday party three years ago. It was love at first sight! From the first moment we spoke we did not stop seeing each other.

Julia è molto bella, ha i capelli scuri, la pelle chiara ed è di media statura. I suoi occhi sono grandi e marroni e ha un sorriso perfetto.

Julia is very beautiful, she has dark hair, fair skin and she's of medium height. Her eyes are big and brown and she has a perfect smile.

Per me è la donna più bella del mondo. Inoltre, è molto affascinante e ha un grande senso dell'umorismo e intelligenza.

To me, she is the most beautiful woman in the world. Also, she is very charming, and has a great sense of humor and intelligence.

Dopo alcuni mesi di appuntamenti e di conoscerci, abbiamo deciso di sposarci.

After a few months of dating and getting to know each other we decided to get married.

Le nostre famiglie dicevano che era troppo presto per sposarsi e che avremmo dovuto aspettare un po', ma eravamo sicuri che volevamo passare il resto della nostra vita insieme.

Our families said that it was too early to get married and that we should wait a little while, but we were sure that we wanted to spend the rest of our lives together.

Non abbiamo visto alcun motivo per rimandare il nostro matrimonio. Ci siamo sposati due anni fa in una bellissima e grande festa. Abbiamo avuto più di cento ospiti e una cena lussuosa e indimenticabile che ricorderemo per sempre.

We saw no reason to postpone our wedding. We got married two years ago in a beautiful and big party. We had over a hundred guests and a luxurious and unforgettable dinner that we will remember forever.

Ma la cosa più incredibile è stato l'abito da sposa di Julia, molto moderno ed elegante, creato da uno stilista francese.

But the most incredible thing was Julia's wedding dress, very modern and elegant, the creation of a French designer.

Viviamo insieme da due anni ormai e non potremmo essere più felici. Abbiamo gusti e interessi molto diversi, ma ci amiamo così tanto che non importa.

We have lived together for two years now and we couldn't be happier. We have very different tastes and interests, but we love each other so much that it doesn't matter.

A Julia piace andare a ballare e cantare al karaoke, ma quello che ama di più è lo shopping. Julia ama essere alla moda e vestirsi bene.

Julia likes to go out dancing and singing karaoke, but what she loves most is shopping. Julia loves to be fashionable and to dress well.

Andiamo al centro commerciale ogni fine settimana e lei compra sempre un nuovo vestito o gioielli, sa molto di stile e mi aiuta a scegliere le mie cravatte e le mie camicie perché non capisco molto di quelle cose.

We go to the mall every weekend and she always buys a new dress or jewelry, she knows a lot about style and helps me choose my ties and shirts because I don't understand much of those things.

Preferisco invece passare il mio tempo a fare escursioni in montagna o in spiaggia.

Instead, I prefer to spend my time hiking in the mountains or on the beach.

Julia lavora come segretaria in un'importante azienda nel centro di Napoli e io sono un'insegnante di biologia in una scuola alla periferia della città.

Julia works as a secretary in an important company in the center of Napoli and I am a biology teacher in a school on the outskirts of the city.

Mi piace molto il mio lavoro perché sono appassionato di scienza e mi piace molto insegnare ai miei studenti.

I really like my job because I am passionate about science and I really like teaching my students.

A volte non studiano molto, ma con un piccolo sforzo è possibile renderli interessati all'apprendimento.

Sometimes they don't study much, but with a little effort it is possible to make them interested in learning.

La scorsa domenica Julia si è svegliata molto malata, ha avuto un fortissimo mal di testa tutto il giorno e non riusciva a dormire la notte. Ero molto preoccupato per la sua salute e il giorno dopo sono andato con lei in ospedale in modo che un medico la visitasse.

Last Sunday Julia woke up very ill, she had a very bad headache all day and could not sleep at night. I was very concerned about her health and the next day I went with her to the hospital for a doctor to examine her.

L'ospedale più vicino è a un'ora di macchina, quindi mentre eravamo in viaggio abbiamo ascoltato un intero album del nostro cantante preferito, il canadese Michael Bublé.

The closest hospital is an hour away by car so while we were on our way we listened to an entire album by our favorite singer, the Canadian Michael Bublé.

C'erano molti pazienti in ospedale e abbiamo dovuto aspettare due ore prima che un dottore vedesse Julia. Dopo aver esaminato Julia, il medico ha detto: "Congratulazioni, sarete genitori".

There were many patients in the hospital and we had to wait two hours for a doctor to see Julia. After examining

Julia, the doctor said, "Congratulations, you will be parents."

Non ci potevo credere. Questa notizia è stata del tutto inaspettata, ma siamo stati molto felici di ricevere questa buona notizia.
I couldn't believe it. This news was totally unexpected, but we were very happy to receive this good news.

Abbiamo passato il viaggio di ritorno a casa chiedendoci quale nome dare al bambino. È stato molto difficile raggiungere un accordo ma alla fine abbiamo deciso che lo chiameremo Tommaso se è un maschio e Greta se è una ragazza.
We spent the way back home wondering what name to give the baby. It was very difficult to reach an agreement but in the end we decided that we will call him Thomas if it's a boy and Stacey if it's a girl.

Quando siamo tornati a casa abbiamo cenato e abbiamo iniziato a programmare i cambiamenti che faremo nella nostra casa per accogliere il nuovo membro della famiglia.

When we got home we had dinner and began to plan the changes that we will make in our house to welcome the new member of the family.

La nostra casa non è molto grande ma è molto carina. La casa è su due piani, al primo piano c'è un soggiorno, una sala da pranzo e la cucina.

Our house is not very big but it is very pretty. The house has two floors, on the first floor there is a living room, a dining room and the kitchen.

Al secondo piano c'è il bagno e ci sono due camere da letto, io e Julia dormiamo in quella più grande e nella più piccola ora c'è una scrivania e un computer, ma quando nascerà il bambino questa piccola stanza sarà la camera da letto.

On the second floor there is the bathroom and there are two bedrooms, Julia and I sleep in the largest one and in the smallest there is now a desk and a computer, but when the baby is born this small room will be the bedroom.

Abbiamo deciso di aspettare per sapere se il bebè sarà un maschio o una femmina per iniziare a fare i cambiamenti in camera e acquistare la culla e gli indumenti per neonati.

We decided to wait to know if the baby will be a boy or a girl to start making changes in the room and buy the crib and baby clothes.

Ieri siamo tornati dal dottore e abbiamo avuto un'altra grande sorpresa. Saranno gemelli!

Yesterday we went to the doctor again and we had another big surprise. They will be twins!

Non potevamo crederci, la nostra famiglia raddoppierà tra pochi mesi, forse è una buona idea trasferirsi in una casa più grande, con più spazio per far giocare i bambini.

We could not believe it, our family is going to double in size in a few months, perhaps it is a good idea to move to a bigger house, with more space for the children to play.

Bisognerà anche comprare due lettini e raddoppiare i vestiti, ora sono due piccole creature!

It will also be necessary to buy two cribs and double the clothes, now they are two little creatures!

Trovare l'amore a Cefalù?
Finding love in Cefalù?

Alessandra è una donna americana di ventotto anni, vive a New York, ma la sua famiglia è italiana e le sue radici italiane sono una parte innegabile della sua vita.

Alessandra is a twenty-eight year old American woman, she lives in New York, but her family is from Italy and her Latin roots are an undeniable part of her life.

Tuttavia, non ci ha mai pensato molto, tranne quando alcuni amici le hanno chiesto dell'origine della sua famiglia.

However, she never thought much about it, except when some friends asked her about the origin of her family.

Alessandra aveva vissuto solo i primi due anni della sua vita in Italia. La sua infanzia e adolescenza sono state trascorse a New York. È sempre stata una bravissima studentessa, la migliore della sua classe, e quando ha deciso cosa fare in futuro, ha deciso di studiare diritto.

Alessandra had only lived the first two years of her life in Mexico. Her childhood and adolescence were spent in New York. She was always a very good student, the best in her class, and when deciding what to do in the future, she decided to study law.

Dato che era molto concentrata sui suoi studi, non usciva molto o aveva molti amici, ma i suoi sforzi sono stati ripagati e durante gli studi ha ottenuto ottimi voti.
As she was very focused on her studies, she didn't go out much or have many friends, but her efforts paid off and throughout her studies she achieved excellent grades.

Negli anni Alessandra è diventata un eccellente avvocato e ora lavora in uno studio legale a Manhattan.
Over the years Alessandra became an excellent lawyer and now works at a law firm in Manhattan.

Il lavoro di Alessandra è molto impegnativo e stimolante. Ogni giorno si alza molto presto per andare a lavorare. Inizia ogni giornata con una doccia fredda e musica rock.
Alessandra's job is very demanding and challenging. Every day she gets up very early to go to work. She starts each day with a cold shower and rock music.

La sua colazione consiste in toast con uova strapazzate con caffè e succo d'arancia. Dopo colazione si veste e prende la metro per andare al lavoro.

Her breakfast consists of toast with scrambled eggs with coffee and orange juice. After breakfast she gets dressed and takes the subway to go to work.

Alle cinque del pomeriggio finisce il lavoro e torna a casa. Di solito cena a casa da sola o con un amico. Nei fine settimana le piace fare jogging a Central Park la mattina e nel pomeriggio andare al cinema o visitare un museo con gli amici.

At five in the afternoon she finishes work and returns home. She usually dines at home alone or with a friend. On weekends she likes to go jogging in Central Park in the mornings and in the afternoons go to the movies or visit a museum with friends.

La sua vita è un po' routine, ma ama quanto sia impegnativo il suo lavoro e essere d'aiuto ai suoi clienti, e lo stipendio è molto buono.

Her life is a bit routine, but she loves how challenging her job is and being helpful to her clients, and the salary is very good.

Una domenica pomeriggio, dopo aver fatto un po' di shopping, Alessandra ha ricevuto una telefonata inaspettata da qualcuno che non vedeva da molto tempo, era sua zia Vittoria.

One Sunday afternoon, after doing some shopping, Alessandra received an unexpected call from someone she hadn't seen for a long time, it was her Aunt Vittoria.

La zia Vittoria era tornata a vivere in Italia qualche anno fa e da allora non si erano parlati più di un paio di volte al telefono. Zia Vittoria ha invitato Alessandra a trascorrere le vacanze nella sua casa di Cefalù.

Aunt Vittoria had returned to live in Italy a few years ago and since then they had not spoken more than a couple of times on the phone. Aunt Vittoria invited Alessandra to spend the holidays at her home in Cefalù.

Alessandra ha accettato immediatamente l'invito. Come poteva rifiutare? Non vedeva sua zia Vittoria da molti anni e non era mai stata a Cefalù.

Alessandra accepted the invitation immediately. How could she refuse? She had not seen her aunt Vittoria in many years and she had never been to Cefalù.

Così, dopo alcune settimane, fece domanda per una vacanza, fece i bagagli e prese un volo per la città siciliana. Zia Vittoria l'ha accolta con un grande abbraccio e una grande festa di cibo siciliano.

So after a few weeks she applied for a vacation, packed up and took a flight to the Sicilian city. Aunt Vittoria received her with a big hug and a great feast of Sicilian food.

Nonostante il tempo trascorso senza vedere sua zia, Alessandra si è sentita subito a casa.

Despite the time without seeing her aunt, Alessandra felt at home right away.

Zia Vittoria viveva con il suo compagno Michelangelo in un bellissimo appartamento con vista sul mare. Le spiagge paradisiache di Cefalù sembrano fatte per essere da cartolina.

Aunt Vittoria lived with her partner Michelangelo in a beautiful apartment overlooking the sea. The paradisiacal beaches of Cefalù seem made to be on a postcard.

Le acque turchesi e la bellezza della sua antica architettura ne fanno una meta privilegiata per chi ama il mare e una vacanza rilassante.

The turquoise waters and the beauty of its ancient architecture make it a preferred destination for those who like the sea and a relaxed vacation.

A Cefalù puoi trovare tutto per rilassarti e goderti un piacevole soggiorno.

In Cefalù you can find everything to relax and enjoy a pleasant stay.

Oltre alle spiagge paradisiache e gli edifici storici, ci sono molti piccoli negozi per tutte le tasche e per tutti i gusti.

In addition to the paradisiacal beaches and the historical buildings there are many small shops for all budgets and all tastes.

Inoltre, la notte a Cefalù è molto attiva, l'effervescente vita notturna ha un'atmosfera festosa che non finisce fino al sorgere del sole.

Also, the night in Cefalù is very active, the effervescent nightlife has a festive atmosphere that does not end until the sun rises.

Ma ciò che Alessandra ha trovato più interessante a Cefalù non sono state le spiagge o lo shopping, ma le affascinanti rovine che si trovano nelle vicinanze di Cefalù.

But what Alessandra found most interesting in Cefalù was not the beaches or shopping but the fascinating ruins that are found in the vicinity of Cefalù.

Alessandra è sempre stata interessata all'archeologia e all'architettura dei tempi antichi.

Alessandra was always interested in archeology and architecture from ancient times.

Alessandra è andata a visitare molte rovine greche e romane vicino a Cefalù che ha trovato molto interessanti, ma il suo ricordo più bello è stata la visita al Tempio di Diana.

Alessandra went to visit many Greek and Roman ruins near Cefalù that she found very interesting, but her most beautiful memory was her visit to the Tempio di Diana.

Il "Tempio di Diana" è un famoso monumento megalitico dei tempi antichi, più antico dei Greci e dei Romani! Quindi è molto, molto vecchio. Si trova in una pianura sul lato ovest della 'Rocca', la bellissima montagna di Cefalù.

The 'Temple of Diana' is a famous megalithic monument from ancient times, more ancient than the Greeks and Romans! So it is very, very old. It is located on a plain on the west side of the 'Rocca', the beautiful mountain in Cefalù.

Nei pressi del tempio ci sono ruderi di mura difensive costruite nel corso dei secoli, oltre a ruderi di altri piccoli edifici. Alessandra ha passato ore a girovagare per il Tempio e dintorni.

Nearby the temple, there are ruins of defensive walls built over the course of the centuries, as well as ruins of other small buildings. Alessandra spent hours wandering around the Temple and its surroundings.

E' anche presente una cisterna posta su un fondale profondo, che ospita una piccola pozza d'acqua utilizzata fin dall'antichità per immagazzinare l'acqua. A causa della presenza di questa piccola pozza d'acqua, gli archeologi ritengono che il tempio fosse legato al culto dell'acqua.

There is a cistern located on a deep, which has a small pool of water used since ancient times to store water. Due to the presence of this small pool of water, archeologists think the temple was linked to the worship of water.

Fu mentre Alessandra scattava alcune fotografie di questo bellissimo posto che accadde l'evento più importante del suo viaggio in Sicilia.
It was while Alessandra was taking some photographs of this beautiful place that the most important event of her trip in Sicily occurred.

Un uomo le ha chiesto se poteva farle una foto e lei l'ha fatto. Poi hanno iniziato a parlare e conoscersi.
A man asked if he could take a picture of her and she did. Then they started talking and getting to know each other.

Si chiamava Pietro ed era un medico americano che viveva anche a New York ed era in vacanza in Italia. Era molto alto e aveva capelli biondi e occhi azzurri.
His name was Pietro and he was an American doctor who also lived in New York and was on vacation in Italy. He was very tall and had blond hair and blue eyes.

Alessandra lo trovò molto attraente e gli diede il suo numero di telefono. Il giorno dopo, di ritorno a Cefalù, si sono dati appuntamento in un lussuoso ristorante.

Alessandra found him very attractive and gave him her phone number. The next day, back in Cefalù, they had a date at a luxurious restaurant.

L'appuntamento è stato molto romantico, il ristorante aveva un'ottima atmosfera e una gastronomia molto sofisticata. Hanno bevuto vino e mangiato aragoste e ostriche.

The date was very romantic, the restaurant had a great atmosphere and a very sophisticated gastronomy. They drank wine and ate lobster and oysters.

Dopo cena sono andati a fare una passeggiata lungo la spiaggia di Cefalù. Cosa potrebbe esserci di meglio di questo appuntamento con Pietro?

After dinner they went for a walk along the shore of Cefalù's beach. What could be better than this date with Pietro?

Alessandra aveva iniziato ad emozionarsi e immaginava come sarebbe stato continuare a uscire con Pietro a New York, forse lui poteva essere il suo ragazzo e poi chi lo sa? Forse vivere insieme, ma presto le sue illusioni si sarebbero scontrate con la realtà.

Alessandra had begun to get excited and imagined what it would be like to continue dating Pietro in New York, maybe he could be her boyfriend and then who knows? Maybe living together, but her illusions would soon collide with reality.

Mentre camminavano lungo la spiaggia, Pietro le disse che era sposato. Questo è stato un duro colpo per la povera Alessandra.

As they walked along the beach, Pietro told her that he was married. This was a great blow to poor Alessandra.

Diventò molto triste, ma finse di non preoccuparsene in modo che Pietro non notasse la sua delusione.

She became very sad, but pretended not to care so that Pietro would not notice her disappointment.

Il giorno dopo Pietro la chiamò di nuovo per chiederle di uscire, ma Alessandra non accettò e si scusò dicendo che aveva già un appuntamento.

The next day Pietro called her again to ask her out, but Alessandra did not accept and excused herself saying that she already had an engagement.

Le erano rimasti solo un paio di giorni di vacanza a Cefalù, quindi Alessandra ha deciso di trascorrere gli ultimi giorni con sua zia Vittoria.

She only had a couple of vacation days left in Cefalù so Alessandra decided to spend the last few days with her aunt Vittoria.

Era stato bello avere l'illusione di aver trovato un ragazzo così bello in un posto così affascinante, ma Alessandra rifletté che c'erano molti pesci nel mare e non aveva senso lamentarsi di una delusione in amore.

It had been nice to have the illusion of having found such a handsome boyfriend in such a fascinating place, but Alessandra reflected that there were many fish in the sea and there was no point in lamenting a disappointment in love.

Tra un paio di giorni sarebbe tornata a casa e avrebbe iniziato una nuova vita, chissà se l'amore della sua vita l'aspettava dietro l'angolo?

In a couple of days she would go back home and start a new life, who knows if the love of her life was waiting for her around the corner?

Alberto o Giacomo?
Alberto or Giacomo?

Ciao Piera! Come stai? Sto molto bene, come sai, sono arrivata a Firenze sei mesi fa e amo la città.
Hello Mariah! How are you? I'm very well, as you know, I arrived in Florence six months ago and I love the city.

Sai quanto amo l'arte e qui ci sono tanti bei capolavori, dal David di Michelangelo alla Primavera di Boticelli, è impossibile annoiarsi. È anche un luogo eccellente per gli amanti del gelato.
You know how much I love art and here there are so many beautiful masterpieces, from Michelangelo's David to Boticelli's Spring, it's impossible to get bored. It is also an excellent place for ice cream lovers.

Ci sono così tante gelaterie a Firenze, puoi trascorrere settimane assaggiando tutto il delizioso gelato qui. E sai quanto amo il gelato.
There are so many ice cream places in Florence, you can spend weeks tasting all the delicious ice cream here. And you know how much I love ice cream.

Mi sono divertita molto, e anche il mio nuovo lavoro è interessante e la paga è buona, molto meglio rispetto al mio lavoro precedente. Non posso lamentarmi.

I've had a great time, and also my new job is interesting and the pay is good, much better than in my previous job. I cannot complain.

La verità è che ti scrivo per raccontarti cosa mi è successo negli ultimi mesi in relazione alla mia vita sentimentale in modo che tu possa aiutarmi a prendere una decisione.

The truth is that I am writing to tell you what has happened to me in recent months in relation to my love life so you can help me make a decision.

Da quando eravamo a scuola mi hai sempre dato ottimi consigli quindi mi fido molto della tua opinione. Farò quello che mi dici!

Since we were in school you have always given me very good advice so I trust your opinion a lot. I will do what you tell me!

Allora, arrivo subito al punto. Accade così che nelle ultime settimane ho incontrato due ragazzi molto interessanti. Mi piacciono davvero entrambi. Sono molto diversi, ma mi piacciono entrambi. Il problema è che non so quale mi piace di più. Che problema!

Well, I'll get right to the point. It so happens that in the last few weeks I have met two very interesting guys. I really like them both. They are very different, but I love them both. The problem is that I don't know which one I like best. What a problem!

Uno si chiama Alberto: molto bello. L'ho conosciuto in un bar, è un musicista, suona la chitarra in un gruppo, scrive poesie e canta. È un grande artista, molto creativo e di talento. Ha viaggiato in tutto il mondo e ha vissuto a Parigi e Barcellona, parla perfettamente spagnolo e francese.

One is called Alberto: very handsome. I met him in a bar, he is a musician, and he plays guitar in a group, writes poetry and sings. He is a great artist, very creative and talented. He has traveled all over the world and has lived in Paris and Barcelona, he speaks Spanish and French perfectly.

Ha anche gli occhi azzurri e lunghi capelli biondi, mi ricorda molto Kurt Cobain e sai quanto mi piaceva lui. Alberto è sicuramente un sogno, tutto ciò che mi piace in un uomo.

He also has blue eyes and long blonde hair, he reminds me a lot of Kurt Cobain and you know how much I liked him. Alberto is definitely a dream, everything I like in a man.

Alberto è fantastico ma, non lo so, a volte sembra un po' indifferente e poco interessato ad avere una relazione seria. Ad esempio, non mi chiama mai, io chiamo sempre.

Alberto is fantastic but, I don't know, sometimes he seems a bit indifferent and little interested in having a serious relationship. For example, he never calls me, I always call.

Inoltre viaggia tutto il tempo con la sua band, quindi non ha molto tempo da passare con me...

He's also traveling all the time with his band so he doesn't have much time to spend with me...

Ma in questi mesi abbiamo fatto tante cose insieme: siamo andati a teatro, al cinema, ai concerti, a ballare. Sa anche ballare il tango e sai quanto mi piace ballare!

But in recent months we have done a lot of things together: we have gone to the theater, to the cinema, to concerts, to dance. He also knows how to dance tango and you know how much I like to dance!

Dato che Alberto è così creativo, ha composto una canzone per me, l'abbiamo suonata insieme, io al piano e lui alla chitarra, e suona molto bene. Nessuno aveva mai composto una canzone per me, Alberto è così romantico e appassionato, mi fa sentire davvero speciale.

As Alberto is so creative, he has composed a song for me, we have played it together, me on piano and he on guitar, and it sounds very good. No one had ever composed a song for me, Alberto is so romantic and passionate, he makes me feel very special.

Bene, ora vi parlerò dell'altro mio amico: Giacomo. Giacomo è totalmente diverso da Alberto. In realtà, io e Giacomo in qualche modo siamo simili, perché anche lui è un ingegnere (ha studiato in Inghilterra come me per due anni) ed è molto concentrato sul suo lavoro. È anche piuttosto ambizioso, come me.

Well, now I will tell you about my other friend: Giacomo. Giacomo is totally different from Alberto. Actually, Giacomo and I are alike in some ways, because he is also an engineer (he has studied in England like me for two years) and he is very focused on his work. He is also quite ambitious, like me.

Fisicamente, Giacomo non è attraente come Alberto. Nonostante abbia solo trent'anni, è già un po' calvo e poco atletico. Ma ha un bel sorriso e uno straordinario senso dell'umorismo, quando sono con lui rido sempre.

Physically, Giacomo is not as attractive as Alberto. Despite being only thirty years old, he is already a bit bald and not very athletic. But he has a beautiful smile and an extraordinary sense of humor, when I'm with him I'm always laughing.

La verità è che mi sono divertita molto con lui. Giacomo ama andare al ristorante e mangiare bene, quasi ogni fine settimana andiamo in un nuovo ristorante.

The truth is that I had a great time with him. Giacomo loves to go to restaurants and eat well, almost every weekend we go to a new restaurant.

Abbiamo mangiato di tutto, dal cibo cinese a quello francese. Inoltre mi ha invitato a mangiare a casa sua e ho conosciuto tutta la sua famiglia, sono tutti molto simpatici!

We have eaten everything from Chinese to French food. In addition, he has invited me to eat at his house and I have met his whole family, they are all very nice!

Giacomo è un tesoro, mi chiama tutti i giorni. Qualche giorno fa mi ha detto che è molto innamorato di me. So cosa stai pensando, Alberto non ha detto niente sull'essere innamorato; E se n'è andato anche perché ha un tour di due mesi in Europa.

Giacomo is a sweetheart, he calls me every day. A few days ago he told me that he is very much in love with me. I know what you're thinking, Alberto hasn't said anything about being in love; And he has also left because he has a two-month tour in Europe.

Penso di conoscere già i consigli che mi darai, dimentica Alberto e inizia una relazione seria con Giacomo. Ma è molto complicato, mi piace molto Alberto.

I think I already know the advice you will give me, forget Alberto and start a serious relationship with Giacomo. But it's very complicated, I really like Alberto a lot.

So che non potrei avere un rapporto stabile con lui, perché viaggia sempre e non sembra essere molto interessato a me, ma i pochi momenti che posso condividere con lui mi sembrano un sogno. Potrebbe essere che io sia innamorata di lui?

I know that I could not have a stable relationship with him, because he always travels and does not seem to be very interested in me, but the few moments that I can share with him I feel like in a dream. Could it be that I am in love with him?

Quando Giacomo mi ha detto che mi amava, non gli ho risposto. Non sarebbe onesto dirgli che lo amo anch'io. Penso che potrebbe essere necessario per me trascorrere un po' di tempo da sola a riflettere su quali sono i miei sentimenti e su cosa voglio veramente fare.

When Giacomo told me that he loved me, I didn't answer him. It would not be honest to tell him that I love him too. I think it may be necessary for me to spend some time alone reflecting on what my feelings are and what I really want to do.

Allora, aspetterò la tua risposta in modo che tu mi consigli cosa fare, sei la mia migliore amica e mi fido della tua saggezza e buon giudizio.

Well, I'll wait for your answer so that you advise me what to do, you are my best friend and I trust your wisdom and good judgment.

Ho scritto così tanto su me stessa! Non dimenticarti di raccontarmi come stanno andando i tuoi studi in Australia e come va la tua vita sentimentale, l'ultima volta mi hai detto che uno dei tuoi compagni di classe ti aveva invitato ad uscire un paio di volte al cinema.

I have written so much about myself! Don't forget to tell me how your studies are going in Australia and how your love life is going, the last time you told me that one of your classmates had invited you to go out a couple of times to the movies.

Come è andata a finire? Stanno ancora uscendo insieme? Dimmi tutto, sai quanto mi piace conoscere le storie d'amore dei miei amici.

How did that turn out? Are you still dating? Tell me everything, you know how much I like to know the love stories of my friends.

Abbracci,
Hugs,

Chiara

Intervista a Pietro Abrami
Pietro Abrami Interview

Pietro Abrami è un importante attore italiano, ha anche lavorato con grande successo in Australia, negli Stati Uniti e in altre parti del mondo.
Pietro Abrami is an important Italian actor, he has also worked with great success in Australia, the United States and other parts of the world.

Attualmente vive in Costiera Amalfitana con la sua bellissima moglie Anna. In questa intervista impareremo qualcosa in più su questo attore di successo, sulla sua vita personale e sui suoi sogni per il futuro.

He currently lives on the Amalfi Coast with his beautiful wife Anna. In this interview we will learn a little more about this successful actor, his personal life and his dreams for the future.

Com'è una giornata tipo per Pietro Abrami?
What is a typical day for Pietro Abrami like?

Se non sto lavorando a un film, la mia vita è del tutto normale. Mi alzo presto e faccio colazione. Poi leggo il giornale. A volte con mia moglie andiamo a fare una passeggiata e se c'è il sole nuotiamo un po' sulla spiaggia, è il bello di vivere in Costiera Amalfitana.

If I'm not working on a movie, my life is completely normal. I get up early and have breakfast. Then I read the newspaper. Sometimes with my wife we go for a walk and if it's sunny we swim a bit on the beach, it's the good thing about living on the Amalfi Coast.

Mi piace molto cucinare, quindi di solito passo molto tempo in cucina, ma odio lavare i piatti. Io e mia moglie pranziamo sempre insieme, poi facciamo un pisolino.

I really like to cook, so I usually spend a lot of time in the kitchen, but I hate doing the dishes. My wife and I always have lunch together, then take a nap.

La sera tardi di solito andiamo al cinema o andiamo a mangiare in un ristorante. Di tanto in tanto invitiamo i nostri amici a cena.

Later in the evening we usually go out to the movies or go to eat at a restaurant. From time to time we invite our friends to dinner.

A cosa stai lavorando attualmente?

What are you currently working on?

Ora mi sto preparando per recitare in un film di fantascienza su un viaggio su Marte. Il mio personaggio è molto interessante, ma preferisco tenerlo segreto. Inoltre, sto lavorando a una soap opera, interpretando il ruolo principale.

Now I am preparing to act in a science fiction movie about a trip to Mars. My character is very interesting, but I prefer to keep it a secret. Also, I'm working on a soap opera, playing the lead.

Preferiresti lavorare in televisione o al cinema?

Would you rather work on television or in the cinema?

Entrambi hanno il loro fascino, ma personalmente preferisco il cinema, perché le questioni sono più complesse e impegnative. Quando ero piccolo volevo fare l'attore televisivo, ma negli ultimi anni ho scoperto che il cinema è la mia passione.

Both have their appeal, but personally I prefer the cinema, because the issues are more complex and challenging. When I was little I wanted to be a television actor, but in recent years I have discovered that cinema is my passion.

Qual è la cosa più pericolosa che hai fatto nel tuo lavoro di attore?

What is the most dangerous thing that you have done in your work as an actor?

Ho fatto molte cose pericolose! Una volta in Africa ho dovuto recitare insieme a un leone. All'inizio avevo molta paura, ma poco a poco mi ci sono abituato e poi non ho più avuto paura.

I've done a lot of dangerous things! Once in Africa I had to act together with a lion. At first I was very scared, but little by little I got used to it and then I was no longer scared.

Ho anche recitato sott'acqua in alcune scene e sono stato in un incendio. Ma senza dubbio la parte più impegnativa del lavoro di un attore è passare molte ore a lavorare. Lavoro da 20 ore senza fermarmi!

I have also acted underwater in some scenes and I've been in a fire. But without a doubt the most challenging part of an actor's job is spending many hours working. I have been working for 20 hours without stopping!

Che progetti hai per la prossima vacanza?
What plans do you have for the next vacation?

Con mia moglie viaggeremo in Europa per un mese. Andremo in molti paesi, Francia, Croazia, Svizzera e molti altri. Abbiamo già prenotato hotel e alcuni voli, ci piace pianificare in anticipo ogni cosa che faremo.

With my wife we are going to travel to Europe for a month. We will go to many countries, France, Croatia, Switzerland and many others. We have already booked hotels and some flights, we like to plan in advance each thing we will do.

Siamo molto entusiasti di questo viaggio, è la prima volta che viaggiamo in Europa insieme, quindi è qualcosa di speciale.

We are very excited about this trip, it is the first time we are travelling in Europe together so it is something special.

C'è qualcosa nella tua carriera di attore che non hai ancora fatto che ti piacerebbe fare?

Is there anything in your acting career that you haven't done yet that you would like to do?

Mi piacerebbe recitare in teatro, poiché per tutta la mia carriera mi sono esibito davanti a una telecamera, ma mai per un pubblico dal vivo.

I would like to act in the theater, since all my career I have performed in front of a camera, but never for a live audience.

Lo so, è strano che un attore non si sia mai esibito in un teatro, ma è così che sono andate le cose per me, ho iniziato in televisione e poi ho subito iniziato a recitare nei film, quindi non ho mai avuto l'opportunità di esibirmi sul palco.

I know, it's weird that an actor has never performed in a theater, but that's how things have turned out for me, I started in television and then immediately started acting in movies, so I never had the opportunity to perform on stage.

C'è qualcosa di speciale nell'esibirsi per un pubblico dal vivo e penso che sia necessario per il mio sviluppo professionale e personale.
There is something special about performing for a live audience and I think it is necessary for my professional and personal development.

Sappiamo già che preferisci non parlare in dettaglio della tua vita personale, ma qual è il rapporto che hai con tua moglie?
We already know that you prefer not to talk in detail about your personal life, but what is the relationship you have with your wife like?

Beh, come hai detto tu mi piace mantenere la mia vita privata davvero privata. Non sono come quegli attori che traggono vantaggio dall'esporre le loro intimità.

Well, like you said I like to keep my private life really private. I am not like those actors who benefit from exposing their intimacies.

Basti pensare che abbiamo un ottimo rapporto con Anna, con alti e bassi come tutte le coppie, ma siamo uniti da grande amore e impegno per un progetto di vita comune.
Suffice it to say that we have an excellent relationship with Anna, with ups and downs like all couples, but we are united by great love and commitment to a common life project.

Avere figli fa parte di quel progetto?
Is having children part of that project?

Certo, è qualcosa di cui abbiamo discusso con Anna, ma al momento con quanto siamo impegnati non mi sembra una buona idea.
Of course, it is something that we have discussed with Anna, but at the moment with how busy we are it does not seem like a good idea.

Credo che avere figli sia un'enorme responsabilità e vorrei poter dedicare più tempo alla crescita dei miei figli di quanto potrei in questo momento. Il lavoro di un attore può essere molto impegnativo.

I believe that having children is a huge responsibility and I wish I could spend more time raising my children than I could right now. The work of an actor can be very demanding.

Tornando alla tua vita professionale, che consiglio daresti a un attore che sta iniziando la sua carriera?

Going back to your professional life, what advice would you give to an actor who is starting his career?

Per prima cosa è importante istruirsi, prendere lezioni di recitazione e danza. Leggi anche libri di storia del teatro e molti copioni.

First it is important to educate yourself, take acting and dance classes. Also read theater history books and many scripts.

Secondo, devi andare a quante più audizioni possibile, non importa quanto piccolo o strano sia il ruolo.

Second, you need to go to as many auditions as possible, no matter how small or strange the role is.

E infine, chiunque desideri una carriera come attore o attrice deve imparare a gestire il rifiuto costante.

And finally, anyone who wants a career as an actor or actress has to learn to deal with constant rejection.

Recitare può essere una vita molto dura, poiché c'è molta concorrenza e i ruoli buoni non sono molti, quindi un attore alle prime armi deve avere la forza di non considerare un "no" come un fallimento o un rifiuto personale da parte del direttore del casting, ma come esperienza di apprendimento.

Acting can be a very hard life, as there is a lot of competition and the good roles are not many so a beginning actor has to have the strength not to consider a "no" as a failure or a personal rejection on the part of the casting director, but as a learning experience.

Ricordi di mia nonna
Memories of my grandmother

Mia nonna mi ha insegnato tante cose: come cucinare, leggere e scrivere. Ma la cosa più importante che ho imparato da lei e che ha definito il resto della mia vita è come dipingere, è grazie a lei che sono diventata una artista.
My grandmother taught me many things: how to cook, read and write. But the most important thing that I learned from her and that defined the rest of my life is how to paint, it is because of her that I became an artist.

Mia nonna si chiamava Micaela come me ed è morta due anni fa, ma la ricordo ogni giorno ad ogni pennellata.
My grandmother was called Micaela like me and she passed away two years ago, but I remember her every day with every brushstroke.

Dipingeva sempre dei quadri ad olio e da piccola passavo ore a guardare la tela bianca trasformarsi gradualmente in un'immagine chiara e riconoscibile mentre in sottofondo suonava la musica preferita di mia nonna: Mozart.

She was always painting some oil painting and as a child I spent hours watching the white canvas gradually transform into a clear and recognizable image while in the background my grandmother's favorite music played: Mozart.

Tutta la mia famiglia è americana, ma mia nonna Micaela era italiana. Come è arrivata negli Stati Uniti questa ragazza italiana?
My whole family is American, but my grandmother Micaela was from Italy. How did this Italian girl come to the United States?

Per capirlo, devi andare al passato e ricordare la seconda guerra mondiale. Dopo questa guerra molti italiani stavano affrontando terribili difficoltà economiche, tanti di loro emigrarono verso l'America e altre parti del mondo.
To understand it, you have to go to the past and remember the Second World War. After this war many italians were facing terrible economic hardship, so many of them emigrated towards America and other parts of the world.

Un gran numero di uomini, donne e bambini sono stati costretti a emigrare in altri paesi in cerca di opportunità e di una vita migliore. New York è stata una delle città che hanno accolto un gran numero di italiani.

Large numbers of men, women and children were forced to migrate to other lands in search of opportunities and a better life. New York was one of the cities that received a large number of Italians.

Quando mia nonna è arrivata in America, aveva otto anni. Accompagnata da suo padre e sua madre, era arrivata dopo un lungo viaggio di trenta giorni in battello a vapore.

When my grandmother arrived in America, she was eight years old. Accompanied by her father and mother, she had arrived after a long thirty-day journey by steamboat.

Mia nonna mi ha detto che dopo aver passato così tanto tempo a vivere su una nave in mezzo al mare è stato molto emozionante arrivare finalmente a New York e calpestare la terra.

My grandmother told me that after spending so much time living on a ship in the middle of the sea it was very exciting to finally arrive in New York and step on land.

All'inizio, come mi disse, era stato un po' difficile abituarsi al suo nuovo paese, la lingua che le persone parlavano era diversa e alcune cose sulla cultura del paese le sembravano strane, ma a poco a poco si è abituata alla sua nuova paese e, quando è diventata adolescente, non si sentiva più una straniera e parlava un inglese perfetto.

At first, as she told me, it had been a bit difficult to get used to her new country, the language people spoke was different and some things about the country's culture seemed strange to her, but little by little she got used to her new country and, when she became a teenager, she did not feel like a foreigner anymore and she spoke perfect English.

Mia nonna si è sposata giovanissima, a diciassette anni. Tutto è iniziato quando la famiglia si è trasferita in un nuovo quartiere di New York, mio nonno era un vicino di casa che si è innamorato di mia nonna a prima vista, quindi scriveva le sue lettere d'amore che lasciava sotto la porta.

My grandmother married very young, at seventeen. It all started when the family moved to a new neighborhood in New York, my grandfather was a neighbor who fell in love with my grandmother as soon as he saw her, so he used to write her love letters that he left under the door.

Lei doveva nascondere le lettere in modo che i suoi severi genitori non le trovassero.

She had to hide the letters so that her strict parents wouldn't find them.

Nonostante gli sforzi di mia nonna, un giorno suo padre vide il vicino lasciare una delle lettere e ha letto la lettera. Era furioso! Il vicino stava seducendo sua figlia! A quei tempi i genitori erano molto iperprotettivi con le loro figlie.

Despite my grandmother's efforts, one day her father saw the neighbor leaving one of the letters and read it. He was furious! The neighbor was seducing his daughter! In those days parents were very overprotective with their daughters.

Una volta scoperta la storia d'amore, i genitori di mia nonna hanno dato alla giovane coppia due opzioni: interrompere questo scambio di lettere d'amore o sposarsi.

Once the romance was discovered, my grandmother's parents gave the young couple two options: stop this love letter exchange or get married.

Hanno scelto questa seconda opzione. Devo ringraziarli perché altrimenti non sarei mai nata.

They chose this second option. I must thank them because otherwise I would never have been born.

I miei nonni non si sono mai pentiti della loro decisione e vissero felici per decenni fino a quando morirono entrambi nello stesso anno, separati solo da pochi mesi.

My grandparents never regretted their decision and lived happily for decades until they both died the same year, only separated by a few months.

È stato poco dopo la nascita del suo primo figlio che mia nonna Rosa ha iniziato a disegnare e dipingere. Aveva cinque figli, a quei tempi era normale avere cinque o più figli.

It was shortly after the birth of her first child that my grandmother Rosa began to draw and paint. He had five children, in those times it was normal to have five or more children.

La seconda di quei bambini era mia madre. Dopo aver fatto le faccende domestiche, mia nonna trascorreva alcune ore del pomeriggio dedicate ai suoi interessi artistici.

The second of those children was my mother. After doing housework, my grandmother spent a few hours in the afternoon dedicated to her artistic interests.

Essere madre, casalinga e artista non è stato facile ed è stato solo quando i suoi figli se ne sono andati che ha iniziato a dedicare più tempo alla pittura.

Being a mother, a housewife and an artist was not easy and it was only when her children left that she began to spend more time on painting.

La casa dove vivevano i miei nonni non era molto grande, ma mia nonna è riuscita a dare spazio alla sua creatività.

The house where my grandparents lived was not very big, but my grandmother managed to make room for her creativity.

Quando i suoi figli sono usciti di casa, la cameretta dei bambini è diventata l'atelier di mia nonna. Era una stanza molto luminosa e colorata, piena di vita e c'era sempre musica nell'aria.

When her children left home, the children's bedroom became my grandmother's atelier. It was a very bright and colorful room, full of life and there was always music in the air.

Era piena di dipinti di mia nonna e degli oli che usava per dipingere. Aveva anche carboncino, pastelli e acquerelli, ma li usava un po' meno.

It was full of paintings from my grandmother, and the oils she used to paint. She also had charcoal, pastels, and watercolors but she used them a little less.

Non so quando ha iniziato a dipingere o come l'ha imparata, secondo lei non ha mai avuto un insegnante o un'educazione artistica, anche se considerando quanto bene lo facesse, era un po' difficile da credere.

I don't know when she started painting or how she learned it, according to her she never had a teacher or an art education, although considering how well she did it, that was a bit hard to believe.

In ogni caso, diceva sempre di se stessa che era un'artista autodidatta e non aveva imparato da nessuno se non dalle opere di altri artisti, guardando e copiando i grandi maestri.

In any case, she always said of herself that she was a self-taught artist and had not learned from anyone other than the works of other artists, watching and copying the great masters.

Amava gli impressionisti francesi, in particolare Monet e Renoir. Anche il cubismo di Picasso e le visioni surrealiste di Dalí. Aveva diversi libri con riproduzioni dei suoi dipinti.

She loved the French Impressionists, especially Monet and Renoir. Also the cubism of Picasso and the surrealist visions of Dalí. She had several books with reproductions of his paintings.

Leggendo questi libri di mia nonna ho imparato molto di storia dell'arte da bambina, tant'è che quando ho iniziato a studiare arte all'università sapevo già praticamente tutto quello che ho studiato al corso di Storia dell'Arte.

Reading these books from my grandmother I learned a lot about art history when I was a child, so much so that when I started studying art at university I already knew practically everything I studied in Art History class.

Mia nonna mi ha lasciato questi ricordi e molte conoscenze artistiche, ma ha lasciato anche molti dipinti. Ricordo che dipingeva cose in cucina che disponeva in diverse posizioni: un pomodoro, un vaso di succo, delle tazze.

My grandmother left me these memories and a lot of artistic knowledge, but she also left many paintings. I remember her painting things in the kitchen that she arranged in different positions: a tomato, a vase of juice, some cups.

A volte chiedeva a me oa mia madre di sederci per ore e ci dipingeva. Disegnava e dipingeva molto bene qualsiasi cosa, dalla natura morta ai ritratti.

Sometimes she would ask me or my mother to sit for hours and she would paint us. She drew and painted anything very well, from still life to portraits.

Oggi ho ancora un ritratto che mia nonna fece di me e mia madre, anche il paesaggio di una spiaggia che dipinse durante una delle sue vacanze a Coney Island.

Today I still have a portrait that my grandmother made of my mother and I, also a landscape of a beach that she painted on one of her vacations on Coney Island.

Mia nonna Micaela è il tesoro più prezioso della mia infanzia che ancora oggi conservo nella memoria. E anche se mi manca in ogni momento, sento che mi accompagna ogni giorno con la sua eredità e i suoi insegnamenti.

My grandmother Micaela is the most precious treasure of my childhood that I still keep in my memory today. And although I miss her at all times, I feel that she accompanies me every day with her legacy and teachings.

Sono sicura che se non fosse stato per lei non mi sarei dedicato all'arte, quindi ogni volta che affronto la tela bianca ringrazio mia nonna per essere esistita.

I'm sure that if it weren't for her I wouldn't have dedicated myself to art, so every time I face the white canvas I thank my grandmother for having existed.

Un intervista di lavoro
A job interview

Adele uscì dalla vasca e dopo aver avvolto un asciugamano intorno alla vita, si avvicinò allo specchio e si disse:

Adele got out of the bathtub and after wrapping a towel around her waist, she walked in front of the mirror and said to herself:

"Guardati Adele, sei impressionante e il colloquio di lavoro di oggi sarà sicuramente perfetto e otterrai quella posizione, ti adatti perfettamente a quello che stanno cercando".

"Look at you Adele, you look impressive and today's job interview will surely be perfect and you will get that position, you fit perfectly with what they are looking for".

In realtà, era molto nervosa per questa intervista, ma quelle parole l'hanno aiutata a darle un po' di fiducia in più.

Actually, she was very nervous about this interview, but those words helped give her some additional confidence.

Adele aveva 28 anni e da quando si era laureata in amministrazione aveva lavorato nella stessa azienda con grande successo, tuttavia era disoccupata da sei mesi.

Adele was 28 years old and since she graduated in administration she had worked in the same company with great success, however she had been unemployed for six months.

Aveva perso il lavoro a causa di un ridimensionamento dell'azienda che era sull'orlo del fallimento.

She had lost her job due to a downsizing of the company that was on the verge of bankruptcy.

Adele è uscita dal bagno ed è andata in camera da letto, dove ha scelto i vestiti da indossare, ha optato per qualcosa di semplice e classico, un abito nero molto elegante.

Adele left the bathroom and went to the bedroom, where she chose what clothes to wear, she decided on something simple and classic, a very elegant black suit.

Aveva comprato le scarpe il giorno prima ed erano belle e sofisticate. Guardò l'orologio ed era ora di sbrigarsi: in un'ora aveva il colloquio e da casa sua al luogo dell'appuntamento ci vollero circa 50 minuti di metropolitana.

She had bought the shoes the day before and they were beautiful and sophisticated. She looked at the clock and it was time to hurry: in an hour she had the interview and from her house to the place of the appointment it took about 50 minutes by subway.

Tornò in bagno, si lavò i denti e si truccò velocemente e infine il profumo; una fragranza non troppo appariscente. Era un colloquio di lavoro, non un appuntamento!

She went back to the bathroom, brushed her teeth, and quickly applied some makeup and finally the perfume; a not too flashy fragrance. It was a job interview, not a date!

Dopo aver dato un'ultima occhiata allo specchio, è uscita di casa e ha preso la metropolitana. Non era l'ora di punta, quindi c'era un posto libero e Adele si sedette comodamente.

After taking one last look in the mirror, she left the house and took the subway. It wasn't rush hour so there was a free seat and Adele sat down comfortably.

Per liberarsi dei suoi nervi, ha deciso di ascoltare una meditazione guidata che lei usava per rilassarsi e dormire.

To get rid of her nerves, she decided to listen to a guided meditation that she used to relax and sleep.

In pochi minuti si sentiva già molto rilassata, lentamente il rilassamento aumentava, il suo respiro diventava più lento e profondo. Lentamente si addormentò, persa in un sonno profondo.

In a few minutes she already felt very relaxed, slowly the relaxation increased, her breathing became slower and deeper. Slowly she fell asleep, lost in a deep sleep.

Fu due ore dopo che un impiegato della metropolitana la svegliò. Adele, appena si è svegliata, ha guardato l'orologio, erano le 5 e l'intervista era alle 4!

It was two hours later that a subway worker woke her up. Adele, as soon as she woke up, looked at her watch, it was 5 o'clock and the interview was at 4 o'clock!

Cosa fare? Adele guardò il suo telefono e vide che c'era un messaggio: "Signorina Adele, purtroppo e dato che non ha partecipato al colloquio la posizione per la quale stavamo considerando è già stata assegnata ad un'altra persona, per favore non si preoccupi di venire, poiché puntualità e responsabilità sono requisiti necessari per la posizione. "

What to do? Adele looked at her phone and saw that there was a message: "Miss Adele, unfortunately and since you did not attend the interview the position for which we were considering you has already been assigned to another person, please do not bother to come, since punctuality and responsibility are necessary requirements for the position."

Adele era molto triste e arrabbiata con se stessa, era troppo tardi per fare qualcosa. Così ha deciso di scendere alla prossima stazione e bere qualcosa.

Adele was very sad and angry with herself, it was too late to do anything. So she decided to get off at the next station and have a drink.

Questo era uno dei quartieri più ricchi della città. Adele viveva lontano e non veniva mai qui, quindi sembrava una buona opportunità per distrarsi dalla brutta situazione che stava attraversando.

This was one of the richest neighborhoods in the city, Adele lived far away and never came here so it seemed like a good opportunity to distract herself from the bad situation she was going through.

Una volta fuori, è andata in un bar vicino all'uscita della metropolitana e ha ordinato un whisky con ghiaccio. L'atmosfera era molto piacevole, c'era un'illuminazione calda che metteva in risalto la ricca trama dei mobili in pelle e mogano.

Once outside, she went to a bar near the subway exit and ordered a whiskey on the rocks. The atmosphere was very pleasant, there was warm lighting that brought out the rich texture of the leather and mahogany furniture.

Si rimproverava ancora di aver preso la cattiva decisione di ascoltare quella meditazione guidata in un momento come quello, ma a poco a poco il whisky diminuì la sua preoccupazione.

She still reproached herself for having made the bad decision to listen to that guided meditation at a time like this, but little by little the whiskey lessened her concern.

A pochi passi, al bar, c'era un uomo che la fissava da diversi minuti. Adele si sentì un po' spaventata perché il suo sguardo era molto persistente.

A few feet away at the bar was a man who had been staring at her for several minutes. Adele felt a little scared because his gaze was very persistent.

Cosa vorrebbe quest'uomo? Sarebbe interessato a lei? Era qualcuno che aveva incontrato prima ma non ricordava? Molte domande e ipotesi le riempirono la mente.
What would this man want? Would he be interested in her? Was it someone she had met before but didn't remember? Many questions and hypotheses filled her mind.

Alla fine, l'uomo le si avvicinò e si sedette accanto a lei. Indossava un abito di ottima qualità senza cravatta, un orologio Rolex e un profumo che Adele non riusciva a identificare ma era senza dubbio molto costoso.
Finally, the man walked over to her and sat down next to her. He wore a very good quality suit without a tie, he wore a Rolex watch and a perfume that Adele could not identify but was undoubtedly very expensive.

-Scusatemi signorina- disse l'uomo- mi chiamo Martin Roberts e sono un direttore del casting per una compagnia cinematografica. Sei un'attrice?

-Excuse me young lady- said the man- my name is Martin Roberts and I am a casting director for a film company. Are you an actress?

- Io, un'attrice? Haha, no, lavoro nell'amministrazione - ha risposto Adele.

- Me, an actress? Haha, no, I work in administration - Adele answered.

-Beh, non importa, come ti chiami?

-Well, that doesn't matter, what is your name?

-Adele.

-Adele.

- Piacere di conoscerti Adele. Come dicevo, sono un direttore del casting e stiamo cercando una nuova attrice per un ruolo da protagonista in un film ad alto budget.

-Nice to meet you Adele. As I was saying, I am a casting director and we are looking for a new actress for a leading role in a very high budget movie.

È una commedia romantica che sarà girata in diverse località del mondo. Penso che tu, Adele, tu abbia l'aspetto perfetto per il ruolo che stiamo cercando, bella ed elegante, con un tocco di malinconia.

It is a romantic comedy that will be shot in different locations around the world. I think you, Adele, have the perfect appearance for the role we are looking for, beautiful and elegant, with a touch of melancholy.

Per quanto riguarda la tua mancanza di esperienza, quello è secondario, con qualche mese nella nostra talent academy sarà sufficiente. Saresti interessata a questa opportunità?

Regarding your lack of experience, that is secondary, with a few months in our talent academy it will be enough. Would you be interested in this opportunity?

Adele è rimasta senza parole, ha riso e poi ha detto di sì con grande entusiasmo. Martin Roberts le ha dato il suo biglietto da visita e hanno fissato un appuntamento per fare un test della telecamera in studio il giorno successivo.

Adele was speechless, she laughed and then said yes with great enthusiasm. Martin Roberts gave her his card and they made an appointment to do a camera test in the studio on the next day.

Quando Martin Roberts ha detto addio, Adele ha bevuto un altro whisky per festeggiare e ha preso la metropolitana per tornare a casa.
When Martin Roberts said goodbye, Adele had another whiskey to celebrate and took the subway back home.

Sulla via del ritorno pensò che se quel pomeriggio non si fosse addormentata e se non si fosse persa il colloquio di lavoro, non sarebbe mai stata in quel bar per farsi scoprire da quell'uomo.
On the way back she thought that if she hadn't fallen asleep this afternoon and if she hadn't missed her job interview, she would never have been to that bar to be discovered by that man.

La vita è pazzesca! Quello che si era detta davanti allo specchio quella mattina era verissimo, ma non nel modo in cui lo immaginava. Chi avrebbe potuto immaginare che oggi, addormentandosi, avrebbe avuto un cambiamento così grande nella sua vita?

Life is crazy! What she had said to herself in front of the mirror this morning was very true, just not in the way she imagined it. Who could have imagined that today, by falling asleep, she would have such a big change in her life?

Tutto è stato fantastico e incredibile, l'unica certezza è che domani avrebbe mosso i primi passi nella sua nuova carriera. I suoi amici le avevano sempre detto che era molto attraente e aveva una bellezza hollywoodiana, ma non l'aveva mai preso troppo sul serio.

Everything was amazing and incredible, the only certainty is that tomorrow she would take her first steps in her new career. Her friends had always told her that she was very attractive and had a Hollywood beauty, but she had never taken it too seriously.

Era stata una giornata troppo interessante ed era già stanca, arrivata a casa si sdraiò nel suo comodo letto con pace e gioia, domani iniziarebbe la sua nuova vita di attrice.

It had been too interesting a day and she was already tired, arriving home she lay down in her comfortable bed with peace and joy, tomorrow she would begin her new life as an actress.

STORIES IN ITALIAN

Vacanze a Rimini

Il mio nome è Lorenzo Costa e ho vent'anni. Sono nato a Firenze, ma vivo a Roma da più di dieci anni. Studio ingegneria all'università e mi piace molto praticare sport come il calcio e la pallavolo, e nei fine settimana mi piace passare ore a giocare ai videogiochi con i miei amici.

La mia vita è un po' noiosa perché passo molto tempo a studiare, ma l'estate scorsa è stata molto divertente. A febbraio sono andato in vacanza con alcuni amici a Rimini. Rimini è una città molto turistica sulla costa adriatica con bellissime spiagge, un'ottima opzione per trascorrere una bella estate in un luogo affascinante.

A Rimini ci sono molti centri commerciali, bar, discoteche e luoghi di intrattenimento per tutti i gusti. I miei amici ed io abbiamo affittato un appartamento un appartamento vicino al lungomare per una settimana.

È un piacere trascorrere del tempo con i tuoi amici in una città così bella e con una vista spettacolare sul mare. I tramonti sono molto belli!

Siamo un interessante gruppo di amici. Claudia ha ventun anni e anche lei è di Roma. Studia ingegneria con me e nel tempo libero ama cucinare. Ho provato i piatti di Claudia e sono buonissimi, Claudia è un'ottima cuoca e una ragazza molto simpatica, ma è un po' timida e introversa.

Samuele è di Milano, ha vent'anni e studia medicina, ma la sua passione sono le auto sportive. È molto socievole, ama le feste e conoscere nuove persone.

Infine c'è Alfredo, è uno studente di interior design ed è molto interessato alla moda e alle ultime tendenze. Io ei miei amici ci conosciamo da un paio d'anni e, nonostante abbiamo interessi molto diversi, andiamo molto d'accordo, quindi vivere con loro per una settimana è stato molto bello.

Il primo giorno della nostra vacanza è stato molto buono. La mattina ci siamo alzati molto presto per sfruttare al massimo la giornata. Siamo andati in spiaggia, siamo andati in mare e abbiamo nuotato per ore, poi io e Samuele abbiamo giocato a pallavolo mentre Claudia e Alfredo prendevano il sole.

A mezzogiorno faceva molto caldo e siamo tornati al nostro appartamento. Con un piccolo aiuto da parte nostra, Claudia ha preparato dell'ottimo pesce e patatine per il pranzo e poi abbiamo fatto un pisolino fino alle sei del pomeriggio.

La prima sera della nostra vacanza abbiamo deciso di andare in un bar vicino, ma Claudia non voleva andare. Claudia ha detto che era molto stanca e assonnata. Samuele, Alfredo e io abbiamo passato una serata molto divertente, abbiamo bevuto molta birra e parlato fino a tardi, ma ci siamo sentiti un po' male perché Claudia era sola nell'appartamento mentre ci siamo divertiti molto.

Come ho già detto, Claudia non è molto socievole e non ama molto uscire, probabilmente la sua stanchezza era solo una scusa per restare a casa. Il secondo giorno di vacanza siamo andati anche al mare. La sera, con molta fatica, siamo riusciti a convincere Claudia ad accompagnarci a una festa elettronica sulla spiaggia. Eravamo tutti molto contenti che Claudia fosse con noi questa volta!
Claudia non sa molto di moda e stile, quindi Alfredo l'ha aiutata a scegliere cosa indossare e come truccarsi. Dopo questa trasformazione, Claudia sembrava bellissima, sembrava davvero una star di Hollywood.
Quando siamo andati alla festa c'era molta gente, era piena di giovani e meno giovani. Tutti erano venuti perché un DJ molto famoso era stato invitato a suonare alla festa.

La musica era molto buona e l'atmosfera era rilassata. Sentivamo tutti che venire alla festa era stata un'ottima decisione. I ragazzi e io abbiamo deciso di andare a ballare, ma Claudia non voleva. Claudia è così timida! Non le piace ballare e lei rimase seduta a bere qualcosa mentre noi siamo andati a ballare.

Dopo poco più di un'ora ci siamo stancati di ballare e siamo tornati dove avevamo lasciato Claudia, ma non siamo riusciti a trovarla. Dov'era la nostra amica? Eravamo molto spaventati e temevamo il peggio. L'abbiamo chiamata molte volte ma non ha risposto al telefono. Avevamo molta paura che le fosse successo qualcosa. Abbiamo cercato Claudia tra la folla e chiesto a molte persone se avevano visto una come lei, ma nessuno ci ha dato informazioni utili e non siamo riusciti a trovarla.

Dopo un paio d'ore la festa finì e la gente iniziò a tornare a casa. C'era già pochissima gente e poi l'abbiamo vista: Claudia era con un ragazzo, lo baciava! È stato un grande sollievo e allo stesso tempo una grande sorpresa vedere la nostra timida amica così affettuosa con uno sconosciuto.

Dopo averci visto, Claudia si è scusata per non aver risposto al telefono perché la musica della festa era così alta che non l'ha sentita. L'unica cosa che contava per noi era avere la nostra amica sana e salva.

Più tardi, Claudia e il suo nuovo amico si sono scambiati i numeri di telefono e si sono salutati con un bacio. Mentre tornavamo al nostro appartamento, Claudia ci ha raccontato del suo nuovo amico Louis.

Quella sera, quando l'abbiamo lasciata per andare a ballare, Louis è venuto a salutare Claudia e ha iniziato a parlarle. Nonostante la timidezza di Claudia, a poco a poco sono diventati amici e più che amici.

Louis è un ragazzo alto e molto attraente, ha ventiquattro anni ed è francese, ma è in vacanza in Italia, è anche un bravissimo poeta che ha vinto concorsi di poesia nel suo paese.

Il giorno successivo abbiamo deciso di andare a San Marino che è poco distante da Rimini. San Marino è un paese indipendente completamente circondato dall'Italia, è uno dei paesi più piccoli del mondo. Quella mattina abbiamo preso un autobus e in circa un'ora siamo arrivati.

La Città di San Marino è piena di antichi edifici, ristoranti e negozi per i turisti, oltre a diversi musei, e offre splendide viste sulle città e sulla campagna circostanti.

Ci sono pochissime auto a San Marino e le strade sembrano molto medievali, come se il tempo non fosse passato qui. Una delle cose che ci è piaciuta di più sono state le mura della città che puoi scalare e percorrerla in alcuni punti.

Abbiamo trascorso oltre due ore esplorando San Marino e girovagando per i suoi affascinanti vicoli. Ci siamo fermati a bere un caffè quando improvvisamente Samuele si è accorto che Claudia non era con noi. Claudia si era persa di nuovo?

Non di nuovo! L'abbiamo cercata ma non era da nessuna parte. Poi l'abbiamo cercata in un piccolo giardino e finalmente l'abbiamo trovata, era sotto un albero con Louis. Spiegò che Louis era venuto a cercarla per uscire quella sera a un bar a Rimini.

Chi l'avrebbe mai detto? La nostra timida amica ha trovato il suo primo amore estivo in questa vacanza e ha trascorso il resto dei giorni con lui.

Alla fine della settimana Louis doveva partire per Parigi e noi per Roma, così Claudia e Louis si salutarono, promettendo che l'anno prossimo si sarebbero incontrati di nuovo qui.

Non so se Louis e Claudia manterranno la loro promessa di rivedersi a Rimini il prossimo anno. Chi lo sa? Sarà più di un amore estivo?

Non lo so, ma Samuele, Alfredo e io andremo probabilmente da qualche altra parte la prossima vacanza. Ci sono così tanti posti interessanti da scoprire!

Il quindicesimo compleanno della mia migliore amica

Mi chiamo Martina, ho quindici anni e vivo a Milano. Vivo con mio padre, mia madre e mio fratellino di dieci anni.

Abbiamo anche un piccolo cane di nome Cesare e due canarini in gabbia. Mi piace sentirli cantare la mattina!

I miei genitori sono venuti dal Messico quando erano bambini piccoli e la nostra famiglia mantiene ancora vive molte delle tradizioni del nostro background messicano.

Come ho detto all'inizio, ho quindici anni, questa è un'età molto importante nella cultura messicana.

In Messico, quando una ragazza compie quindici anni, si celebra una grande festa. Questa festa di compleanno si chiama "quinceañera" che in spagnolo significa "ragazza di quindici anni".

La festa inizia con l'arrivo della quinceañera, che indossa un abito realizzato appositamente per l'occasione, di solito un disegno ispirato agli abiti usati nelle danze antiche europee.

L'idea è che in questo giorno speciale ogni ragazza dovrebbe avere la fantasia di sembrare e sentirsi una bellissima principessa.

I festeggiamenti iniziano con l'ingresso della ragazza accompagnata dalla musica e dagli applausi degli invitati. Poi inizia il valzer, in cui la ragazza balla prima con il padre e poi con parenti e amici. Naturalmente c'è anche un grande banchetto in cui si fanno brindisi in onore della "quinceañera".

La "quinceañera" è senza dubbio una festa indimenticabile per ogni ragazza.

Qualche mese fa ho avuto la mia quinceañera, tuttavia non voglio parlarvi della mia festa, ma della quinceañera della mia migliore amica Beatrice che è stata lo scorso fine settimana.

Io e Beatrice siamo compagni di classe e stiamo sempre insieme, andiamo molto d'accordo.

Volevo avere un bell'aspetto per la quinceañera della mia amica, quindi il giorno prima ero andata al centro commerciale a comprare un vestito nuovo da indossare alla festa.

Quel giorno mi sono alzata molto presto per andare a comprare un vestito e degli accessori. Ero accompagnata da mia madre, lei va sempre a fare spese con me. C'erano così tanti bei vestiti di tutti i colori, era molto difficile sceglierne uno.

Alla fine, dopo aver passato ore nel camerino, la mia scelta è stata un vestito rosso. Il rosso è il mio colore preferito e il design del vestito era molto moderno ed elegante. Tuttavia, c'era un piccolo problema: l'abito era molto, molto stretto.

Mia madre mi ha consigliato di scegliere un vestito un po' più comodo in modo che potessi godermi di più la festa, ma ho pensato che fosse un'occasione speciale e che valesse la pena essere un po' a disagio per avere un bell'aspetto.

Più tardi, sono andata al negozio di scarpe e ho comprato dei tacchi rossi che stavano perfettamente con il mio vestito. Alla fine sono andata in gioielleria e ho comprato un paio di orecchini e una collana d'argento. Era tutto molto bello!
Il giorno dopo, poco prima della quinceañera della mia amica, sono andata al salone di bellezza. Là mi hanno truccato, mi hanno dipinto le unghie e mi hanno pettinato i capelli. Quando ho finito mi sono guardata allo specchio e penso di non essere mai stata così bella prima.

Quando Beatrice fece il suo ingresso nella sua quinceañera, tutti furono colpiti da quanto fosse carina. Indossava un abito di pizzo rosa, sembrava una vera principessa.

Tutto è andato alla perfezione e abbiamo iniziato a cenare. Il cibo era delizioso! C'erano salmone alla griglia e aragosta ripiena. Amo il pesce e i frutti di mare, quindi ho mangiato molto. Dopo cena era ora di ballare.

Mi sentivo molto bene con il mio vestito rosso, ma siccome avevo mangiato tanto e il vestito era molto stretto, ora mi sentivo molto a disagio.

Non riuscivo quasi a respirare, ma non mi importava perché Daniele, il ragazzo più bello della scuola, mi aveva invitato a ballare. Dan è molto alto, intelligente e un ottimo giocatore di tennis. È il ragazzo perfetto!

La verità è che riuscivo a malapena a muovermi, ma ero così entusiasta di ballare con il ragazzo che mi piaceva che ho fatto del mio meglio per sembrare naturale.

Era orribile perché Daniele voleva ballare e io sembravo una mummia nonostante i miei sforzi per ballare normalmente.

Poi è successa la cosa peggiore che poteva accadere: la cerniera del mio vestito si è rotta. Una scena dell'orrore!

Ho dovuto smettere di ballare e sono andata a sedermi rossa come un pomodoro. Poi ho salutato velocemente Daniele e Beatrice e ho lasciato la festa in taxi.

Sono uscita molto imbarazzata con il mio vestito rosso strappato. La quinceañera di Beatrice è finita per essere un'esperienza orribile per me, quando sono tornata a casa ho chiuso la porta della mia camera da letto e ho pianto molto.

Anche il giorno dopo mi sentivo molto male, ma poi ho parlato di quello che mi era successo con mia madre e mi sono sentito un po' meglio.

Questo è successo lo scorso fine settimana, da allora sono stata a casa sperando che tutti abbiano dimenticato quello che è successo. È così imbarazzante! Non credo di essere mai stata così imbarazzata prima.

Ma almeno tutto questo mi ha aiutato a imparare due cose: primo, ascoltare il consiglio di mia madre e, secondo, non comprare mai più un vestito troppo stretto, per quanto bello.

La famiglia cresce

Mi chiamo Francesco, ho trent'anni e vivo con mia moglie Julia, ventinovenne, a Napoli, in Italia.

Sono italiano, ma mia moglie è francese, è venuta a Napoli con la sua famiglia quando aveva quattordici anni.

Nonostante abbia vissuto in Italia per molti anni, ha ancora un po' di accento francese, che mi piace molto.

Julia e io ci siamo conosciuti alla festa di compleanno di un amico comune tre anni fa. Fu amore a prima vista! Dal primo momento in cui abbiamo parlato non abbiamo smesso di vederci.

Julia è molto bella, ha i capelli scuri, la pelle chiara ed è di media statura. I suoi occhi sono grandi e marroni e ha un sorriso perfetto.

Per me è la donna più bella del mondo. Inoltre, è molto affascinante e ha un grande senso dell'umorismo e intelligenza.

Dopo alcuni mesi di appuntamenti e di conoscerci, abbiamo deciso di sposarci.
Le nostre famiglie dicevano che era troppo presto per sposarsi e che avremmo dovuto aspettare un po', ma eravamo sicuri che volevamo passare il resto della nostra vita insieme.

Non abbiamo visto alcun motivo per rimandare il nostro matrimonio. Ci siamo sposati due anni fa in una bellissima e grande festa. Abbiamo avuto più di cento ospiti e una cena lussuosa e indimenticabile che ricorderemo per sempre.

Ma la cosa più incredibile è stato l'abito da sposa di Julia, molto moderno ed elegante, creato da uno stilista francese.

Viviamo insieme da due anni ormai e non potremmo essere più felici. Abbiamo gusti e interessi molto diversi, ma ci amiamo così tanto che non importa.

A Julia piace andare a ballare e cantare al karaoke, ma quello che ama di più è lo shopping. Julia ama essere alla moda e vestirsi bene.

Andiamo al centro commerciale ogni fine settimana e lei compra sempre un nuovo vestito o gioielli, sa molto di stile e mi aiuta a scegliere le mie cravatte e le mie camicie perché non capisco molto di quelle cose.

Preferisco invece passare il mio tempo a fare escursioni in montagna o in spiaggia.

Julia lavora come segretaria in un'importante azienda nel centro di Napoli e io sono un'insegnante di biologia in una scuola alla periferia della città.

Mi piace molto il mio lavoro perché sono appassionato di scienza e mi piace molto insegnare ai miei studenti.

A volte non studiano molto, ma con un piccolo sforzo è possibile renderli interessati all'apprendimento.

La scorsa domenica Julia si è svegliata molto malata, ha avuto un fortissimo mal di testa tutto il giorno e non riusciva a dormire la notte. Ero molto preoccupato per la sua salute e il giorno dopo sono andato con lei in ospedale in modo che un medico la visitasse.

L'ospedale più vicino è a un'ora di macchina, quindi mentre eravamo in viaggio abbiamo ascoltato un intero album del nostro cantante preferito, il canadese Michael Bublé.

C'erano molti pazienti in ospedale e abbiamo dovuto aspettare due ore prima che un dottore vedesse Julia. Dopo aver esaminato Julia, il medico ha detto: "Congratulazioni, sarete genitori".

Non ci potevo credere. Questa notizia è stata del tutto inaspettata, ma siamo stati molto felici di ricevere questa buona notizia.

Abbiamo passato il viaggio di ritorno a casa chiedendoci quale nome dare al bambino. È stato molto difficile raggiungere un accordo ma alla fine abbiamo deciso che lo chiameremo Tommaso se è un maschio e Greta se è una ragazza.

Quando siamo tornati a casa abbiamo cenato e abbiamo iniziato a programmare i cambiamenti che faremo nella nostra casa per accogliere il nuovo membro della famiglia.

La nostra casa non è molto grande ma è molto carina. La casa è su due piani, al primo piano c'è un soggiorno, una sala da pranzo e la cucina.

Al secondo piano c'è il bagno e ci sono due camere da letto, io e Julia dormiamo in quella più grande e nella più piccola ora c'è una scrivania e un computer, ma quando nascerà il bambino questa piccola stanza sarà la camera da letto.

Abbiamo deciso di aspettare per sapere se il bebè sarà un maschio o una femmina per iniziare a fare i cambiamenti in camera e acquistare la culla e gli indumenti per neonati.

Ieri siamo tornati dal dottore e abbiamo avuto un'altra grande sorpresa. Saranno gemelli! Non potevamo crederci, la nostra famiglia raddoppierà tra pochi mesi, forse è una buona idea trasferirsi in una casa più grande, con più spazio per far giocare i bambini.

Bisognerà anche comprare due lettini e raddoppiare i vestiti, ora sono due piccole creature!

Trovare l'amore a Cefalù?

Alessandra è una donna americana di ventotto anni, vive a New York, ma la sua famiglia è italiana e le sue radici italiane sono una parte innegabile della sua vita.

Tuttavia, non ci ha mai pensato molto, tranne quando alcuni amici le hanno chiesto dell'origine della sua famiglia.

Alessandra aveva vissuto solo i primi due anni della sua vita in Italia. La sua infanzia e adolescenza sono state trascorse a New York. È sempre stata una bravissima studentessa, la migliore della sua classe, e quando ha deciso cosa fare in futuro, ha deciso di studiare diritto.

Dato che era molto concentrata sui suoi studi, non usciva molto o aveva molti amici, ma i suoi sforzi sono stati ripagati e durante gli studi ha ottenuto ottimi voti.

Negli anni Alessandra è diventata un eccellente avvocato e ora lavora in uno studio legale a Manhattan.

Il lavoro di Alessandra è molto impegnativo e stimolante. Ogni giorno si alza molto presto per andare a lavorare. Inizia ogni giornata con una doccia fredda e musica rock.

La sua colazione consiste in toast con uova strapazzate con caffè e succo d'arancia. Dopo colazione si veste e prende la metro per andare al lavoro.

Alle cinque del pomeriggio finisce il lavoro e torna a casa. Di solito cena a casa da sola o con un amico. Nei fine settimana le piace fare jogging a Central Park la mattina e nel pomeriggio andare al cinema o visitare un museo con gli amici.

La sua vita è un po' routine, ma ama quanto sia impegnativo il suo lavoro e essere d'aiuto ai suoi clienti, e lo stipendio è molto buono.

Una domenica pomeriggio, dopo aver fatto un po' di shopping, Alessandra ha ricevuto una telefonata inaspettata da qualcuno che non vedeva da molto tempo, era sua zia Vittoria.

La zia Vittoria era tornata a vivere in Italia qualche anno fa e da allora non si erano parlati più di un paio di volte al telefono. Zia Vittoria ha invitato Alessandra a trascorrere le vacanze nella sua casa di Cefalù.

Alessandra ha accettato immediatamente l'invito. Come poteva rifiutare? Non vedeva sua zia Vittoria da molti anni e non era mai stata a Cefalù.

Così, dopo alcune settimane, fece domanda per una vacanza, fece i bagagli e prese un volo per la città siciliana. Zia Vittoria l'ha accolta con un grande abbraccio e una grande festa di cibo siciliano.

Nonostante il tempo trascorso senza vedere sua zia, Alessandra si è sentita subito a casa.

Zia Vittoria viveva con il suo compagno Michelangelo in un bellissimo appartamento con vista sul mare. Le spiagge paradisiache di Cefalù sembrano fatte per essere da cartolina.

Le acque turchesi e la bellezza della sua antica architettura ne fanno una meta privilegiata per chi ama il mare e una vacanza rilassante.

A Cefalù puoi trovare tutto per rilassarti e goderti un piacevole soggiorno.

Oltre alle spiagge paradisiache e gli edifici storici, ci sono molti piccoli negozi per tutte le tasche e per tutti i gusti.

Inoltre, la notte a Cefalù è molto attiva, l'effervescente vita notturna ha un'atmosfera festosa che non finisce fino al sorgere del sole.

Ma ciò che Alessandra ha trovato più interessante a Cefalù non sono state le spiagge o lo shopping, ma le affascinanti rovine che si trovano nelle vicinanze di Cefalù.
Alessandra è sempre stata interessata all'archeologia e all'architettura dei tempi antichi.

Alessandra è andata a visitare molte rovine greche e romane vicino a Cefalù che ha trovato molto interessanti, ma il suo ricordo più bello è stata la visita al Tempio di Diana.

Il "Tempio di Diana" è un famoso monumento megalitico dei tempi antichi, più antico dei Greci e dei Romani! Quindi è molto, molto vecchio. Si trova in una pianura sul lato ovest della 'Rocca', la bellissima montagna di Cefalù.

Nei pressi del tempio ci sono ruderi di mura difensive costruite nel corso dei secoli, oltre a ruderi di altri piccoli edifici. Alessandra ha passato ore a girovagare per il Tempio e dintorni.

E' anche presente una cisterna posta su un fondale profondo, che ospita una piccola pozza d'acqua utilizzata fin dall'antichità per immagazzinare l'acqua. A causa della presenza di questa piccola pozza d'acqua, gli archeologi ritengono che il tempio fosse legato al culto dell'acqua.

Fu mentre Alessandra scattava alcune fotografie di questo bellissimo posto che accadde l'evento più importante del suo viaggio in Sicilia.

Un uomo le ha chiesto se poteva farle una foto e lei l'ha fatto. Poi hanno iniziato a parlare e conoscersi.

Si chiamava Pietro ed era un medico americano che viveva anche a New York ed era in vacanza in Italia. Era molto alto e aveva capelli biondi e occhi azzurri.

Alessandra lo trovò molto attraente e gli diede il suo numero di telefono. Il giorno dopo, di ritorno a Cefalù, si sono dati appuntamento in un lussuoso ristorante.

L'appuntamento è stato molto romantico, il ristorante aveva un'ottima atmosfera e una gastronomia molto sofisticata. Hanno bevuto vino e mangiato aragoste e ostriche.

Dopo cena sono andati a fare una passeggiata lungo la spiaggia di Cefalù. Cosa potrebbe esserci di meglio di questo appuntamento con Pietro?

Alessandra aveva iniziato ad emozionarsi e immaginava come sarebbe stato continuare a uscire con Pietro a New York, forse lui poteva essere il suo ragazzo e poi chi lo sa? Forse vivere insieme, ma presto le sue illusioni si sarebbero scontrate con la realtà.

Mentre camminavano lungo la spiaggia, Pietro le disse che era sposato. Questo è stato un duro colpo per la povera Alessandra.

Diventò molto triste, ma finse di non preoccuparsene in modo che Pietro non notasse la sua delusione.

Il giorno dopo Pietro la chiamò di nuovo per chiederle di uscire, ma Alessandra non accettò e si scusò dicendo che aveva già un appuntamento.

Le erano rimasti solo un paio di giorni di vacanza a Cefalù, quindi Alessandra ha deciso di trascorrere gli ultimi giorni con sua zia Vittoria.

Era stato bello avere l'illusione di aver trovato un ragazzo così bello in un posto così affascinante, ma Alessandra rifletté che c'erano molti pesci nel mare e non aveva senso lamentarsi di una delusione in amore.

Tra un paio di giorni sarebbe tornata a casa e avrebbe iniziato una nuova vita, chissà se l'amore della sua vita l'aspettava dietro l'angolo?

Alberto o Giacomo?

Ciao Piera! Come stai? Sto molto bene, come sai, sono arrivata a Firenze sei mesi fa e amo la città.

Sai quanto amo l'arte e qui ci sono tanti bei capolavori, dal David di Michelangelo alla Primavera di Boticelli, è impossibile annoiarsi. È anche un luogo eccellente per gli amanti del gelato.

Ci sono così tante gelaterie a Firenze, puoi trascorrere settimane assaggiando tutto il delizioso gelato qui. E sai quanto amo il gelato.

Mi sono divertita molto, e anche il mio nuovo lavoro è interessante e la paga è buona, molto meglio rispetto al mio lavoro precedente. Non posso lamentarmi.

La verità è che ti scrivo per raccontarti cosa mi è successo negli ultimi mesi in relazione alla mia vita sentimentale in modo che tu possa aiutarmi a prendere una decisione.

Da quando eravamo a scuola mi hai sempre dato ottimi consigli quindi mi fido molto della tua opinione. Farò quello che mi dici!
Allora, arrivo subito al punto. Accade così che nelle ultime settimane ho incontrato due ragazzi molto interessanti. Mi piacciono davvero entrambi. Sono molto diversi, ma mi piacciono entrambi. Il problema è che non so quale mi piace di più. Che problema!

Uno si chiama Alberto: molto bello. L'ho conosciuto in un bar, è un musicista, suona la chitarra in un gruppo, scrive poesie e canta. È un grande artista, molto creativo e di talento. Ha viaggiato in tutto il mondo e ha vissuto a Parigi e Barcellona, parla perfettamente spagnolo e francese.

Ha anche gli occhi azzurri e lunghi capelli biondi, mi ricorda molto Kurt Cobain e sai quanto mi piaceva lui. Alberto è sicuramente un sogno, tutto ciò che mi piace in un uomo.

Alberto è fantastico ma, non lo so, a volte sembra un po' indifferente e poco interessato ad avere una relazione seria. Ad esempio, non mi chiama mai, io chiamo sempre.

Inoltre viaggia tutto il tempo con la sua band, quindi non ha molto tempo da passare con me...

Ma in questi mesi abbiamo fatto tante cose insieme: siamo andati a teatro, al cinema, ai concerti, a ballare. Sa anche ballare il tango e sai quanto mi piace ballare!

Dato che Alberto è così creativo, ha composto una canzone per me, l'abbiamo suonata insieme, io al piano e lui alla chitarra, e suona molto bene. Nessuno aveva mai composto una canzone per me, Alberto è così romantico e appassionato, mi fa sentire davvero speciale.
Bene, ora vi parlerò dell'altro mio amico: Giacomo. Giacomo è totalmente diverso da Alberto. In realtà, io e Giacomo in qualche modo siamo simili, perché anche lui è un ingegnere (ha studiato in Inghilterra come me per due anni) ed è molto concentrato sul suo lavoro. È anche piuttosto ambizioso, come me.

Fisicamente, Giacomo non è attraente come Alberto. Nonostante abbia solo trent'anni, è già un po' calvo e poco atletico. Ma ha un bel sorriso e uno straordinario senso dell'umorismo, quando sono con lui rido sempre.
La verità è che mi sono divertita molto con lui. Giacomo ama andare al ristorante e mangiare bene, quasi ogni fine settimana andiamo in un nuovo ristorante.

Abbiamo mangiato di tutto, dal cibo cinese a quello francese. Inoltre mi ha invitato a mangiare a casa sua e ho conosciuto tutta la sua famiglia, sono tutti molto simpatici!

Giacomo è un tesoro, mi chiama tutti i giorni. Qualche giorno fa mi ha detto che è molto innamorato di me. So cosa stai pensando, Alberto non ha detto niente sull'essere innamorato; E se n'è andato anche perché ha un tour di due mesi in Europa.

Penso di conoscere già i consigli che mi darai, dimentica Alberto e inizia una relazione seria con Giacomo. Ma è molto complicato, mi piace molto Alberto.

So che non potrei avere un rapporto stabile con lui, perché viaggia sempre e non sembra essere molto interessato a me, ma i pochi momenti che posso condividere con lui mi sembrano un sogno. Potrebbe essere che io sia innamorata di lui?
Quando Giacomo mi ha detto che mi amava, non gli ho risposto. Non sarebbe onesto dirgli che lo amo anch'io. Penso che potrebbe essere necessario per me trascorrere un po' di tempo da sola a riflettere su quali sono i miei sentimenti e su cosa voglio veramente fare.
Allora, aspetterò la tua risposta in modo che tu mi consigli cosa fare, sei la mia migliore amica e mi fido della tua saggezza e buon giudizio.

Ho scritto così tanto su me stessa! Non dimenticarti di raccontarmi come stanno andando i tuoi studi in Australia e come va la tua vita sentimentale, l'ultima volta mi hai detto che uno dei tuoi compagni di classe ti aveva invitato ad uscire un paio di volte al cinema.

Come è andata a finire? Stanno ancora uscendo insieme? Dimmi tutto, sai quanto mi piace conoscere le storie d'amore dei miei amici. Abbracci,

Chiara

Intervista a Pietro Abrami

Pietro Abrami è un importante attore italiano, ha anche lavorato con grande successo in Australia, negli Stati Uniti e in altre parti del mondo.

Attualmente vive in Costiera Amalfitana con la sua bellissima moglie Anna. In questa intervista impareremo qualcosa in più su questo attore di successo, sulla sua vita personale e sui suoi sogni per il futuro.

Com'è una giornata tipo per Pietro Abrami?

Se non sto lavorando a un film, la mia vita è del tutto normale. Mi alzo presto e faccio colazione. Poi leggo il giornale. A volte con mia moglie andiamo a fare una passeggiata e se c'è il sole nuotiamo un po' sulla spiaggia, è il bello di vivere in Costiera Amalfitana.

Mi piace molto cucinare, quindi di solito passo molto tempo in cucina, ma odio lavare i piatti. Io e mia moglie pranziamo sempre insieme, poi facciamo un pisolino.

La sera tardi di solito andiamo al cinema o andiamo a mangiare in un ristorante. Di tanto in tanto invitiamo i nostri amici a cena.

A cosa stai lavorando attualmente?

Ora mi sto preparando per recitare in un film di fantascienza su un viaggio su Marte. Il mio personaggio è molto interessante, ma preferisco tenerlo segreto. Inoltre, sto lavorando a una soap opera, interpretando il ruolo principale.

Preferiresti lavorare in televisione o al cinema?

Entrambi hanno il loro fascino, ma personalmente preferisco il cinema, perché le questioni sono più complesse e impegnative. Quando ero piccolo volevo fare l'attore televisivo, ma negli ultimi anni ho scoperto che il cinema è la mia passione.

Qual è la cosa più pericolosa che hai fatto nel tuo lavoro di attore?

Ho fatto molte cose pericolose! Una volta in Africa ho dovuto recitare insieme a un leone. All'inizio avevo molta paura, ma poco a poco mi ci sono abituato e poi non ho più avuto paura.

Ho anche recitato sott'acqua in alcune scene e sono stato in un incendio. Ma senza dubbio la parte più impegnativa del lavoro di un attore è passare molte ore a lavorare. Lavoro da 20 ore senza fermarmi!

Che progetti hai per la prossima vacanza?

Con mia moglie viaggeremo in Europa per un mese. Andremo in molti paesi, Francia, Croazia, Svizzera e molti altri. Abbiamo già prenotato hotel e alcuni voli, ci piace pianificare in anticipo ogni cosa che faremo.

Siamo molto entusiasti di questo viaggio, è la prima volta che viaggiamo in Europa insieme, quindi è qualcosa di speciale.

C'è qualcosa nella tua carriera di attore che non hai ancora fatto che ti piacerebbe fare?

Mi piacerebbe recitare in teatro, poiché per tutta la mia carriera mi sono esibito davanti a una telecamera, ma mai per un pubblico dal vivo.

Lo so, è strano che un attore non si sia mai esibito in un teatro, ma è così che sono andate le cose per me, ho iniziato in televisione e poi ho subito iniziato a recitare nei film, quindi non ho mai avuto l'opportunità di esibirmi sul palco.

C'è qualcosa di speciale nell'esibirsi per un pubblico dal vivo e penso che sia necessario per il mio sviluppo professionale e personale.

Sappiamo già che preferisci non parlare in dettaglio della tua vita personale, ma qual è il rapporto che hai con tua moglie?

Beh, come hai detto tu mi piace mantenere la mia vita privata davvero privata. Non sono come quegli attori che traggono vantaggio dall'esporre le loro intimità.

Basti pensare che abbiamo un ottimo rapporto con Anna, con alti e bassi come tutte le coppie, ma siamo uniti da grande amore e impegno per un progetto di vita comune.

Avere figli fa parte di quel progetto?

Certo, è qualcosa di cui abbiamo discusso con Anna, ma al momento con quanto siamo impegnati non mi sembra una buona idea.

Credo che avere figli sia un'enorme responsabilità e vorrei poter dedicare più tempo alla crescita dei miei figli di quanto potrei in questo momento. Il lavoro di un attore può essere molto impegnativo.

Tornando alla tua vita professionale, che consiglio daresti a un attore che sta iniziando la sua carriera?

Per prima cosa è importante istruirsi, prendere lezioni di recitazione e danza. Leggi anche libri di storia del teatro e molti copioni.

Secondo, devi andare a quante più audizioni possibile, non importa quanto piccolo o strano sia il ruolo.

E infine, chiunque desideri una carriera come attore o attrice deve imparare a gestire il rifiuto costante.

Recitare può essere una vita molto dura, poiché c'è molta concorrenza e i ruoli buoni non sono molti, quindi un attore alle prime armi deve avere la forza di non considerare un "no" come un fallimento o un rifiuto personale da parte del direttore del casting, ma come esperienza di apprendimento.

Ricordi di mia nonna

Mia nonna mi ha insegnato tante cose: come cucinare, leggere e scrivere. Ma la cosa più importante che ho imparato da lei e che ha definito il resto della mia vita è come dipingere, è grazie a lei che sono diventata una artista.

Mia nonna si chiamava Micaela come me ed è morta due anni fa, ma la ricordo ogni giorno ad ogni pennellata.

Dipingeva sempre dei quadri ad olio e da piccola passavo ore a guardare la tela bianca trasformarsi gradualmente in un'immagine chiara e riconoscibile mentre in sottofondo suonava la musica preferita di mia nonna: Mozart.

Tutta la mia famiglia è americana, ma mia nonna Micaela era italiana. Come è arrivata negli Stati Uniti questa ragazza italiana?

Per capirlo, devi andare al passato e ricordare la seconda guerra mondiale. Dopo questa guerra molti italiani stavano affrontando terribili difficoltà economiche, tanti di loro emigrarono verso l'America e altre parti del mondo.

Un gran numero di uomini, donne e bambini sono stati costretti a emigrare in altri paesi in cerca di opportunità e di una vita migliore. New York è stata una delle città che hanno accolto un gran numero di italiani.

Quando mia nonna è arrivata in America, aveva otto anni. Accompagnata da suo padre e sua madre, era arrivata dopo un lungo viaggio di trenta giorni in battello a vapore.

Mia nonna mi ha detto che dopo aver passato così tanto tempo a vivere su una nave in mezzo al mare è stato molto emozionante arrivare finalmente a New York e calpestare la terra.

All'inizio, come mi disse, era stato un po' difficile abituarsi al suo nuovo paese, la lingua che le persone parlavano era diversa e alcune cose sulla cultura del paese le sembravano strane, ma a poco a poco si è abituata alla sua nuova paese e, quando è diventata adolescente, non si sentiva più una straniera e parlava un inglese perfetto.

Mia nonna si è sposata giovanissima, a diciassette anni. Tutto è iniziato quando la famiglia si è trasferita in un nuovo quartiere di New York, mio nonno era un vicino di casa che si è innamorato di mia nonna a prima vista, quindi scriveva le sue lettere d'amore che lasciava sotto la porta.

Lei doveva nascondere le lettere in modo che i suoi severi genitori non le trovassero.

Nonostante gli sforzi di mia nonna, un giorno suo padre vide il vicino lasciare una delle lettere e ha letto la lettera. Era furioso! Il vicino stava seducendo sua figlia! A quei tempi i genitori erano molto iperprotettivi con le loro figlie.

Una volta scoperta la storia d'amore, i genitori di mia nonna hanno dato alla giovane coppia due opzioni: interrompere questo scambio di lettere d'amore o sposarsi.

Hanno scelto questa seconda opzione. Devo ringraziarli perché altrimenti non sarei mai nata.

I miei nonni non si sono mai pentiti della loro decisione e vissero felici per decenni fino a quando morirono entrambi nello stesso anno, separati solo da pochi mesi.

È stato poco dopo la nascita del suo primo figlio che mia nonna Rosa ha iniziato a disegnare e dipingere. Aveva cinque figli, a quei tempi era normale avere cinque o più figli.

La seconda di quei bambini era mia madre. Dopo aver fatto le faccende domestiche, mia nonna trascorreva alcune ore del pomeriggio dedicate ai suoi interessi artistici.

Essere madre, casalinga e artista non è stato facile ed è stato solo quando i suoi figli se ne sono andati che ha iniziato a dedicare più tempo alla pittura.

La casa dove vivevano i miei nonni non era molto grande, ma mia nonna è riuscita a dare spazio alla sua creatività.

Quando i suoi figli sono usciti di casa, la cameretta dei bambini è diventata l'atelier di mia nonna. Era una stanza molto luminosa e colorata, piena di vita e c'era sempre musica nell'aria.

Era piena di dipinti di mia nonna e degli oli che usava per dipingere. Aveva anche carboncino, pastelli e acquerelli, ma li usava un po' meno.

Non so quando ha iniziato a dipingere o come l'ha imparata, secondo lei non ha mai avuto un insegnante o un'educazione artistica, anche se considerando quanto bene lo facesse, era un po' difficile da credere.

In ogni caso, diceva sempre di se stessa che era un'artista autodidatta e non aveva imparato da nessuno se non dalle opere di altri artisti, guardando e copiando i grandi maestri.

Amava gli impressionisti francesi, in particolare Monet e Renoir. Anche il cubismo di Picasso e le visioni surrealiste di Dalí. Aveva diversi libri con riproduzioni dei suoi dipinti.

Leggendo questi libri di mia nonna ho imparato molto di storia dell'arte da bambina, tant'è che quando ho iniziato a studiare arte all'università sapevo già praticamente tutto quello che ho studiato al corso di Storia dell'Arte.

Mia nonna mi ha lasciato questi ricordi e molte conoscenze artistiche, ma ha lasciato anche molti dipinti. Ricordo che dipingeva cose in cucina che disponeva in diverse posizioni: un pomodoro, un vaso di succo, delle tazze.

A volte chiedeva a me oa mia madre di sederci per ore e ci dipingeva. Disegnava e dipingeva molto bene qualsiasi cosa, dalla natura morta ai ritratti.

Oggi ho ancora un ritratto che mia nonna fece di me e mia madre, anche il paesaggio di una spiaggia che dipinse durante una delle sue vacanze a Coney Island.

Mia nonna Micaela è il tesoro più prezioso della mia infanzia che ancora oggi conservo nella memoria. E anche se mi manca in ogni momento, sento che mi accompagna ogni giorno con la sua eredità e i suoi insegnamenti.

Sono sicura che se non fosse stato per lei non mi sarei dedicato all'arte, quindi ogni volta che affronto la tela bianca ringrazio mia nonna per essere esistita.

Un intervista di lavoro

Adele uscì dalla vasca e dopo aver avvolto un asciugamano intorno alla vita, si avvicinò allo specchio e si disse:

"Guardati Adele, sei impressionante e il colloquio di lavoro di oggi sarà sicuramente perfetto e otterrai quella posizione, ti adatti perfettamente a quello che stanno cercando".

In realtà, era molto nervosa per questa intervista, ma quelle parole l'hanno aiutata a darle un po' di fiducia in più.

Adele aveva 28 anni e da quando si era laureata in amministrazione aveva lavorato nella stessa azienda con grande successo, tuttavia era disoccupata da sei mesi. Aveva perso il lavoro a causa di un ridimensionamento dell'azienda che era sull'orlo del fallimento.

Adele è uscita dal bagno ed è andata in camera da letto, dove ha scelto i vestiti da indossare, ha optato per qualcosa di semplice e classico, un abito nero molto elegante.

Aveva comprato le scarpe il giorno prima ed erano belle e sofisticate. Guardò l'orologio ed era ora di sbrigarsi: in un'ora aveva il colloquio e da casa sua al luogo dell'appuntamento ci vollero circa 50 minuti di metropolitana.

Tornò in bagno, si lavò i denti e si truccò velocemente e infine il profumo; una fragranza non troppo appariscente. Era un colloquio di lavoro, non un appuntamento!

Dopo aver dato un'ultima occhiata allo specchio, è uscita di casa e ha preso la metropolitana. Non era l'ora di punta, quindi c'era un posto libero e Adele si sedette comodamente.

Per liberarsi dei suoi nervi, ha deciso di ascoltare una meditazione guidata che lei usava per rilassarsi e dormire.

In pochi minuti si sentiva già molto rilassata, lentamente il rilassamento aumentava, il suo respiro diventava più lento e profondo. Lentamente si addormentò, persa in un sonno profondo.

Fu due ore dopo che un impiegato della metropolitana la svegliò. Adele, appena si è svegliata, ha guardato l'orologio, erano le 5 e l'intervista era alle 4!

Cosa fare? Adele guardò il suo telefono e vide che c'era un messaggio: "Signorina Adele, purtroppo e dato che non ha partecipato al colloquio la posizione per la quale stavamo considerando è già stata assegnata ad un'altra persona, per favore non si preoccupi di venire, poiché puntualità e responsabilità sono requisiti necessari per la posizione. "

Adele era molto triste e arrabbiata con se stessa, era troppo tardi per fare qualcosa. Così ha deciso di scendere alla prossima stazione e bere qualcosa.

Questo era uno dei quartieri più ricchi della città. Adele viveva lontano e non veniva mai qui, quindi sembrava una buona opportunità per distrarsi dalla brutta situazione che stava attraversando.

Una volta fuori, è andata in un bar vicino all'uscita della metropolitana e ha ordinato un whisky con ghiaccio. L'atmosfera era molto piacevole, c'era un'illuminazione calda che metteva in risalto la ricca trama dei mobili in pelle e mogano.

Si rimproverava ancora di aver preso la cattiva decisione di ascoltare quella meditazione guidata in un momento come quello, ma a poco a poco il whisky diminuì la sua preoccupazione.

A pochi passi, al bar, c'era un uomo che la fissava da diversi minuti. Adele si sentì un po' spaventata perché il suo sguardo era molto persistente.

Cosa vorrebbe quest'uomo? Sarebbe interessato a lei? Era qualcuno che aveva incontrato prima ma non ricordava? Molte domande e ipotesi le riempirono la mente.

Alla fine, l'uomo le si avvicinò e si sedette accanto a lei. Indossava un abito di ottima qualità senza cravatta, un orologio Rolex e un profumo che Adele non riusciva a identificare ma era senza dubbio molto costoso.

-Scusatemi signorina- disse l'uomo- mi chiamo Martin Roberts e sono un direttore del casting per una compagnia cinematografica. Sei un'attrice?
- Io, un'attrice? Haha, no, lavoro nell'amministrazione - ha risposto Adele.
-Beh, non importa, come ti chiami?
-Adele.

- Piacere di conoscerti Adele. Come dicevo, sono un direttore del casting e stiamo cercando una nuova attrice per un ruolo da protagonista in un film ad alto budget.

È una commedia romantica che sarà girata in diverse località del mondo. Penso che tu, Adele, tu abbia l'aspetto perfetto per il ruolo che stiamo cercando, bella ed elegante, con un tocco di malinconia.

Per quanto riguarda la tua mancanza di esperienza, quello è secondario, con qualche mese nella nostra talent academy sarà sufficiente. Saresti interessata a questa opportunità?

Adele è rimasta senza parole, ha riso e poi ha detto di sì con grande entusiasmo. Martin Roberts le ha dato il suo biglietto da visita e hanno fissato un appuntamento per fare un test della telecamera in studio il giorno successivo.

Quando Martin Roberts ha detto addio, Adele ha bevuto un altro whisky per festeggiare e ha preso la metropolitana per tornare a casa.

Sulla via del ritorno pensò che se quel pomeriggio non si fosse addormentata e se non si fosse persa il colloquio di lavoro, non sarebbe mai stata in quel bar per farsi scoprire da quell'uomo.

La vita è pazzesca! Quello che si era detta davanti allo specchio quella mattina era verissimo, ma non nel modo in cui lo immaginava. Chi avrebbe potuto immaginare che oggi, addormentandosi, avrebbe avuto un cambiamento così grande nella sua vita?

Tutto è stato fantastico e incredibile, l'unica certezza è che domani avrebbe mosso i primi passi nella sua nuova carriera. I suoi amici le avevano sempre detto che era molto attraente e aveva una bellezza hollywoodiana, ma non l'aveva mai preso troppo sul serio.

Era stata una giornata troppo interessante ed era già stanca, arrivata a casa si sdraiò nel suo comodo letto con pace e gioia, domani iniziarebbe la sua nuova vita di attrice.

Printed in Great Britain
by Amazon

FRAGMENTED

Pete McHugh

First published in March 2024 by Watermelon Press

Copyright © 2024 by Pete McHugh

This book is a work of fiction and the product of the author's imagination.

However, some of the events described did occur, most of the locations and settings are real, and *elements of some* of the characters are based on real people.

All rights reserved.

No part of this book may be used or reproduced in any form whatsoever without written permission except in the case of brief quotations in critical articles or reviews.

For more information

www.pete-mchugh.com

For Frankie & Norrie

"So we beat on, boats against the current, borne back ceaselessly into the past."

F.S. Fitzgerald, The Great Gatsby

OUT OF THE BLUE

DUBLIN

March 1996

1.

OUT OF THE BLUE, Pops ended his Alzheimer's life. That day, when he couldn't solve even one of the *Simplex* crossword clues, that's when he made his mind up. He couldn't go on, not if he was going to lose his mind. His mind, of all things.

Two months later, the grieving Hogan siblings gathered in the Sandymount family home for one of Joey's legendary Lebanese mezzes. Five chaotic lives, each at crisis point, colliding briefly in the bubbling cauldron of a family meal. Tensions were already on a rolling boil when Joey dropped the bombshell that Christy was splitting up with Maud after thirteen years of marriage and four kids.

'Sorry man, sorry. It just slipped out.' What with the illness, Joey's conversation filter was a bit off these days, but hey, these things are best out in the open. 'It's not as if —'

'Go on, Joey, say it out loud. Tell everyone, off you go,' Christy invited through gritted teeth.

'Cool, cool. You can only bottle things up for so long, especially with . . . you know, us opening all these wine bottles,' Joey giggled, finger twisting his curly, brown hair.

'Funny, Joey. Hilarious. What a fecking comedian.'

'Shit, Christy. That's terrible,' Sam looked across at Maud, who was gulping her wine. 'And Maud, too. Shit.'

'Is this for real? Where has this come from?' Bee placed a consoling hand on Christy's arm.

Head bowed, Christy struggled to muster any energy in his

voice. 'Yeah, well, we've been having some problems for a while. But we don't need you lot running an intervention, alright?'

'Paranoia, man, there's no plans for anything like that. We've enough dirty laundry hanging on the line as it is.' Damien flipped a cigarette through the air, trapped it between his lips, and flicked his Zippo to light it.

'Very theatrical, Damien.'

'Sorry, Christy, I'm just trying to help you and Maud out.' Joey lit a fresh cigarette off the butt that smouldered in his yellowed fingers. 'What more can I say?'

'Maybe nothing,' Christy spat with venom. 'Why not try that for a while?'

'Roger dodger, message received and understood.'

Maud refilled her wine glass and sighed, 'This is all so pathetic.'

'What's so pathetic?'

'You're so pathetic.'

Christy sighed deeply. 'I do love you, Maud, I do.'

'I do, I do, I do. La dee fucking dah.'

'The problem is Maud, these days I really can't stand you.'

Any further talk was smothered by Maud, off on a slurry rant about unreliable men and how in the end, 'they all end up being unfaithful'. Pity, Christy thought, she'd been doing so well, off the drink more than a year, until Pops died, presenting her with the alcoholic's perfect lame excuse to tumble off the wagon, 'just until I get over the shock'. And that was swiftly followed by the sizeable aftershock of her cheating husband going off with some young wan at work.

As Joey and Bee cleared away the dips and pitta and brought on bowls of rice and salads, Christy pushed back from the table and went for a piss in the back garden. He was seething with Joey for mouthing off, but he was also annoyed with himself for allowing the worrying thought into his head: maybe he'd made a very big mistake. Why, now that he finally had the freedom he'd craved for ages, was he feeling crippled by doubt? He would miss the kids something awful: the bedtime stories, the racket around the breakfast table, the pickups from the school bus. And Sadie was becoming more demanding – had recently even said something about starting their own family. It was all happening too fast. For all her faults, Maud was the only one who really got him. During the breakup talk, they'd said the most horrible things to each other, but after he'd felt almost liberated, knowing there was nothing worse left to be said. And a lot of what he'd said wasn't even true. They do say you should never make an important decision when you're grieving.

Soon, the clamour for airtime around the table resumed, each talking over the other, a constant flow of interrupted stories and friendly conversations snatched between heated disputes. In a rare lull, Sam pitched into the haze of cigarette smoke. 'Guys, guys, I've got some news. Shush Damien. Quiet everyone! I've got some big news.' An expectant hush before Sam continued, 'For a change, it's a good news story. Well, actually, Greta and I have some good news.'

'No way, man, you're joking. That's amazing.'

'Oh wow. Oh wow. Greta, as in Greta Newport? Like, this is going to be a UN kids' wedding? There's a first.'

'Isn't it a bit soon? You only met up at that reunion, what? A year ago?'

'One jumps into marriage, one jumps out, eh?'

'Not helpful, Joey.'

'Yeah, well, as the song goes, I didn't know I was looking for love. I sure as hell ain't wasting any more time now that I've found it.' Sam smiled widely, revealing his shiny gold tooth.

'Can someone pass the tabouleh?'

'I knew there was something up. I mean, Sam not dressed head to toe in black? The colourful shirt is clearly Greta's influence.'

Christy caught Maud's eye, clocked her twinkle of amusement, and then looked away, troubled by the thrill of knowing they were both thinking the same thing.

'Well, I pity that poor girl, the poor crathur. Does she have any notion what she has ahead of her?'

'Maud, please. Respect.'

'It's fine. Thanks, everyone,' Sam said, clinking his glass against the raised glasses around the table. 'The wedding is at the end of the year. I'd like you all there, but if it's going to involve thumbscrews, don't bother.' He scooped up a mouthful of tahini-covered kofte. 'And then, more good news, we're moving to the countryside. We're looking for a place in Mayo, somewhere on a lake. The easy life from here on.'

'Sam the fisherman, hanging up his camera.'

Since leaving Dublin aged twenty, Sam had lived a nomadic life, wandering from one shithole warzone to the next, wherever men were fixed on blowing each other up and tearing lives apart. But now he'd had enough. He was ending his harrowing journey through the darkness of human destruction, and though he'd survived, the damage done was deeply embedded. Nowadays, it would be called PTSD; back then, it wasn't called anything much, maybe a bit of combat stress or shellshock. Besides, all photojournalists seemed to be a bit crazy to start with. 'Actually, I've got a gig with Bord Fáilte, photographing landscapes for their brochures, selling the dream to tourists.'

'The west is the best, and Mayo is the best of the west.'

'Man, oh man, there's a lot of moving parts in this plan, Sam.'

'You'll be needing cash then, to buy your pad in Mayo, won't you? Here's the question. Where's that money coming from?'

'Fucks sake, Damien, leave off.'

However, Damien had his point to make, had been waiting for just such an opening. Damien was the oldest, the tallest, and the least interesting of the brothers. In a few years, he would also become the richest Hogan by some distance, a winner-all-right who rode the emerging Celtic Tiger tsunami to its peak, but at this dinner, he was still just a hopeful property speculator with a debt-laden nightclub empire perilously close to the abyss. 'I'm serious people. None of you want to talk about it, the big bad elephant stinking up the room, so I have to be the one to bring it up. What's happening with selling this house?'

'Nothing, Damien. That's what's happening. Nothing.' Bee's fiery blue eyes stared him down. She got up to change the music, with a dismissive, 'It's way too early.'

'Ah, listen, someone back me up here. Surely you can see doing nothing makes no sense.' Damien scanned the faces staring at him. 'Pops is gone, and his will is very clear on the —'

'How do you know what his will says?'

'Are we getting into this now?'

'Don't be stupid, Bee, of course I know what's in his will. We —'

'You're being a gobshite, Damien, just calm down.'

'Don't talk to me like that, please. You're all living in a dream world. Carpe the day, people.'

Maud was unimpressed with the butchered Latin. 'What a fucking eejit, just listen to yourself for a moment.'

'Let's keep it civil, please. Ceasefire declared.' Christy, ever the peacemaker. 'Lower your weapons. We're all family here.'

'That's probably the problem.'

'The family that eats together fights together.'

'Glad we can all agree on something. Damien's the world's worst brother; go on, I can take it. Everyone roll up and hop on board the most fantastical beat-your-brother-up bandwagon.'

'Is anyone even interested in eating this lovely food Joey made?' Bee implored as she passed around the platter of meat and fish. Her painted fingernails were a similar shade of orange as the tint in her buzz cut. The butterfly and bee tattoos on either side of her neck were a nod to her boxing hero, rather than anything to do with her name. 'Or do we all just want to have a big shouting match and then bugger off home.' Her voice faltered. 'It'd be so nice if we could for once have a family meal that didn't descend into a kill fest.'

'What d'ya expect? It's a Hoganfest.'

'Loving this fattoush, man. Katera kwaias, shukran. Bee, could you pass it on.'

'You promised you wouldn't do this, Damien; you promised you wouldn't bring the will up.'

'I'm sorry, but whoopity doo, I don't give a fuck. This is important to me. Me and Pops talked about it many times. He, for one, was very supportive of the business I'm trying to build. He said to me late one night that he was happy to fund me, part of what I need at least.'

'Oh really? What else did he say to you late one night, in the wee hours, when no one else was around? Did he confess to stealing Shergar?'

Joey was enjoying the show and thought he'd toss some more fuel on the fire. 'Newsflash, newsflash. Guess who Damien thinks should be the ringmaster? Go on, guess who? It's going to blow your tiny mind.'

'Shut up, Joey. At least one of us is trying to make some money in this family instead of spending all his hard-earned cash.'

'Fuck you, Damien, you . . . you . . . you're like an anxiety fountain. Aggro comes pouring out every time you open your mouth.'

'You know what, good luck motherfucker. You're going to need it.'

'Actually, I have to agree with Damien,' Sam piped up as he picked at the trails of candlewax dripping onto the table. His eyes twitched in his long, weathered face. 'I could use whatever's due to me.'

'I can't fucking believe this. Now you too, Sam.'

'Easy for you to say. I'm broke, Bee, stone cold broke. How am I ever going to afford —'

'Hey, what is this, a fucking snake pit?' Damien banged his fist down on the table. 'You all want a piece? Here, I'll cut off my fingers, and you can each take one home with you, then maybe you'll leave me alone.'

'Hmmm, that sounds tasty,' Joey said as he moved around the table, refilling everyone's glasses.

'Are we finally going to get an apology, Damien?'

'Fuck you. I'm sorry to be the one. It's just—'

'OK, OK, listen. Can we get back up, guys? Everyone stop talking.' Joey held his hands up, palms facing down. 'That's not backing up Sam; stop with the fucking faces. Enough with this grubby money-grabbing conversation; it's doing my head in. Let's listen to the music. Everybody chill.'

'What, so we're all going to play happy families now?'

Right on cue, the chorus of *Let It Be* kicked in. 'Ha, Pops' favourite.' Christy smiled as he sucked on a cigarette with scabby lips, blistered from chewing.

'Can you believe his funeral playlist – of course, he had to have a Beatles song, but followed by Handel's *Messiah* and *Nearer my God to Thee*? Come on!'

'Typical Pops, all organised, the funeral running order, the playlist, everything precisely written down.'

'Hard to believe he's gone, just like that,' Damien said, clicking his fingers. 'Physically he was never in better shape.'

'Yea but that's not what this illness is about, is it?' Bee said. 'It used to annoy him, people saying, "Ah shur, he's only a bit forgetful, doesn't that happen to the best of us? None of us are getting any younger". He knew this wasn't a normal ageing thing. People focus on the wrong thing, the physical side, because that's all they can see. Just a couple of weeks ago, he came home fuming after playing tennis, saying Jimmy was going on, "By God, you're doing great there PJ, running around the court like a young lad". But that's not the point. The point is that he had lost the ability to count the points. He literally couldn't keep the score in a simple tennis match anymore.'

'At least he wasn't all alone at the end. Fair play to you Bee and Joey.'

A murmur of agreement rippled around the table.

'Gee, thanks Damien. You're all heart.'

'No, seriously, I mean it Bee. And Joey. It's a hell of a thing you guys did.'

'Well, he did also ask you to be there,' Bee replied.

'I know. I'm sorry . . . I . . . I just couldn't do it.'

'To be honest, I'm not sure I could have either,' Christy said, almost a whisper. 'Even if I didn't have the excuse of being in Israel.'

'It's weird,' Sam jerked his head and squinted. 'All the dead bodies I've seen, all those people who've died right in front of me, you'd think I'd be up for it, no bother. But I couldn't have sat there and watch Pops go.'

'It's just us now.'

The room fell silent. Christy took hold of the hands either side of him, and the others joined in, forming a rectangle of linked hands around the table.

'He was . . .' Bee coughed to clear her throat. 'He was so freaked out about losing the ability to make his own decisions. I remember him saying that once that's taken out of your hands, it won't ever come back. Then it's up to some medic to make the calls, and he's going to totally cover his ass and take the safe option, which is to do nothing. Or more likely, lock him up in a home somewhere.' She paused, then continued, a shake in her voice, 'His exact words were, "I'm not prepared to spend any part of my life in a care home. No fucking way is that ever fucking happening to me." That's when I knew, hearing that word come out of Pops' mouth — the career diplomat, the man who never, ever, ever cursed: he was going to take things into his own hands.'

'Good on him. It takes real balls to do what he did.'

'Extraordinary mental strength and willpower is what you mean, I think Joey,' Maud said, as she topped up their glasses.

'Why did the coroner have to record a verdict of suicide? It's so wrong,' Christy said. 'I know that technically it's correct, but there should be a distinction between a young person who's in a terrible place in their life and who kills themselves out of desperation and a sixty-four-year-old man with an incurable illness who's decided his time has come.'

'Are we telling people he took his own life?'

'Of course we are.'

'Absolutely. We have nothing to be ashamed of.'

'He talked a lot about it, about wanting to fly the flag for self-deliverance,' Bee said, tears in her eyes. 'He supported a change in the law allowing a doctor, in specific circumstances obviously, to administer the appropriate drugs like any other medical procedure. That's the premise —'

'That's the catch though, isn't it? What are the specific circumstances?'

'Excuse me. I'm talking Christy. That's the premise behind the assisted dying movement, allow people to end their own life with dignity, at a time of their choosing and with their family around so they can say goodbye properly, without fear of recrimination. That would be the civilised thing.'

'Exactly. I don't think Pops should be bracketed with other tragic cases because it's not a tragedy,' Joey said as he locked eyes with Bee. 'He had a very happy life, and we're all very proud of him.'

'Don't they have that in Switzerland? A place you can go and they put you to sleep?'

'And the Netherlands, haven't they legalised euthanasia?'

'They have. Along with drugs and prostitution.'

'Gerr up ya boy ya.'

'Quiet, gombeen.'

'That wasn't an option for Pops, they don't take foreigners. And they only permit it for people with terminal illnesses. Mental illness doesn't make the grade.'

'Jesus, you make it sound like he failed to get into some exclusive club.'

'Well, you know . . .'

'He was so happy going back on the fags after years of quitting. Free of worry about the damage that smoking would do to him.'

'Hear, hear,' Christy said as he lit a cigarette and passed the pack around.

'It was all part of taking back some control, taking big life decisions again.'

'Yeah, like deciding to kill himself.'

'Shut the fuck up, Damien.'

'At least he's reunited with his beloved again, thank God,' Maud said, looking at the picture of Ma on the wall, smiling down at them, one of the hundreds of photographs Bee had filled the house with to keep Pops' memory active. Ma's family was always plagued by high blood pressure and circulation problems, so Pops had been on constant alert for any stroke symptoms, especially when she was running around pregnant in the scorching Middle East heat. She'd insisted on having summer babies, claiming they were cheerier than those born in winter. All Pops' misdirected vigilance and the killer cancer snuck unnoticed into her pancreas. Taken after a mercifully brief struggle, her body imploded more from the treatment than the illness itself. He'd never loved another after her, never found any woman who came close, who wouldn't sully his lovely memories of Maeve. Unlike the behaviour of his son.

Gathering everyone together for this dinner had been the wrong move; emotions were still too raw, with the family dynamic thrown out of kilter. It was too soon, just as Bee had feared, but Joey wouldn't listen. He went on and on about collective healing and making the most of their limited time with each other. Since they'd lost Pops, everything was so utterly pointless. Lost, what a stupid expression, like she'd misplaced her keys or couldn't find the dog. None of the others had to deal with the racket going on in her head. Death cert, cops' questions, autopsy report, life insurance policies, the will, why was she the one having to deal with all that crap? It was the sort of situation you read about, something that happened to other people. But it was happening to *them*, and it turned out the Hogans didn't have some magic pass, allowing them to skip over this unpleasant part of the story. The family had always worked this way: Bee has her shit together, she knows what's what, she'll sort things out. Well, this time, she was really struggling.

All the things that just eight weeks ago had seemed important, the vital small moments that formed her daily routine – the three meals a day, the bike ride to work, the meeting up with friends, the sparring in the boxing ring – all of it was now irrelevant. It was like a double death; Pops was gone, but her own life had been snuffed out, too. She was trapped in a disorienting, unfamiliar limbo land, warily waiting for a return to some semblance of normality. Their having-your-parents-alive phase was over; it was just the five of them now, and Bee wasn't sure the pruned family tree was strong enough to withstand this much shaking.

The smallest thing sent her into a panic. Only yesterday, an old man with a stick walking the promenade, and she had to park up, stupidly bawling her eyes out. Or when she turned the TV on, and there was University Challenge. Pops used to love watching the sneering Jeremy Paxman asking the questions; one time he was over the moon when he got nine answers right! Or that plastic supermarket bag blowing in the wind, which got stuck on the telegraph pole and flapped noisily, taunting her, reminding her. She was exhausted from the accumulation of sleepless nights. All she wanted was to get a million miles away from these people, these siblings over whom she had never been given a choice. Still. No matter how much she wanted to sever all ties and run away, no matter how tempting they all made that proposition, without getting all Godfather-like, family is family. The bonds between them, forged in the crucible of a UN childhood from those shared formative experiences in the Middle East, were diamond-tough. And UN blue blood coursed through their veins, feeding fierce loyalties and an often cruel love.

Whenever Pops was asked how he'd ended up in a thirty-five-year career tramping across the Middle East, trying to keep the peace between the Israelis and Arabs, he always went back to that day in The Railway Bar, him clearing glasses and emptying ashtrays for loose change. The youngest of seven children, Pops had left school at just thirteen to help his ageing parents with chores around their subsistence farm and to take on whatever odd jobs would earn the family some additional money. In the corner of the pub, three auld fellas, one of whom was the local Garda Superintendent, were nursing pints and chewing the cud. Pops overheard one of the fellas say to the Superintendent: 'Wouldn't that PJ Hogan make a fine Garda? Just look at the height on him.' Pops liked to call it career guidance 1950s style: in those days, you needed to be six-foot-plus to join the Irish police. Between the jigs and the reels, Pops completed his training at the Garda College in Templemore three years later and landed up as a rookie in Donnybrook Garda station, where he spent five uneventful years until historic events halfway across the globe conspired to launch him on a whole new adventure.

In October 1956, a political crisis erupted following Egypt's nationalisation of the Suez Canal, the prime route for oil shipments from the Arabian Gulf to Europe. The Israeli army, ever eager for an opportunity to expand its bootprint, pushed into Egypt, and soon British and French troops were dispatched to re-take the Canal. Following a ceasefire agreement, the United Nations was asked to provide an international peacekeeping force to supervise the withdrawal of all foreign troops. Instead of turning as usual to the big superpowers, the UN asked non-aligned countries to fulfil the mandate. Ireland, a politically neutral country that had only joined the UN the previous year, was one of the first countries approached. Pops was sipping a pint in Ashtons of Donnybrook with his Garda colleagues when he saw the Irish Press advert looking for staff to resource the mission. Preference would be given to English speakers and those with police or other security training. And the starting salary was almost equivalent to that of the Chief of Irish Police.

Within six months, Pops and nine other Guards were boarding a plane to Heathrow and from there onto Tel Aviv; over the following three years, nearly fifty Gardaí joined the UN, each one as untravelled as the other. Pops loved to tell the tale of one of his buddies leaping from his seat as the plane banked to the right on approach to Ben Gurion Airport and roaring at the others to get over to the left side of the plane to prevent it from crashing.

Moving to Dublin from rural Leitrim in the 1950s might have been a huge deal for a young country lad, but going to Israel (the Holy Land, of all places!) was off the scale. Pops would talk of landing in a brown, arid land so unlike the lush green, fertile fields of home. The sting on his face from that scalding heat. Pungent smells from unfamiliar foods. Incessant noise from manic traffic, driving on the right side of the road. Strange faces everywhere, turbaned Arabs and curly-haired orthodox Jews in black garb and fancy hats. And so many towns and villages whose names (Bethlehem, Nazareth, Galilee) were very familiar to a Catholic, Bible-reading boy.

Maeve, whom he'd married just before leaving, joined him four months later when he'd found suitable accommodation in the Sheikh Jarrah neighbourhood of East Jerusalem. The four Hogan children soon followed, each born one year apart, Irish quadruplets. Maeve wasn't one for hanging around when she set her mind to something, and she kept going until she got her daughter. As the children grew up, there were occasional, unintentional reminders of their parents' affection pecking order, which ran in the reverse of their ages: out in front, beloved Bee, tomboyish and unconventional, an independent, adventurous spirit with a zest for life; next, easy-going Christy, who came out of the womb on a wave of laughter and always had a good word to say about everybody; then chilled Sam, taciturn and thoughtful, a restless loner; and finally Damien, self-centred and aloof, conventionally ambitious and constantly striving to please his father. Later on, cousin Joey was thrown into the mix when aged five and an only child, his parents were killed in a car crash. Devastated by the death of his brother, Pops assumed his obligations and adopted Joey, decreeing that, 'A fragmented family comes together in times of need'. Maeve was more sanguine and told everyone, 'Another son, a twin for Christy.' Everyone loved Joey, with his good looks, warm smile, and engaging personality, even if he was a magnet for trouble. Whenever there was a familial drama, Joey was inevitably bouncing around its epicentre, leaving only walk-on parts for everyone else.

A year after Maeve's early death, Pops retired, but he struggled with transitioning from such a stimulating, varied career and never really settled back into Dublin life. Bee had watched with growing horror as his forgetfulness turned into an Alzheimer's diagnosis. For the last year, she'd put her promising boxing career on hold to take care of him and soften his loneliness. As his mind deteriorated, she wasn't really surprised by his decision; they both knew how Alzheimer's would play out. Even still, it was a hell of a shock when he took hold of her hand one evening over supper and said, 'You'll have to help me kill myself, Bee.'

That was how he said it, all matter of fact, stripped of emotion.

And from there, the plan developed.

Over time, having agreed on the desired outcome, they worked through the thorny topic of how to do it. Pops had done his research and discovered that it's actually not so easy to kill yourself. Certainly not if you want to be sure of not screwing it up, of not surviving with some severe impairment, maybe partly paralysed or with even worse brain damage than he already had. He laid it all out for Bee. 'Watching TV and movies, we're brainwashed by the mirage of a fast, painless death. Spy movie baddies are forever popping a cyanide capsule and keeling over dead in five seconds. The actor stuffs his head in an oven or runs a pipe from the car exhaust and turns on the engine. And everything's sorted, hunky dory, end of story. That's a complete fantasy. Total make-believe.'

Bee's head was spinning, so much to take in. The fact that Pops wanted to kill himself. That he wanted her to help him. That they had to run through all these macabre scenarios, picturing her father dying in all these different ways. Or not dying, it turned out, because they're all such ineffective means of killing yourself. That didn't stop Pops talking about it, his bushy Magnum PI moustache bouncing as he spoke, 'Taking bleach or any kind of poison can be a long, horrible death, vomiting and awful pain, from the acid burning the throat and stomach. Hanging might work, but it's a slow death, and unless the rope breaks the neck, I might survive, potentially with an even more messed-up brain.'

'Daddy, please, can you not do this? Just stop with all the gruesome stuff.'

'I know it's difficult for you to listen to all this pet, but I need you to understand that I've looked at all the options, and there's only one that works, without leaving a mess behind for someone to clean up.'

'I really don't want to be thinking about any of this, let alone talking about it. I'm not even sure what I'm supposed to do with all this.'

'Lethal injection is the perfect way to die if —'

'Oh, great, the perfect solution. Can't wait to hear it.'

'Well, perfect in theory, but you must get the mix of chemicals right. You often hear about these executions in America going wrong and the prisoners needing several hits before they die. In any case, there's no way of getting a doctor to administer the meds; not in Ireland, where they'd be liable to themselves. Especially with a mental illness, you're just supposed to tolerate it. It's not a good enough reason to stop living.' He paused briefly. 'I just want you to know I'm not approaching this half-cocked, that I've really thought it through. I read about the whole thing in a book, it's very —'

'A fucking book? You're basing this massive decision, this literally life-and-death decision, on something you read in a book?'

'A book, yes, Bee. A very authoritative book. Many books, in fact. The critical issue is that there mustn't be any hint of another person helping someone to kill themselves; otherwise, that individual is subject to prosecution. Even if there are any suspicions, don't forget you're innocent until proven guilty; it's up to the investigators to find evidence of wrongdoing. And we're not going to leave room for even a scintilla of suspicion. Say nothing. Silence is your best protection.'

Joey had gotten involved by chance, a fillip to Bee who wasn't sure could face it all by herself. When Christy and Maud returned to Israel, after their scouting-a-move-back-to-Ireland-trip ended in a 'forget it', Joey decided to hang around in Dublin for a while. In the following weeks, he spent most of his time with Pops, two lost souls rattling around the three-storey Sandymount house, so many ghosts from happier times. Conversation flowed easily, the pair united by their shared distress at losing control over their lives to a damaged mind, with having their futures dictated by daily medication and a monster list of side effects. It wasn't as if the pills were going to fix anything for either of them. All they did was moderate the symptoms; in Pops' case, possibly give him a few more months of still being able to take a shit without needing help.

Getting struck down so young with Alzheimer's had hit Pops hard, a man of his intellect, with a brain that thrived on stimulation, suddenly having to deal with mental shutdown. Early onset, rapidly turning to severe. Pops hinted at it a few times, things like: 'I'm not going to make it to the end'; another time: 'I'm going to have to do something to end this'. Then one day, he filled Joey in on his plan and asked for his help.

'But you've got years left in you,' Joey pleaded.

'Exactly, and that's what I'm afraid of.' Pops had a way of speaking that drew you in, his voice soft, like you're having a cosy chat around the fireplace. 'Picking the right moment to go is terribly difficult. Too soon and you've given up perfectly good time, when you could still have a reasonable quality of life. But with this heinous disease, this invasive, relentless illness, too late is much worse. We can't sugar coat it, Joey, I'm literally losing my mind. It's disappearing right before us, washing away like names scratched in the sand by the shoreline.'

Ghastly as it had been for Joey and Bee to sit there and watch Pops end his life, there was never any acceptable alternative. No way were they allowing him to die all alone, without a loved one by his side. For practical reasons, their presence ensured it wasn't a botched self-deliverance; they could have intervened if anything went wrong, although Pops had been adamant: helping him in any way opened them up to criminal liability.

Of course, the police had to be involved, to establish for certain that it wasn't a murder, especially as the siblings gained financially from Pops' death. But calling 999 first off and reporting a dead body was tantamount to suggesting a crime had been committed, so they'd agreed the safe play was to call Dr Mason, his GP, to inform him of the death and start the paper trail. After a final scan of the room for anything incriminating and, with a nod to Bee, Joey composed himself and picked up the phone.

No need to give any details, just that they'd found Pops sitting peacefully in his chair, on the coffee table beside him a half-empty whiskey tumbler, with four cigarette butts in the ashtray, and his handwritten note titled "My Final Exit", with the wording the three of them had drafted: he wasn't depressed and this wasn't a spontaneous decision; over time, he had decided to end his life because he couldn't face a life so diminished by Alzheimer's; he was ready to go, and he asked people to accept his decision without anger or unhappiness. The note also detailed the method he had used to kill himself and confirmed that he had acted alone: he had not in any way been persuaded by someone else to take his own life, nor had he been helped by anyone in performing the actions taken. There were instructions for the paramedics in the event he was found in a coma, referring them to the Do Not Resuscitate notice he had lodged with Dr Mason. Alongside, he had left five envelopes, one for each of the children, containing identical letters explaining the reasoning behind his decision and apologising that he couldn't warn them in advance in case they tried to stop him. This last element was typical belt and braces Pops: the three siblings living in Dublin at the time were fully aware of his intentions.

Seated on the sofa opposite Pops, with Bee's hand in his, waiting for the doctor to show up, Joey struggled to calm his shaking body. He rubbed a sleeve across his eyes and sighed deeply.

'Ha, I've only just noticed,' Bee said. 'He got his haircut today.'

'Oh right, yeah, the long hair didn't really work, did it?'

They both smiled, flashing back to the last night's supper, when Pops had tied his hair into a pony-tail and danced around the kitchen, doing his Nana Mouskouri impersonation. He'd been growing it since the day he decided on this course, one final act of rebellion for a man who'd worn short back and sides all his life.

'Do you ever know what life will throw at you?' Bee said.

'Don't you go through an awful lot in a lifetime,' they parroted in harmony, laughing at the memory of Pops' favourite expression.

They hugged briefly, then Bee got up to put the kettle on. Joey leaned back on the sofa and closed his eyes, pondering his own life and how he'd got to here from there. And where was there? At what point had his carefree, easy life shifted tracks?

In retrospect, he could see the fuse was lit that morning thirteen years ago, when the letter from the Dean of English had arrived in the post, even though at the time it really was no big deal. Back then, Joey was in the final year of an English degree at Trinity College, and he'd been earning some useful money from a side hustle writing essays for first- and second-year English students, one hundred punts a pop. But some clown got pulled up and questioned over his unusually erudite submission and expeditiously ratted Joey out. When the Dean's letter arrived, Joey knew the jig was up. Minimum, he'd be suspended, and his finals deferred for a year, but more likely, they'd expel him. Rather than waiting for the university's move, he split before anyone started messing with his options. He was done with university and there was a big world out there to explore. That inauspicious decision, taken with scant consideration, had inexorably altered the course of all their lives, and the consequences reverberated still, unseen and lethal, like fallout from an out-of-control fission reaction.

TAKE IT AS IT COMES

The Doors

LEBANON

March 1984 to June 1985

2.

ALMONDS ROASTING AND LAMB KEBABS SIZZLING on a charcoal brazier filled Joey's nostrils. Exhaust fumes belched from idling cars and rattling lorries. Horns blared, and car stereos pounded, snaring his eardrums. A pack of skeletal dogs barked at passers-by as they scavenged in a rubbish heap. Two street hawkers bellowed from opposite corners of a busy street junction: 'Marlboro, Kent, Rothmans' fighting for customer attention with 'Johnnie Walker, Gordon's, Smirnoff'. From behind his mirrored shades, the scene was yellow and fogged with sweat. Joey strode along rue Makhoul, flip-flops clapping. Ahead, a raucous argument had broken out at a sandbagged militia checkpoint. He turned right onto a side street, which led to a souk. At the entrance, an enterprising vendor rattled off his simple sales pitch: 'Glass for houses, glass for cars'. Business as a glazier in a war zone was obviously brisk, Joey thought as he pushed the shades onto his head, scraping back the jumble of sweaty brown hair.

Inside the souk, a heaving mass of humanity jostled under the corrugated plastic roof. A web of electric cables clung to its underside, powering a network of light bulbs that hung over the stalls. Two wide-hipped women in long, dark galabeyas passed alongside, bum cheeks wobbling like blancmanges. Joey followed in their slipstream until the dense press of bodies bottlenecked outside a stall selling old-style women's underwear and men's pyjamas. A trolley of hessian sacks had tipped over and coated the ground in a layer of flour. Alongside, a tall, officious man barked instructions, but no one seemed persuaded by his route out of the jam. Dodging down an alleyway, Joey overtook a navy-robed woman, arms swinging Spinney's supermarket shopping bags. An olive-skinned man with an eagle-nose in a jowly face called out as he pointed at a tower of sesame seed flatbreads piled high on his handcart. Joey smiled and continued to a street corner coffee shop.

On the way in, he passed a group of old men sitting on plastic chairs, smoking hubbly bubbly and drinking coffee. One of them called out some sort of greeting, and Joey mumbled, 'Ahlen' as he crossed the sticky linoleum to the only available table. From the waiter — quick to introduce himself as Ali and to welcome Joey to his fine country — he ordered a coffee. Despite his limited English, Ali soon had Joey signed up for a *Man'oushe* (explaining that 'it is very popular with all Lebanese for breakfast') and a *Jallab* ('very fresh fruit drink, with very much ice, and on top, nuts and raisins'). Floor-to-ceiling mirrors covered the back wall, giving the interior an illusion of depth. On the wall opposite, a fading poster of a swimsuit-clad Farrah Fawcett grinned toothily. Below her, a bearded youth slammed his hands against the pinball machine and, with a roar, stormed off.

In the sudden quiet, Joey closed his eyes and let his mind wander. Breakfasting in civil war-ravaged Lebanon. Who'd have thought he'd land up here? Until he dropped out of university, Joey did at least have a loose life plan: finish his English degree, maybe get a job as a journalist, maybe write a novel, maybe get into teaching, maybe do some academic research. He'd been into English ever since his secondary school teacher had kindled his imagination and prised his eyes open to the magical prose of Fitzgerald and Waugh, the heady pleasures of Austen, and the poems of Kavanagh, Keats, and Dickinson. Now, he was on a very different track, unfamiliar in so many ways, although it wasn't Joey's first time in Beirut. When the UN Hogans (as they were known within the wider Hogan clan) adopted him, he joined the nomadic family on their travels across the Middle East, until aged twelve he and Christy were sent to the same Irish boarding school as Damien and Sam. After that, time with Ma and Pops was limited to Christmas and summer holidays, when the three brothers (and later Bee) and Joey transited through Heathrow on their way to some exotic, often dangerous, location. As Pops progressed up the UN ranks, he secured increasingly prestigious postings: Transport Officer in Damascus, Head of Security in Cairo and Jerusalem, then his appointment as the head honcho CAO in Beirut for three years until he was shipped off to head up the mission in Pakistan, his current post. As the last one in, Joey often felt like an outsider, although his sense of detachment was tempered with gratitude that he was even part of this strange family. Nonetheless, it would have been reassuring to occasionally hear some loving words from Pops, maybe something like, 'I'm proud of you, son, well done'. That was now even more unlikely after Joey's phone call when he announced over a hissing line from Paris to Rawalpindi that he had packed in university. Pops was quick to cut him loose. 'If you're going to squander all those years of education . . . and you're not going to put the brains that God has given you to good use . . . a decent university degree was the least I could have expected in return . . . and you seem to have no interest in establishing a conventional career . . .' Joey had tuned out as the monologue rambled on.

His hunger sated, Joey left the café, puffing a fourth cigarette in a futile attempt to smoke off the layer of sticky, cardamom-flavoured coffee that lined his throat. Crossing the street, he noticed a portly, bearded man dressed in a sack-cloth tunic and a straw-hat shading gold-rimmed sunglasses on his head. He was sweeping the pavement in front of a makeshift home: latticed metal poles interlaced with palm leaves, and inside was a wood-framed hessian bed and a paraffin stove.

'Good morning, good sir,' Beardy called out in a booming, affected English accent. 'Look! Up there.' He pointed skywards, and their eyes followed a Peregrine falcon as it shifted from hover to plummet and whooshed down to pick off a scuttling rodent. 'Aha, banzai!' the man roared as he held out his hand. 'By the way, my name is Adolf. Please sit, and we will have a coffee.'

Great, another coffee, this time with a loony, bird-spotting street bum. 'Ah, no, thank you, not today. I'm in a hurry, maybe another time.'

'No problem, another time, I am always here,' Adolf said, already back to sweeping butts and spent matches into a neat pile on the pavement.

Joey figured he'd done enough exploring for his first morning and trudged up the hill towards Sam's apartment. At the top, he stopped to take in the view. The Mediterranean Sea was framed by two high-rise buildings and on the horizon a line of ships stuttered across the sweeping arc of Beirut's azure bay. Just yesterday, he'd arrived by ferry into the port of Jounieh after a short crossing from Cyprus, the safest route into Lebanon. From there, bathed in glorious early afternoon sunshine, his fin-tailed Mercedes 200 shared taxi had joined the chaotic coastal route south to Beirut. In the backseat, he was squeezed between a bulky woman in a full-body black dress, with a headscarf covering her entire head save for two dark eyes, and a squat man sweating profusely in a beige safari suit. The Merc belted along, doing over one hundred and forty clicks per hour, scrambling for road position with luridly painted lorries and battered cars, all with the same speed imperative. Off in the distance, a cable car ferried passengers up to the snow-capped mountain peaks, providing a serene backdrop to the turbulent traffic flow. The Sannine Heights was known as the only place you could still find the Lebanese national emblem, cedar trees, that had survived for thousands of years but were now decimated by disease, deforestation, and, of course, the incessant war. As the taxi entered the northern outskirts of the city, Joey was struck by the geographical similarities between Beirut and Dublin: both constrained by mountains on one side and the sea on another, although Beirutis had the better boast: in the morning, they could swim in the Med and then head up the snowy mountain slopes for skiing in the afternoon.

Panting and sweating, hair stuck to the back of his neck, Joey climbed the stairs to Sam's fourth- floor-apartment, downtown in the Hamra district. Like its neighbours, the exterior of the apartment block bore the scars of war, its walls chipped by bullets and pockmarked with shell holes. From the building opposite, dark cavities gaped like empty eye sockets where windows should be, and shredded blue awnings fluttered in the light morning breeze. Joey peeled off his shorts and tee-shirt and took a quick shower. After a Lipton's tea, Sam suggested they visit the scene where it had all kicked off for him, where he took the now famous photographs for the International Herald Tribune that hung on the wall opposite Joey's new bed.

'When I got here, the top five storeys had been blown off and moved maybe twenty feet sideways,' Sam said, pointing straight ahead. The March noon heat wrapped the sweaty black shirt tight as a bandage around his slender torso. 'All that was left was a massive smoking crater and a pile of rubble. Over there is where I took that shot of the paratrooper, crawling through a haze of smoke, a wounded colleague on his back.'

At 6 a.m. on October twenty-third, 1983, in a synchronised attack, two suicide bombers blew up the Drakkar building, which served as the French battalion headquarters, and shortly afterwards, the US Marines' headquarters near the airport. Sam was on the scene within an hour, snapping the photographs he had been destined to take ever since his fifteenth birthday when Maeve raided her rainy-day kitty to buy his first camera. He still had it, a Pentax K1000, 35mm SLR — Sam had reeled off the peculiar sequence of numbers and letters so often that they tripped off Joey's tongue without effort. In his head, he could hear Sam banging on, 'Listen to that cloth blind shutter, still firing after all these years,' as his snapping finger produced that distinctive click-click-pachuum coda to the camera recording a new image for posterity.

Since that birthday, Sam had looked only forward, through his camera lens, into a career that became a vocation, his mission in life. He watched movies about photographers, he devoured books about cameras, he studied coffee-table albums of famous photographs. School was never his thing but with photography, he found something that used different parts of his brain, that only required him to juggle visual images in his head, not crunch numbers into each other or assemble words into sentences. Once he turned sixteen, Sam quit school and worked his way through a series of photography jobs, searching for his angle, once it didn't involve wedding photos, debs' parties, and happy family snaps. He found it in 1979, aged eighteen. For a fortnight after its release, he went to see *Apocalypse Now* every day, dozing through the early story until Martin Sheen nears his journey's end and meets Dennis Hopper's photojournalist character. After that, 'Photojournalism is the life for me' became Sam's mantra. Whereas his friends plastered posters of Liverpool and Leeds, or Led Zeppelin and the Stones, across their bedroom walls, Sam had a huge print of Robert Capa's photo of the falling Spanish Civil War soldier. On the opposite wall, he blue-tacked a similar-sized print of Eddie Adams' snapshot of the handcuffed Vietcong prisoner, a pistol inches from his temple, seconds from execution. These were Sam's heroes, the fearless, driven men who ventured into dangerous warzones to record the unfolding horrors and dispatch the photos home for everyone to see.

'It was total devastation everywhere,' Sam continued, 'like nothing you can ever imagine. Bits of metal shutters ripped off by the force of the explosion and buried in a tree trunk as if someone had thrown them like a hatchet. Ripped-off legs and arms mixed up with building debris and furniture scraps, all scattered in the mud. Horrendous.' He paused and stared at Joey. 'I got some of my best shots that day. You've seen the one of the French army officer, with his war medals pinned to his breast and his head blown apart?'

'Yeah, sure, I remember. Lovely, not.'

Sam looked away to his left, where the wreck of the Drakkar building still stood, a gaping hole in the centre and the wing on one side completely missing. Joey had seen the entire sequence of his brother's photos; every scene suffused with a curtain of smoke so thick it shut out the sun. Moments of black and white action frozen on colour film. Slabs of concrete hanging precariously from the upper floors. Two frames later, those slabs collapsing as the outside walls sheared off the main building, as if sliced by a machete. In the next frame, a huge dust cloud from the fallen debris, and as the cloud cleared over subsequent frames, reminders of human existence: tables, chairs, and filing cabinets pinning dead bodies to the ground.

And then the shot that was syndicated around the world: a French paratrooper stooped over, blood pumping from his head, and in the background, a first-floor room, pristinely preserved, all its furniture neatly arranged. Everything in its right place, while the room next door was a jumble of upturned desks, shattered chairs, shredded carpets, and scraps of paper swirling in the wind.

As he walked across the bomb site, with echoes of the devastation all around, Joey could sense the death still rising from the ashen ground. He was shocked by how real the horror was here, even six months later. It was no longer a well composed series of photos but had come back to life in his imagination, this place of gruesome death where once peacekeeping soldiers from a far-off land had innocently gone about their business. The reality that Beirut was a dangerous place struck him forcibly; here he was plunged deep into a warzone when just last week he was sipping coffee with his aunt on the Champs Élysées. Suddenly, it wasn't so easy to act all cool and who cares. He was glad when Sam suggested they move on.

Down towards the bar and restaurant area of Hamra, the early afternoon sun was burning off the smoke haze that hovered over the city. A pair of cockerels crowed, drowning out the blaring car horns and the muezzin's call to prayer.

Later that night, Joey lay stretched out on the leather sofa, facing the chrome and glass shelving unit that lined an entire wall of Sam's sparsely furnished apartment. In the bedroom there was two single beds and a creaky pine wardrobe, although most of

Sam's clothes were in a heap on the floor. The kitchen was kitted out with all the mod cons, but none looked like they'd seen any recent action. The rest of the apartment was open-plan with sliding French doors leading onto the balcony and randomly scattered Damascus rugs covering the stone-tiled floor. There was a leather camel stool and a wobbly table with four rush-seat chairs at one end of the room; the sitting area at the other end contained the only item of real value in the whole apartment, a top-of-the-range Sony stereo system, into which Sam loaded an AC/DC cassette.

'I tell you, Sammy, snagging this job with Liban à l'Etranger is about the only thing that's worked out for me recently. It's like some sudden, strange alignment of the stars, the gods forming a conspiracy to fix up something good for me.'

Sam sat in the armchair across from Joey and huddled over the fumy paraffin heater, a tumbler of Johnnie Walker cupped in his hand. The nights were still cold, even after a hot day. 'I wouldn't read too much into it, just a bit of good fortune after a run of real bad.'

Aunty Cissie's husband, Loic, had set the whole thing up. After leaving Dublin, Joey was living on the streets of London when Maud chanced upon him one day, hustling outside Hamleys. As she told it, 'I don't know what it was, if it wasn't the holy man himself up above, that made me turn back to take a closer look. And there in front of me was the poor crathur like I'd never seen him before.' During his first week sleeping rough, Joey was unconscious on the hard ground of the Waterloo underpass when someone stole the backpack containing his meagre collection of belongings: some faded photos of the good times in St Jude's, his passport and bank card, his address book and three cassette tapes. Now that she'd found him, Maud wasn't letting him go again, and she dragged Joey home with her. In time, she persuaded him to visit Cissie in Paris to recuperate with his favourite aunt while he figured out what to do next. He and Loic got talking one night about Lebanon and Sam's work there as a photojournalist. Joey had a way with the written word, but he had put limited effort into developing that talent, and its potential had languished until luck, that most powerful of forces, weighed in behind it. Turned out Loic had some useful connections: his grandfather had lived in Beirut back in the days when France still had some political influence over Lebanon. Loic made some phone calls, pulled in a few favours, and next thing, Joey had himself a six-month contract as the guy on the ground for Liban à l'Etranger. Like all the Hogans, Joey was always alive to the opportunity in a problem.

'That's for sure. Cheers to the end of bad shit happening and me now going on a winning streak.' Joey held his whiskey glass aloft. 'Been meaning to ask, what's with the gold tooth?'

'Another of my big finds in Beirut, a good, cheap dentist to sort out my mess of teeth.'

'Looks good, very Goldfinger!' Joey glugged back his whiskey. 'What about a Lebanon history lesson then, headlines only.'

'Ah, right, your primer so you can write all these insightful stories for this magazine I've never heard of?' Sam's scruffy, fair hair, tucked behind his jug ears, had grown longer, and his oval face, tanned and acne-free, had lost the scornful demeanour of his Dublin days.

'Don't be such a fucking snob, Sammy. The magazine's very popular with the Lebanese expat community in France.

'But you're going to have to write in French?'

'Relax, it's all sorted. It was a condition of Loic's. Before he recommended me for the job, he signed me up for a total immersion French language course. I did get an A in the leaving cert, you know.'

'In fairness, you were always good with languages.'

'Before I left, they did all these test articles and said my French was well up to the task. It's not as if they have many alternative candidates.'

'That's for sure.'

'The idea is to cover the war from the perspective of ordinary people, you know, how it affects them day-to-day, their personal stories. Not all that journalistic bullshit recording history as it happens, about this bomb here, that many dead there, this militia group did that. Just the experiences of everyday common people like you and me.'

'Ha, common people like us. That's a laugh.' Sam lit a Marlboro and tossed the pack over to Joey. 'Still can't get over how you blagged this job with no track record in journalism?'

'Well, I did get three-quarters of my English degree completed.' Joey grinned back at him. 'I mean, it's no skin off their nose; they only pay per article, so if I don't deliver, there's no cost to them.'

'A history lesson, then? Okay. Where to start? First, you need to forget about figuring out who all the militias and ethnic groups are. Or which one's in bed with whom or which political party is supposedly in power. Basically, it's a totally fragmented population, broadly divided into Christians, Muslims, and Palestinians, each split into hundreds of factions, and all the factions fight each other nearly all the time.'

'This is Christians in the sense that the Godfather was a Christian.'

'You got it. Then you've got all these big-shot foreign armies who have been coming here for millennia to bring peace.'

'Fighting for peace, like fucking for virginity,' Joey sniggered as he tossed a handful of peanuts into his mouth.

'Exactly. These foreign armies, they roll into town in their tanks and jeeps, overflowing with honourable intentions and noble aspirations. They're greeted by mobs of Lebanese lining the roads and showering them with rice and rose petals — that's the traditional welcome, by the way — because they're so desperate to get rid of whoever it was that last arrived to save them. Lebanon is this great big, fizzing pot of combustible ingredients, churning away until it reaches boiling point and erupts, burning everything that gets in its path.' Sam stubbed out his cigarette and took a sip of Scotch. 'In recent times, we've had the French, the Syrians, even the Israelis got the rice and rose petal treatment when they showed up to boot out the PLO. Then, of course, there's the Americans and our lot, UNIFIL, the United Nations peacekeepers—'

'That's the UN interim force in Lebanon, right? Doesn't interim imply you're not going to hang around for years on end?'

'It's the same with all these' — Sam made rabbit-ear fingers in the air — 'salvation armies. They start out full of optimism, then get bogged down in an unwinnable guerrilla war. They're always humiliated in the end and forced to retreat, creating a vacuum that sucks in the next saviours. What I call the red Leb cycle, circling endlessly from rose petal to bloody nose.'

'Speaking of red Leb,' Joey said, yawning. 'What about the partying?'

A sudden jackhammer rattle of automatic gunfire distracted Sam, and he wandered out to the balcony. Joey joined him as a procession of golden flares flashed across the charcoal sky and exploded, illuminating the empty streets below. 'Whoa, look at that one,' Joey said. 'I thought there was supposed to be a ceasefire.'

Joey was struck again by the proximity of danger in this city. There it was right in front of him, no longer some abstract concept that he read about in the paper or watched on the TV news. It worried him how blasé Sam was about it all, nonchalantly viewing the fireworks show from his balcony, with a drink in his hand. Growing up, Sam had always abhorred any form of violence, never even got into a fight at school. Now people shooting at each other had become a form of evening entertainment for him.

'Ceasefire my ass,' Sam scoffed. 'When a militia calls for a ceasefire, basically what they mean is: Hey, we're running a bit low, so we need some time to go restock our ammo. But don't go away; we'll soon be back. For more mindless, pointless fighting.'

Sam leaned over the railings for a better view and continued, 'Yeah, the partying is good in Beirut; no shortage of weirdos, that's for certain. But I really feel like I'm involved in something here, making a difference. Sometimes, it can be hard to take. You know, like that scene at Drakkar today, reminders of death everywhere.'

'Yeah, I'm a bit freaked out by it all, to be honest.'

'Quite a change from Dublin. You'll get used to it pretty quickly, mark my words. Tell me, what's been happening back home with the sibs?'

Not long ago, they'd all lived together in St Jude's, a five-bedroom semi-detached house in a quiet Dublin suburb. When Christy was accepted for a Law degree in Trinity, he figured that, with few friends in Dublin, his best chance of getting to know people was to get a house share. Neighboured on one side by an aged couple and on the other by two elderly sisters, and colonised in the immediate vicinity by a bevy of home-proud young families, St Jude's reputation as a student party house was already well established by the time Joey moved in. As the one who found the house, Christy got the largest bedroom, on the first floor. Damien had the bedroom next door, and Sam was in the boxroom across the hall, affectionately known as "the Brewery" (it housed the hot press where novice attempts at home brewing occasionally produced a drinkable beverage). Their friend Maud from Limerick, whom they'd known all their lives, slept in the large, converted attic space, a bedroom where both Damien and Joey sometimes took some comfort. Joey was on the ground floor, in a converted garage, pleased to be away from the others and living in a house named after the patron saint of hopeless cases (poetic karma, he called it).

'The big news I have for you is that Christy and Maud just got married a couple of months ago.'

Sam turned towards Joey, his mouth agape. 'No fucking way, how did that come about?'

'Who knows, I was as surprised as you. Seems they got it together soon after I left Dublin.'

'So, they were only going out, what? Barely six months. And then they got married?'

'It was a registry office job. Very hush, hush. No one was invited besides the two witnesses.'

'Something's cooking there for sure. You mustn't forget that Maud grew up on a farm, surrounded by animals mating and birthing like clockwork every year. I guess her own body clock was ticking, and she wanted the gold-ring thing to settle down with a good man who'd give her a posse of wee ones.'

'There ya go, that's the other bit of news. They've just had a baby, a little girl called Kathleen.'

'Why did I not know anything about this?'

'You are stuck out here in the middle of nowhere, Sam, in a country with famously poor lines of communication.'

'I know, but still.' Sam gazed out at the cloudless, now dark sky and fell silent. 'So that makes us both uncles, of course. How weird.'

'Tell me about it. Very fucking weird.'

'Maud was always obsessed with you, Joey. Totally obsessed.'

'Leave off. She certainly never showed any of that sort of interest in Christy.' Joey was distracted by a fresh trail of fiery bullets lighting up the sky. He shook his shoulders and rubbed his arms. 'I'm getting cold, man. Fancy rolling another one? I'll get us some jumpers.'

'Mind the rocks,' Sam called out as Joey stumbled past the row of geranium pots lining the front of the balcony. The gutter outlets were blocked at either end with large rocks to prevent rats from coming up through the drainpipes. Long-tailed rats thrived in Beirut, grown pot-bellied and brazen from feasting on the garbage piles littering the streets.

3.

THE COMMODORE HOTEL SERVED AS A SECOND HOME for many westerners living in Beirut (journalists, diplomats, spies, businessmen), all attracted by the hotel's winning formula of ensuring the bar was always open and fully stocked, no matter what was going on outside. Even in the darkest, most dangerous periods of the Lebanese war, the hotel's generator chugged away, powering not only the lights but the telex machine and the DJ's sound system. Guests could order the finest champagnes, vintage Bordeaux, dry-aged Scottish beef, and premium Cuban cigars. At check-out time, regulars were offered the "Commodore Laundry", a special service that condensed their entire bar bill into the room or dining room bill, maybe even into the actual laundry bill, anywhere once it didn't appear itemised on the guest's expenses statement. Fuad, the hotel manager, also known as Mister Fixit, prided himself on fulfilling each and every guest's request, no matter how obscure. Organising a visa renewal or a new press pass, rewiring a telex line to get a news story out, filling a new spectacles prescription, finding a taxi to take you to the place that no one else was willing to go, nothing was impossible. Further colour was provided by Coco, the hotel's resident parrot, famous for whistling the opening bars of Beethoven's Fifth Symphony and for imitating the hissing sound of an incoming mortar shell.

By the time Joey got there, the bar was busy with the cocktail-hour crowd. He ordered a couple of beers and found a corner table, where Sam joined him soon after.

'God, I need this.' Sam gulped down his Tuborg and signalled for another round. 'Another typical day in Beirut. While you've been arsing around, I spent the day looking down a huge well on the beachfront that's stuffed full of long-dead bodies. Some bird catcher discovered it . . . don't ask; I have no idea how or why he catches birds. Anyhow, this guy was walking along doing his thing when he noticed an obnoxious stench. He tracked it to the well, pulled back the lid, and found a body in police uniform, legs facing up and head missing. Below him in the vault were masses of rotting corpses, bones, and body parts everywhere.'

'Jesus! How can these things go on and yet when you look around, everyday life goes on as normal?'

'Most other places would have died away long ago, but the Lebanese, they just take whatever shit's thrown at them. They get on with it and assume things will get better. Exhibit A, look at this tee-shirt' —Sam pointed at the map of Lebanon sketched across his chest, above it a headline that read *10,452 sq. kms* — 'these tee-shirts were all the rage in 1982 after the Israelis retreated. At that point, the Lebanese government was insisting that all 10,452 square kilometres of its sovereign territory would soon be back under Lebanese control. What a fantasy! That scenario has probably never been less likely.'

A short, bald-headed man appeared with a tray of drinks and placed two Tuborgs on the table as Sam made the introductions. 'The famous Mister Fixit,' Joey said. 'A pleasure to meet you. I gather you run the best hotel in Beirut, although as this is also my first hotel in Beirut, I cannot possibly comment.'

'You are too kind, Mr Joey,' Fuad said with a warm smile. 'Please, search the whole of this city, then come back and tell me if you find a better hotel.'

Fuad wandered off to deposit his drinks at other tables, and Joey continued, 'Hey, you know that guy Adolf? The one who lives in the shack thing on rue Sourati? What's the story with him?'

'I dunno. I try to ignore him, though he's always very talkative.'

'Yeah, I can't quite make him out. He's friendly, but is he just a loony? I'm trying to work him into an article. He's always asking questions, passing on snippets he's heard like it's some kind of trade, an information exchange.' Joey paused, distracted by a noisy group standing near the bar. 'Okay, enough of all the war stuff' — eyes scanning the room — 'Tell me who the hell is that chick?'

'Ah, you noticed her. Lena, Lena Sarkis. She's a local journo with the Associated Press. We get on well; she's great fun.' Lena looked early-twenties and dressed in a chic green trouser suit with a lemon chiffon blouse. Black, glossy hair swung freely about her shoulders. 'That guy on her right, Weiner, he's a big-time drug smuggler; they say he accounts for half the Lebanese hashish that makes its way to Europe. The other guy's a famous journo. Come on, I'll introduce you.'

Before they had made it as far as the group, a hand extended towards Joey, followed by a welcoming voice. 'Hi, I'm Vincent Weiner, you know VW, like the car. And this is my British friend, Frisky.' VW's round face was burrowed with deep lines running from dark, deep-set eyes and his forehead wore a permanently puzzled look. He segued into the story of how his family fled Austria towards the end of World War II and ended up in Lebanon where he'd lived ever since. Joey's attention drifted, and he turned to Lena, smiling as he shook her hand.

'I can see you're new to this country, Joey,' Lena said, her voice rasping but warm. 'You should only shake hands with a woman if you already know she is Christian. If she is Muslim, she would be very insulted. To greet a Muslim woman, you should bring your right hand up and hold it over your left breast like this.' Joey stared at her hand as she continued, 'Luckily I am Christian and am not insulted but happy to meet you.'

From nearby, Sam observed the moves he'd seen work a hundred times before. First the grinning, brandy eyes in the heart-shaped face transfix like a serpent spitting venom to paralyse its prey. Then the head-tilt-to-the-right and the heap of brown curls tumble to his shoulders, as he mumbles some inane comment, sotto voce, a smirk in his seductive voice. While most guys agonise over the best chat-up line, by now, the girl's too distracted to even listen to Joey's words. 'So where do you come from, Lena?'

'A small town in the mountains called Aley, but I left it some time ago.' Lena's bright kohl-rimmed eyes looked at Sam as she said, 'Hey, have you heard the rumours that the Israelis have murdered the Imam Harb? We've been hearing that many Shias are deserting the SLA and joining the resistance.'

'What, you mean, you've heard from leftist sources?' Frisky sneered.

'Ha, as if. What does leftist even mean here in Lebanon?' Weiner said. 'How can you get any more left of what goes on here every day?'

'Joey,' Frisky said, 'you need to understand that in Beirut, there is no such thing as *the* truth, just different versions of it.'

Lena caught Joey staring at her and blushed. 'You see, Joey, this is what happens when journalists get together in Beirut. They swap war stories and rumours and bore everyone else around them.'

'Oh, don't mind me, carry on.'

As evening blurred into night, Joey grew more relaxed with this curious crowd so that by the time they moved onto the Your Father's Moustache nightclub, he was in full flow. Even Frisky, the intellectual, aloof London Times war correspondent, was laughing along to Joey's tales of diplomatic shenanigans from his father's postings (Pops was an amusing raconteur and provided Joey with a rich collection of anecdotes to draw on).

The nightclub was busy, with many people clearly here for the dancing. Joey's eye was drawn to a John Travolta lookalike in white trousers and shiny black shoes, hairy chest sprouting over the top of his blue silk shirt. This guy had learnt all the moves and wanted everyone to see them. Beside him, a circle of girls danced around their handbags, hopping from foot to foot and swinging their bent arms, backwards then forwards with a clap, like chickens stretching their wings. Sam wandered off and returned shortly after with Joumana, an attractively built girl with a cheery face. Joumana was a nurse in the AUB Hospital and a long-time friend of Lena's; they had gone to the same convent school and now lived next to each other on rue Bliss.

'Come on, you Irish boys, come dance,' Joumana called out and pulled Sam onto the dance floor. Lena smiled at Joey, removed her heels, and beckoned to follow her.

Now Lena, she could dance. Her curvy body rippled in time to the music, and her lithe feet hopped across the flashing, coloured squares of the dancefloor. She rolled her arms in a wave motion, fingers spread, head shaking, her face hidden behind a curtain of hair. She caught Joey grinning and smiled back, then looked coyly away. Joumana whispered in her ear, and they giggled, Lena's hand covering her mouth. The music slowed, and Joey grabbed Lena's hands, pulling her musky warmth close.

'So does your father have a moustache?' he joked, spinning Lena around the now nearly deserted dance floor.

Lena laughed, her teeth glowing against rouged lips. 'Incredible, Joey. How could you know that? You must have spies following me.'

'I wish'. He held his hand up and twirled Lena, then held her back at arm's length. 'Do you always move so sexily?'

'Sometimes. If I like the company.'

Just then, a noisy group of young people entered the nightclub and distracted Lena. As the group made their way towards a corner booth, a bearded, muscular man looked over and signalled to her.

'Sorry, I must go, Joey. Nice to meet you,' Lena said and strode off to join the group, grabbing her shoes on the way.

Joey sidled back to the others, where Frisky and Weiner were deep in animated conversation. After a while, Joey rolled his eyes at Sam and nodded towards the exit. Walking the quiet streets towards home, Joey was buzzing. 'Jesus, Sammy, that Lena is gorgeous. I think I could be falling in love. Who was the guy who showed up at the end?'

'No idea, man. Lena has a big circle of friends. Joumana said they were going to give her and Lena a lift home.'

'We could have brought them home.'

'You're unreal man. Just arrived and on the pull already. How many times have I heard you say you're falling in love?

Joey laughed and threw his arm around Sam. 'You know Sammy, I can see myself fitting right into this scene in Beirut.'

'Quite possibly, Joey. Though I don't think Lena is your type. Then again, they always seem to end up being your type.'

4.

FROM THE CLIFF TOP IN RAOUCHE, Joey's eyes followed a pair of skiers as they cut between the Pigeon Rocks and emerged at speed on the other side. Further along the coast, the enclosed sea pool at the Bain Militaire was packed with swimmers enjoying the late April heat. It was one of the pleasures of living in Beirut, these expansive vistas out to the horizon, that appear as you round a corner or climb a hill, a welcome relief from the claustrophobic rows of high-rise blocks jutting skywards from narrow streets. The sea's constant presence was somehow reassuring; the locals joked that it was the only one of Lebanon's neighbours never to have invaded.

Joey was early for his lunch date with Lena, five hundred dollars burning a hole in his pocket. The money from the magazine had finally come through, following the favourable reaction to his first article; 'Send us more of the same,' was the message attached with the payment. To kill time, he wandered into the souk nearby and pottered along, making his way to Yusef's stall, a trestle table covered with pirated cassette tapes. 'Look Joey,' Yusef called out. 'Today's special offer, the new Frankie Goes to Hollywood album.' They talked for a while as Yusef blared the album at high volume. 'This song, listen, effendi, it's called *Two Tribes*. I think maybe they have made this song for us in Lebanon.' Joey laughed and ponied up for the cassette; he'd already worn the tape thin on Lloyd Cole's *Are you ready to be heartbroken?* Yusef's recommendation from last week. The thought reminded him . . . Lena.

By the time he got to the restaurant, Lena was waiting outside and, once they were seated, Joey ordered red snapper with fries for them both and a bottle of Chateau Musar White. Lena's face broke into a radiant smile. 'Your Arabic is impressive, Joey.'

'Why, thank you, habibti. I told you I make a good student.' Encouraged by his stumbling attempts with their neighbour Abu Amar, Joey had signed up for a ten-class programme in the International School to "Learn Arabic like a native", at least that was how the sales blurb put it. 'Tell me, how the hell does Yusef manage to get all the latest music, even before it hits the charts in Europe?'

'Yanni, I have no idea; he would never tell me things like that.'

'You Lebanese are incredible. Sometimes, you could be forgiven for thinking there's no war on here at all.'

Suddenly, a passing car backfired, causing Lena to jump. Joey grabbed her hand and used the opportunity to pry a little. 'Do you mind, could you tell me some of your story? Tell me about the time you were most scared when you really didn't think you'd make it.' Like many Lebanese, Lena was reluctant to revisit past events, so her back story trickled out, a gradual drip feed of fragments for Joey to tessellate into a coherent picture.

'Oh, my God, so many scary times. Which was the worst? It's not easy to say. Maybe the day soon after the Civil War started, Black Saturday it was called, December sixth, 1975. That morning, my parents, two brothers, and I were on our way to Hamra for some Christmas shopping. We were driving towards the ring road when we saw a stream of cars speeding in the opposite direction, flashing their headlights and blowing their horns. My father pulled over to investigate. On the other side of the motorway, where it bends back on itself, we could see a Phalangist checkpoint.

Lena scanned the restaurant, then continued in a slow, quiet voice, 'As we watched, the soldiers grabbed two men and a young boy, eleven, maybe twelve, out of the car and took them below, beneath the overpass. There, they cut their throats, from ear to ear, one after the other. I had never even sen someone die before, and now people were being butchered like animals right before my eyes. My father turned the car around, and we raced off in the other direction, just in time, as we learnt later.'

'Oh my god. That's barbaric. Why would they do that?'

'The day before, four Christians had been found dead, and the Phalangists ordered a retaliation, but tenfold. They wanted to kill forty Muslims in retaliation for the death of their four. They set up roadblocks at the eastern end of the motorway and executed the first forty Muslims to arrive. That was the checkpoint we had seen. Of course, then the Muslim militias had to retaliate for that retaliation, so they set up a copy-cat operation, with their own checkpoint at the other end of the motorway. No one knows how many people were killed that terrible day, but for sure hundreds, maybe as many as five hundred.'

Lena's face was drained of colour, a faraway look in her dark eyes. Although it was all a long time ago, the images were clearly still fresh, singed into her then-innocent, thirteen-year-old mind. Joey wondered how you ever recovered from such an experience. He tried to place the scene in a context that he could identify with: heading into Grafton Street with the clan for some Christmas shopping and coming across a checkpoint where a group of thugs are slitting the throats of whoever shows up first. And not a Guard in sight to stop them. It was literally unimaginable. He moved closer and stroked her hand. 'Sorry, never mind, darling. I shouldn't have asked. Let's talk about something else.'

'No, it's good for you to understand how it all started, this war. You know, we have sixteen officially recognised minority groups in Lebanon. Historically, the Christians, particularly the Maronites, were the top dogs; all but two Lebanese presidents have been Maronites. But by the mid-1970s, the population mix had shifted dramatically, and the Christians came under pressure to share power more evenly with the Muslims and Palestinians.'

'Your family is Maronite, right?'

'Yes,' Lena sighed. 'I sometimes feel ashamed that our people decided to take up arms rather than giving in to demands for power sharing. It was a kind of national suicide as all the old political structures crumbled. We Maronites had the attitude that we built Lebanon, and if someone's going to burn it all down, then it will be us. It is so typical of the Lebanese unwillingness to stop and think, a total refusal to ever compromise. And so, one spark in April 1975 sets off a chain reaction of mindless tit-for-tat atrocities that we are still living with ten years later.'

The relevance of the date only hit Joey then. April 1975 was the same month that the Vietnam war ended with the fall of Saigon. One futile war ends, another begins. He refilled the wine glasses as Lena continued, 'And before even the first year of fighting was over, the Lebanese people were no longer calling the shots. Our country became a killing ground, overrun with foreign powers and militia warlords, all sorts of private armies and neighbourhood gangs.'

'It must be very hard to ever forgive people for all the killings that have gone on. I guess I admire anyone who can do that. Otherwise, an eye for an eye for another eye, and before you know it, everyone's blind.'

'You know, Joey, even still, I love all Lebanese peoples the same, without exception,' Lena said as she brought her bunched fingers up to her mouth, kissed them, and then flicked them open like a blossoming flower. Around her tanned wrist, the gold bangles jingled a coda.

He smiled at the extravagant gesture. 'My cutie, so loving, so wonderful. I want you to have all my babies.'

Lena recoiled in mock horror, then laughed and said, 'It's funny, you get me talking about the war, and I go on and on but mention anything to do with sex' — her husky voice dropped to a whisper — 'and I shut up. You know, for us Lebanese, sex is the opposite of sport. Everyone talks about sport, especially football, but nobody really plays it here. But with sex, it's completely different; everyone is doing it, but nobody talks about it,' she concluded with a decorous smile.

Joey emptied the last of the wine into their glasses. The peak heat of the day had passed, and a mellow contentment came upon him. God, he loved this woman so much. He was filled with pure, raw desire and leaning over said in a lusty whisper, 'Do you fancy a siesta?' Lena dropped her dark eyes coyly, then looked up. 'Mais bien sûr.'

Driving through the Kantari district, they passed a collapsed building that had recently been bombed or shelled. Joey could never tell from the damage which was which. Probably both. Beirutis were used to living in this peculiar half-light between safety and insecurity, where there's just about enough periods of quiet to get on with daily life but never enough to feel confident it won't all end suddenly. Constant reminders of the everyday dangers were everywhere, warnings of how easily you could find yourself in the wrong place at the wrong time in a city where there were so many wrong places all of the time. And, for the first time in a very long time, Joey now had something precious he didn't want to lose. Work was going great, Lebanon was a buzz, and after only a month, he had fallen for Lena. Big time.

Lena offered him something very exciting, the lure of a lifestyle that appealed to his childhood memories of the Middle East, when he was happiest, and life was uncomplicated. She was a real beauty, vivacious and easy company. She made limited demands on him and gave him plenty of room to do his thing. She had a self-sufficiency like he'd never encountered, unlike all those needy women back home. Twenty-three years old and for the first time, he was struck by a new kind of love; could it be connubial? He was trying to think back to a time in his life when he'd felt happier . . . and failing.

'An-Nahar, As-Safir,' roared the newspaper vendor as Joey's Peugeot idled in front of Lena's apartment block. Rue Bliss, mused Joey, how appropriate for Lena's home address, as he leaned forward to peel his sweat-drenched shirt off the sticky leather seat.

Lena appeared in a figure-hugging yellow dress and the usual collection of chunky, rattling jewellery. She smiled, waved at Joey, and click-clacked across the road. Her confidence in his intentions was slowly building, and she had been delighted to hear that his contract with Liban à l'Etranger had been extended for another year.

'Sorry I'm late, habibti. I had to feed the birds and then I couldn't decide which shoes to wear. Do you like the blue?'

'You look gorgeous, my love.' Joey leaned over to kiss her, devouring her musky cologne fragrance. 'And they match perfectly with this,' he said, handing her a shiny lapis lazuli pendant dangling on a silver chain.

'Oh, Joey, it's beautiful,' Lena said and kissed him fully on the lips.

'It's 'cos I love you, baby. Let's hit the trail and get some air into this mobile oven.' He shoved the Peugeot 205 into gear and screeched off, burning rubber in his wake.

All around the traffic was manic as everyone headed for the mountains to escape the stultifying July city heat. It had been a harsh, relentless summer of water shortages, erratic power supplies and closed roads. Tense motorists nudged their cars forward with one fist clenched on the steering wheel, the other hammering on the car horn. By now, Joey had sussed out the Lebanese driving philosophy: keep moving, never let the wheels stop rolling; as soon as there was any danger of coming to a stand-still, the Lebs were up on the pavements, down side alleys, U-turning, lane changing or turning back to find another route. This morning, fuelled by nervousness that the new ceasefire would break and boiled by the sun's sizzle, everyone seemed abnormally frenetic, as they tussled for space on the narrow mountain road. Ahead, a Citroen van collided with a Mercedes sedan but didn't bother to stop. By the side of the road, steam spurted from the bonnet of an overheating lorry. Behind them, two young men in a snarling sports car, soft-top down, nodded their heads in time to national darling Fairouz blasting out *Ya Hawa Beirut* from their car stereo. Finally, the traffic loosened out as the potholed road twisted up the mountainside in a series of hairpins. Sand-filled oil barrels lined the roadside to prevent a fall down the steep slopes. Cicadas hissed from the pine trees, and a sweet pinecone aroma drifted through the open car windows.

'Can't wait to see where you grew up, habibti,' Joey said.

'Yanni, there isn't much left of our home.'

'When do I get to meet your family?'

'Soon, Joey, soon.'

'You're not still worried how they're going to react to you hooking up with some loser Paddy, are you?'

'It's not funny, Joey. My parents are very conventional. You are not the sort of man they had in mind for me. But I make up my own mind on these things.' She smiled and rubbed his hairy thigh. 'Once Papa likes you, the others will follow. And I'm sure you will get on well. He's an intellectual just like you.' She leaned forward and pushed the cassette into the stereo. The slide guitar on *Give Me Love* glided over the acoustic, and they sang along, begging in harmony for some peace in Beirut at least, if not across the globe.

The road into Aley was lined with red-roofed villas that glistened against the rocky mountain slopes. They made their way to Lena's childhood home, a small two-storey villa that stood directly opposite the town hall. Across the road, an old man watched their arrival with interest. His nervous, dark eyes stared out from the blur of white surrounding his head; a white knitted skullcap perched towards the back of his balding head, and a long, fluffy white beard trailed down his chest. Joey parked the Peugeot, and they shuffled hand-in-hand up the path, now overgrown with thorns. Skirting around a pair of ficus trees, they pushed through the gate to the remains of the villa.

'When the shells hit the house, there was dust everywhere,' Lena said when they were inside. 'We couldn't see each other. I could hear coughing and choking for air. That day, all our furniture and belongings, everything, was destroyed. Even the metal bed frames melted from the heat of the explosion.'

They moved towards the back of the villa where the first few steps of the staircase remained, below a hole in the ceiling. 'I remember on the roof up there, my sister and I used to keep pigeons between the oil and the water tanks. We also had two green and yellow parakeets. They were killed that day. Our chickens and rabbits survived, but we let them run away. We didn't want to cage them up again. We left the next day to my uncle who lived further up the mountain in Bhamdoun.' As she spoke, an arrowhead of white pelicans passed across the clear blue sky. Lena's hoarse voice called out, 'Oh Joey, get me out of here. I don't like this place.'

As they made their way back to the car, the old man waved and moved towards them, dragging one foot behind. He was a Druze called Nasseem who had been wounded the day Lena's house was bombed. Two pieces of shrapnel had lodged in his cranium and, as it was too dangerous to extract them, had remained there since. A sizable part of his left leg had also been damaged; at one point, there was a risk it would need to be amputated, but the doctors managed to save it.

Joey stood enthralled as Nasseem continued in stuttering English, 'Yanni, we look different on the outside, but before, the Druze and Christians, we had no problems. We lived happily, side-by-side for many generations, your family and mine. All around here, in Aley and the villages. Together, as brothers, we grew olives and figs, and we had goats in the fields. Now, all the Christians have gone. Too much fighting, God be merciful.'

Back in the car, the young lovers were subdued. The steady chirp of crickets pulsed in the silver birches lining the road. After a while, Joey said, 'I don't know much about the Druze except that they tend to be secretive about their religious practices. But I gather their big thing is reincarnation, which is particularly convenient in Lebanon where living is so precarious. Hey presto, you're back and just start all over again in a new frame of mind.'

'I don't think it works like that, Joey,' Lena snapped. 'Life is unfair and doesn't automatically get better just because you move somewhere different and start up a new life. It's not that simple.'

'No, of course. Sorry. That was stupid of me.'

Try as he might, he couldn't really appreciate what Lena and her family had gone through, creating a new life for themselves in the city after their mountain life was blown up. There was always so much left unsaid with Lena, a wall to her past that she only occasionally allowed him to glance over before pulling back.

As they descended the mountain, Joey's foot glued to the brake pedal, a layer of wispy clouds, rapidly turning to fog, obscured the view back towards Aley. Ahead, they could see Beirut's Legoland of apartment blocks, shimmering in a heat haze, silhouetted against the turquoise Mediterranean. Entering the city's outskirts, the traffic gridlocked; a petrol tanker had rammed a roadside pine tree and doused the road in gasoline. They joined the line of cars snaking around the toppled lorry, wheels mounted for traction on the rocky verge. It was dark by the time they got back to rue Bliss, the daylight prematurely extinguished by a veil of smog that shut out the blood-red sun as it sunk in flames beneath the horizon.

5.

CHRISTY WAS BURSTING WITH EXCITEMENT as the MEA plane from London made its final approach to Beirut Airport. Right up until yesterday, it was touch and go whether he'd get in at all, but suddenly, the shelling stopped, and the airport — accustomed to operating between bouts of fighting — grabbed its chance and quietly reopened. Christy's brain was buzzing with childhood memories of the Middle East, although he could remember little of the family's time in Lebanon. Both he and Sam were born in Beirut, one of Pops' early UN postings. Since then, Christy had only been back once, the summer he finished his Leaving Cert and Pops was back as Beirut CAO. That holiday he fell for the country big time, particularly the people, with their joie-de-vivre and resilience in the face of an escalating civil war. In the intervening five years, the relentless battering of the Lebanese landscape had continued (if anything, conditions had worsened as the rule of law imploded), and he wondered how much of the Beirut he remembered would still exist.

It would certainly be a massive contrast to his life back in lawful London, where he'd left Maud and baby Kathleen; with the twins due in four months, his family life was about to get a lot more complicated, but Maud, fair play, had happily agreed to this two-week trip before all that upheaval. She knew that, for the last two years, there had been a large Joey- and Sam-shaped hole in his life, in both their lives really.

For Christy's first night in Beirut, Joey cooked a chicken curry and as they waited for the food to cook, he dealt with the topic that was front of mind with his two brothers.

'Go on, tell all, Christy. Maud, in the family way when you married, what's that about?' Sam said.

'I know, it's crazy, right? It all happened so quickly. The first time we slept together was the night you left Dublin, Joey. Well, not that much sleeping,' Christy sniggered. 'And then shortly afterwards, Maud found out she was pregnant. There was never any choice; I had to do the decent thing.'

'And Maud got the dependable, faithful husband she always wanted, a good man with a good job and excellent career prospects.' Joey leaned over and topped up their wine glasses. 'And now, here you both are, with a baby girl and twins on the way. Kathleen was my mother's name.'

'Yeah, I know that, but Maud named her after her favourite aunt.'

'Blessed is he amongst women, Christy.'

All this Christy and Maud business felt somehow a bit incestuous; Joey was still getting used to the idea of them having sex at all, let alone there being a big love and marriage thing between them. Love meant different things to different people, but he struggled to see his brother and his new wife anywhere near the Joey and Lena end of the love spectrum. He loved Christy dearly, would have even if they weren't family, but he sure made some strange decisions! Why the hell hadn't they just got rid of the baby? That single decision had sent him down a narrow track to a fun-free life, dominated by rearing kids and slaving to pay off the sizable mortgage on their big house in London. Both still in their mid-twenties and stuck living lives in which so much had been left unexplored.

'And what about you, bro?' Joey continued. 'Is life all you wanted it to be? Are you happy now?'

'You know, I'm grand. Maud wasn't so keen on the move to London, but it's working out well. So how are things with you? Have you found your code to live by? Instead of them ramblings of a has-been rock star who died in his bathtub aged twenty-seven. And him supposedly a lad who specialised in having fun.'

Joey just laughed and said, 'I never take baths now.'

Boy, it was good to be back in the same room with them. Until a year ago, Christy had never been apart from these brothers for any length of time. The last time they'd all been together (it felt like a lifetime ago) was the night of his twenty-first, when Joey was prancing around Dublin, all king of the castle and in his prime. Until his spot of bother in Trinity changed all that and led to him moving halfway across the world to this alien, war-torn place.

28th May 1983 — the portentous day that called a halt to their happy-go-lucky life — started in a pub at lunchtime, like so many others at that time. As founder chairman of the university's Home Brew and Healthfood Society, Joey had convened a meeting for its eight members in O'Neills on Suffolk Street, from where they would begin the hunt for the best pint of Guinness in Dublin. After a suitably liquid route-planning session, Joey led the intrepid researchers (including Christy, whom Joey had invited along as an honorary guest on his birthday) out of the pub and through the snailing mid-afternoon traffic, dodging wiper spray, stick legs pacing out long strides. Whereas all his brothers were tall, the growth gene in Christy went horizontal, leaving him rotund and overweight. He walked with stooped shoulders and the curved look was completed by the John Lennon glasses on his round face.

A young hopeful was busking his way through Neil Young's back catalogue, and his plaintive wail echoed off the church columns opposite. After sampling candidate pints across town, the brothers bailed on the society's pub crawl to meet up with the gang, which had gathered in The Lincoln Inn to celebrate Christy's milestone birthday. By the time they got there, the place was jammers, and a smoky fug hovered over the rolling hubbub of pub chatter. Along the counter, punters called out their orders over the shoulders of the early birds who had secured one of the stools that lined the bar.

Damien was ahead of them, leaning on the bar, arms straight and fingers splayed, his manicured nails displayed like the eyes on a peacock's tail. 'My twist,' he called out, checking his look in the mirror behind the barmen. Damien had the brash arrogance that the offspring of wealthy parents often project as if a birth right. For a long time, he hadn't liked Joey, regarded his addition to the family as a threat, as yet another challenger for his own parents' attention. That changed one day shortly after Joey started in Trinity College when Damien came across him in the student bar reading *Fear and Loathing in Las Vegas*. By the following morning, they'd cooked up a road-trip plan that started with a reproduction of the opening scene in that book, and within a week, they boarded a plane to JFK, where they rented a 1967 Ford Mustang.

On that long, strange, mazy trip across the States, Joey decreed they would make their way to the ocean out west, visiting only low-profile, obscure metropolises and avoiding the predictable entertainment of familiar, mainstream cities. Minneapolis was the surprise highlight of the tour, a city of music packed with dance clubs and live venues, where they saw Prince perform in the First Avenue club, a recording that appeared three years later in the movie *Purple Rain*. From there, they could dredge up only jumbled scraps of memory as they weaved across countless states, nourished by polystyrene coffee, plastic food, and creative drug cocktails. They jammed in a honky tonk bar in Nashville's District area; drank Hurricanes on Bourbon Street in New Orleans; slithered like lounge lizards in Vegas casinos; and partied on LA's Venice Beach in homage to the Doors. Ever since, Joey and Damien's demons had marched in lockstep, united by an apparently limitless capacity for intoxicating substances, even if they had little else in common.

'I'll give Damien a hand. You head on over, Christy,' Joey said.

Shoving through the miasma radiating from the three-deep throng at the bar, and struggling to see through his misted glasses, Christy made his way towards Maud and her bunch of friends seated along the back wall.

'Musha, this is a fine time to be showing up, Mister Hogan,

and it is your own birthday celebration,' Maud exclaimed as she hugged Christy and pecked his cheek. 'This is Eileen, Peg, Ursala, and Babs. I was just telling them about this wan who was having her hair dyed purple and orange in the salon this morning.' And Maud was off with one of her rambling stories, stories that invariably required periodic replays to establish who such-and-such was or how this particular tangent fitted into the overall tale. From experience, Christy knew it was best to hunker down and go with the flow, and he soon found himself laughing along at Maud's tirade about her co-worker, Janine, who was pure, solid useless.

After a while, Joey and Damien broke out of their huddle and joined them. 'Hey, hey Christy, the big two one, what's the plan tonight then?' Damien asked as he rubbed Christy's bum-fluff beard.

'Leave off Damien,' Christy said.

'C'mon girls', Maud said, tucking her wavy, auburn hair behind her ears. 'Shove up in the bed to make some room.'

As everyone squeezed closer on the bench, Christy said, 'Come here, has anyone heard about Sharkey quitting the Undertones? I saw them play earlier this year in Derry, and they were amazing.'

Damien had his own opinion. 'Bollocks. Typical over-hyped band, whose best work turns out to be their first single; *Teenage Kicks* was alright, but why all the fuss? Now they'll spend the rest of their time trying to replicate that one flight close to the sun. Bugger that, I'm much more interested in U2's Red Rocks concert in Colorado. How do we get tickets for that?'

'Brian says he knows someone running that show who can definitely get us in,' Christy said.

'Yeah, sure,' Joey scoffed, 'we've heard before how Brian can help, but it's all hot air, and there'll be enough of that if we ever actually get to Denver.'

'I hear they're planning to film the gig and then release it as a live album,' Damien said.

Joey took that moment to climb onto one of his favourite hobby horses – how much better sixties bands were compared to the current lot, and which of those were top of the pile – and give it a canter around the table. 'Sure, the Beatles wanted to hold your hand while the Stones promised to you sticky fingers, but the Liverpool lads took your mind to places no one else did: from cruising in a yellow submarine around an octopus' garden to following a long and winding road to meet a fool on the hill and on up soaring with Lucy in a sky sparkling with diamonds.'

From there, the talk moved onto a comparison of the merits of American, Irish, and French girls and the national characteristics each of the lads would combine to build their ideal woman. Maud and the girls feigned disgust and, in a giggling chorus, exchanged opinions on which of the four U2 lads they most fancied. Noiselessly, Christy's classmate Bob appeared and hovered on the edge of the group until Joey called for him to squeeze onto the bench. 'Got a little birthday something for you, Christy,' Bob said, a sandy-coloured rat-tail swinging around his shoulders.

Christy ripped open the neatly wrapped small box. 'Boggle! That's mighty Bob. You're the only one who's got me any kind of present, thanks a million. This lot wouldn't give ya the steam off their piss. It's all drink, after drink, after drink with them.'

'Yeah, yeah. Right so, the bumps for Christy,' Joey announced, and with that, an assortment of hands grabbed hold, dragged him prone onto the crowded floor space, and tossed him high in the air until the count reached ten, and Christy's protests had become insistent.

Soon afterwards, Sam, who was back for two weeks R&R from the Middle East, appeared before them, dressed shoulder to toe in his customary black and moaning about, 'Bloody students. I got stuck talking to some blonde Biology bore in the Buttery bar' – he pushed his way onto a low stool beside Joey – 'banging on about how far behind she was on course assignments and all the lectures she had missed because of all the partying. These self-important student types do my head in. Think the whole world rotates around their silly university life.' With his tanned face, fair hair and tall, muscular body, Sam was Adonis-like, and attracted girls wherever he went.

'OK, calm down dude, don't be a buzzkiller.' Christy laughed. 'We're here to have a good time celebrating my twenty-first birthday.'

'Sammy, my preeetty boy,' Joey slurred as he hugged him. 'We've missed you. Join in the fun. Let's all have a snifter.'

'You're locked, asshole. And fading fast from the look of it. What we need is a little mood changer.'

'Good plan, the famous Sam mood changer,' Joey said as he drained his Guinness.

Emerging from the melee around the bar, a tray of tequila shots balanced above his head, Sam made his way to the thirsty mob which had expanded to occupy the whole of the pub's back room. As they cleared away the overflowing ashtrays and discarded pint glasses, he lined up the shot glasses on the Formica table, and everyone tucked in. One tray soon turned into another, and then more pints.

After pubs closed, they ended up back home in St Jude's, where the scene was way mellow. A bunch of people were smoking hash and watching Easy Rider on VCR, but once the acid trip scene was over, Joey lost interest and began pacing. He went to look out the front sitting room window, captivated by the enormous full moon hanging in the ink-black sky. 'Hey Damien, come over here. What d'ya see?'

'I see a big fat full moon,' Damien replied.

'Nah, I mean around it. Look!' – Joey opened the window and pointed – 'Picture an L before the O of the moon, then the letters RELEI after it. It's the Lorelei, man, our siren calling out to us. Can you dig?' Just then, two cloud formations coalesced, narrowing the moonbeam and spotlighting the mountaintops off in the distance.

'Right so,' Joey announced, 'let's go for a moonlight drive up the mountains.'

No one else thought that was a good idea, but Joey wouldn't be deterred and headed off with Damien and John, the house cocker spaniel. At the dog naming ceremony, going with the suggestion to call him John rather than say Spot or Rover, or even the obvious Rusty, had seemed a funny idea, and by the time the joke had worn stale, the dog was used to it, so the name stuck.

Maud and her new boyfriend Kevin were canoodling in the corner. Sam was flaked out in a beanbag, headphones on, busily stacking a chillum. Christy was collapsed on the sofa beside him, on his arm a pretty blonde he'd met in the Pink Elephant. The chillum did the rounds, skipping Maud, who only smoked 'an occasional joint on special occasions'. The smoke clearly didn't agree with Kevin, who greened instantly and had to be helped by Sam to Maud's bed. Soon afterwards, Christy retired to his bedroom with his new friend, and that was the last time he'd seen either of them. Sam returned to Beirut the following evening, and Joey left Dublin two days later. Joey was never a big one for goodbyes ('when it's time to go, just leave, why all the fuss?'), and he certainly wasn't one for sharing plans, possibly because he himself rarely knew what his next move was. It was only months later, after Maud found him homeless, wandering the streets of London, that they got the explanation for Joey's hasty departure and his reason for dropping out of Trinity College.

'Good morning, Abu.'

'No, please, Christy, in Arabic ... Assalamu alaykum, peace be with you.'

'Of course. Wa alaykuma assalam.'

'Very good, very good. Come, come over to my apartment for some tea.'

In the week since arriving, Christy had chatted regularly with

Sam and Joey's neighbour, Abu Amar, who took great delight in teaching him every-day Arabic expressions. Abu ran a curtain-making operation from his balcony. Once, he had a large shop in upmarket Hamra, but it was destroyed during the Israeli air raids. Now he had a more modest setup, an open-air sewing workshop, shaded from the elements on the exposed side of his balcony by a dark green awning. Pairs of freshly sewn and pressed curtains hung on a washing line. Rolls of unused fabric were stacked neatly under a white tarpaulin at the far end of the balcony. Most days, Abu sat stitching at his foot-powered sewing machine, one local enterprise that continued working even when the electricity was off.

This was the first time Christy had been invited into Abu's apartment, and once the tea-pouring formalities were completed, he pressed Abu into relating his life story. After Christy had tasted the piping hot and crazily sweet tea and lit the Marlboro that Abu insisted was needed to truly appreciate the tea flavour, he began. 'Back in 1947, I lived in Jaffa. Now it is part of Israel, but then it was called Palestine. The fighting in Jaffa was very bad, and every day more problems, no water, all the time power cuts. Armed Israeli gangs, they killed dogs, cats, even donkeys. They piled them up in the street to create a health problem. They wanted to make us leave. Finally, it became unbearable, and we decided to move away until things improved. We took only a suitcase of clothes, some jewellery, and the papers for two orange groves my family owned.'

'The Israelis behaved like the school bully, pushing the weaker kids out of the way because they wanted to use the playground. It was . . . How you say in English? Ironical, no? After the World War, when the Israelis came out of the concentration camps, they were the refugees, and they arrived in Palestine saying: "We are a people without a land, and we are coming to a land without people." But what about the Palestinian people who were already living on that land? They did not care; they had the backing of the Americans and British, who allowed them to settle into their new state by evicting hundreds of thousands of Palestinians. We were left with nowhere to go. We have been homeless ever since.'

As a result of what became known as the Nakba, Palestinians were scattered throughout the Middle East, the majority to Lebanon, yet another minority group crowding into an already congested country. Thereafter, the Palestinians became a problem no one really wanted to solve; if any Arab country were to integrate the refugees fully into their society, it would only relieve the pressure on Israel to find a long-term solution, one that accommodated the original residents of Palestine.

Abu paused. 'Taib, wait one minute'. He shuffled off and came back a few minutes later with a shabby leather briefcase that he laid on the floor between them. He removed a black satin scarf and unwrapped it. 'This is the key for my house in Jaffa. That day we left, we locked up our house, thinking we would be back in a month, maybe two when the fighting died down. So, yanni, we took the key with us. It still gives me hope that one day, inshallah . . .'

Christy took the ornate key and turned it over in his palm. It felt cool to the touch, the long, gun-metal shaft now badly rusted. The bow was covered in ivory and painted in a pattern of dark swirling lines. Where the hell was his key for St Jude's? Never gave it a second thought. Leaving Dublin for London meant nothing to him, just another place he'd laid his hat for a while. Steeped in the peripatetic nature of UN life, moving on was just how you lived; by the age of twelve, when he was sent to boarding school in Ireland, he'd lived in fifteen different houses. For a while, he found the constancy of the school routine quite stabilising, but the shiftlessness, the need to drift, kicked in again once he started university. He couldn't relate to this obsession people have with owning their own home, nurturing their roots in one location; it was a completely alien concept. House keys come, and house keys go, as regularly as the seasons. Christy snapped his attention back to Abu Amar, who was enjoying his trip down memory lane.

'You know, effendi, I have many friends who also kept their keys when they left Palestine, but now, they have thrown them away. They do not believe we will ever return to our homeland. The Israelis have taken our homes and changed the locks. But me . . . I still hope.'

Abu poked around in the briefcase and, from a pile of papers, pulled out a faded brown British Palestinian passport. 'Look here, the date,' he said, pointing to the last page. There was a dark blue exit visa, recording Abu Amar's departure from Jaffa port.

'When we arrived in Beirut, with my wife and eight-year-old boys, we lived in the Shatila refugee camp. We had a stone hut with only two rooms. For heat, we had a paraffin stove. There was no electricity, just candles for light. We had no running water and had to fight with other refugees to fill our buckets from the one well in the camp. We used to laugh at that because when it rained, there was water everywhere. The clowns who had chosen where to build the camp didn't realise that Shatila lies in a small valley. Of course, when the heavy rains came, there was water everywhere and mixed with the shit from the open sewers. Yanni, what a smell!'

On the morning of the Sabra and Shatila camp massacres, Abu travelled north to Tripoli to collect a shipment of fabric and returned home to a scene of utter horror. Having recently overseen the evacuation of the PLO from Beirut, the Israeli army had vowed to protect the Palestinians who stayed behind, with the help of their Christian allies. However, the Israelis had taken to calling these allies "chocolate soldiers" because they wouldn't join in the fighting; for once, the Phalangist militia thought they'd show everyone what they could do. As they invaded the camps, the Israeli army turned a blind eye as the Phalangists slaughtered legions of innocent men, women, and children. Thereafter, Shatila and Sabra defined the low bar for evil in a war with many candidates for that title.

Christy recalled hearing about the tragedy before; at the time, Pops was in charge of the UN mission in Beirut and was one of the first into the camps the following day. He would never talk about the savagery he encountered, but a year later, he requested a move to Pakistan when an opening came up, about as far from the

Middle East as he could get while still working for the UN.

'Everywhere, there were bodies, many of them rotting,' Abu continued, his eyes tearful. 'I saw one pile of dead young men, their clothes were stretched tight over their flesh. You know, in the heat, the bodies swell up. Their belts, even their watches, cut into their skin. When I got to my home, I found my wife, my two boys in her arms, all dead, lying on the floor for the flies to feast on. There was blood everywhere. My life ended that day. I ran from the camp and have never been back.'

The sheer scale of death in this troubled region horrified Christy. In Lebanon, where there was no police force or legal due process, the concept of bringing criminals to justice simply didn't exist. It was all crime and no time for the perpetrators, and not a crumb of recompense for the victims unless they took matters into their own hands, which itself fuelled the vortex of violence. Fired by the righteousness of a recently qualified and newly employed lawyer, the injustice of this life boiled Christy's blood. But upon reflection later that day, it was specifically his anger at the plight of the Palestinians that struck him. For the first time, he truly understood the trauma of what they'd had to endure, cast out of their homeland and left to fend for themselves, with no one fighting their corner, disposable pawns in the geopolitical game playing out between the power brokers of the Middle East. As a child, he'd never tuned into the history of the place despite being surrounded by the problem. The Hogans had been sheltered from the reality of the Palestinian refugees, insulated in their UN bubble, living amongst the expat community, and adhering to the UN diplomatic directive never to take sides or express views that supported either the Arab or the Israeli perspective. Little did Christy realise then how this innocent conversation with Abu Amar would later fundamentally alter the course of his own life.

6.

COKED UP AND WITH A FULL TANK OF FUEL, Christy, Joey, and Vincent Weiner hit the road early to steal an hour on the sun. Desperate to escape the claustrophobia of high-rise, narrow-streeted Beirut, they were heading south into the Wild West of the Middle East on a mission to meet up with one of Weiner's drug connections and to show Christy some proper warzone territory along the way. Sam had been due to come along with them, but he and Joey had had a blazing row the previous night about Joey scoring yet another kilo of coke. From what Christy could make out, the Weiner connection was a running sore with Sam. Seemingly, at one point, there had been talk of Joey moving in with him, but even Vincent wasn't convinced that was a good idea.

Sam was also concerned about the dangers of driving unchaperoned in south Lebanon since the recent outbreak of suicide bombings, but Joey wasn't having it. 'Sam's turning into a bit of an old woman,' he roared from the front of the car. 'Worrying about everything. Always on at me that I'm overdoing it, that I need to face reality. Well, it's fucking reality I'm trying to get away from! And no better man for company than VW if that's your goal.'

In the middle of yesterday's blowout, Sam had turned on VW and demanded, 'What will you be doing at fifty, Vincent? Still dealing drugs to dope-heads like Joey?'

VW laughed dryly. 'Fifty? I don't see myself living that long. And if I need to quit having fun so I can get through another ten years, you can stick it up your ass.'

Sam had lost it then and fell on top of VW, flailing punches.

When Joey tried to split them apart, he got clobbered in the mouth and chipped a tooth. That ended any talk of them journeying together.

Looking on as an outsider, Joey and Sam's chaotic lives terrified Christy. What disturbed him more than their hardcore levels of intoxication — duty-free booze was pervasive, and premium quality drugs were available on tap — were their motivations. Back in the day, as carefree students with no responsibilities, sculling pints and dropping pills had been about having a laugh and enjoying new experiences. Here, its purpose was to escape from the real world, to numb the fear of daily living with its unceasing presence of danger and threat to life. Like many of the foreign correspondents, they had learnt to medicate themselves and were now high-functioning addicts. Any fun had a dark edge to it and was short-lived.

Joey's behaviour was erratic, often foolhardy, and ridiculously high energy. There had always been a dark side to Sam, but it was now on full display; when talking about the barbarity and mayhem he photographed every day, he was quite blasé and readily admitted he and Joey had become acclimatised to terror and death. 'Seems to me, once you get over the initial shock, living with danger becomes like a fix, a drug you need to have. In Lebanon, we all face life-threatening situations, but we learn to cope somehow. And that life becomes normalised, a sort of buffer between fantasy and reality.' Twice now, Sam had told Christy the story of a friend whose son woke up screaming one stormy night, frightened by the noise of the thunder and lightning and the rain lashing against the apartment windows. She only managed to get the boy back to sleep by convincing him that it wasn't a storm at all but shellfire that he was hearing. That calmed the boy down, and he happily went back to sleep because shellfire was a familiar sound he'd known all his life.

Why were they willing to put up with all this stress? They both talked about their sense of purpose and their belief that journalism was a worthy profession that might even occasionally influence, if not change, the course of events. Consumed by this noble idealism, it was clear to Christy that they had become consumed by the adrenaline of war coverage. From their ringside seats, they were obsessed with drafting the first version of history as it unfolded in front of them. He worried that this constant immersion in the suffering of others, of witnessing the worst of humanity, was the stuff of future nightmares. Christy kept these thoughts to himself, knowing his concerns would fall on deaf ears. Besides, he was reluctant to spoil their limited time together by doing a deep dive into the shambolic state of his brothers' mental health. It reminded him of visiting the parents on school holidays when everyone focussed on just having a good time and not tainting it by talking about any of the bad things that may have happened since they last met up.

On the outskirts of Saida, having navigated the daisy chain of checkpoints blocking the route south of Beirut, VW pulled his blue Mercedes 180 off the road, and they suctioned a thick white line up their already dribbling noses. In the back, Christy was struggling with a bad hangover, dry mouth and the little men with hammers thumping in his head. The rising sun stung his red-webbed eyes and sweat leaked out all over his body. An unusually early heat wave had sent April temperatures soaring. Despite the early hour, it was already hot, and the limited air circulating through the open car windows was warm and humid.

'Yeehah, bet they make some serious gear from all those,' Joey roared out the window at fields of red poppies nodding in the rocky hills. By the road, a sea of crimson and scarlet flowers spilled over stone walls that enclosed rolling fields of dark tobacco.

'Hey, look at that,' VW screamed, 'incoming five o'clock.' On a hill about two miles south, thick spirals of black smoke curled upwards like fingers poking out of the ground, the tell-tale signs of shells landing. Ahead, a curtain of grey smoke hung over the road and obscured their view of Jezzine, a picturesque mountain village. It had recently been overrun by thousands of people whom the Lebanese Red Cross had evacuated from the surrounding villages following a tip-off about an impending militia attack. The Mercedes crawled past masses of refugees camped along the roadside, some of whom turned with interest towards the car.

'Keep driving, Vincent, whatever you do, don't stop!' Joey roared as a man moved to block their progress. VW blasted the horn and edged cautiously past the man, who banged on the car roof and tried to open the back door.

They sped off and soon came across a truck, spun at an angle so that it part-blocked the road. Corpses were piled on its open flat-bed, arms and legs entwined in grotesque embraces. A trail of sandy blood dribbled down the tailgate. 'Oh, my sweet Jesus, what has happened here?' VW whispered as he clasped the steering wheel vice-like and manoeuvred around the stranded truck. Further up the hill, they came upon a lemon orchard where a huge pit was piled high with dead bodies sprinkled with lime to contain the spread of disease. 'This must have been where that truck was coming.'

Rounding a sharp bend, VW braked abruptly to avoid crashing into a three-man checkpoint. Blinded by the glint of the soldiers' AK-47 rifles in the sun, Joey squinted through the windscreen and said, 'Now, which militia are these guys?' Riding a wave of panic, Christy tried to remember whether he'd stashed the bag of speed in the car boot or the foot well under the front seat. On the breast pocket of the approaching soldier, he could make out an insignia, a cedar tree surrounded by a red triangle. 'Phalangists, good one,' Joey said and called out the window, 'Ahlen mo sahlen.'

The short solider moved towards VW's open window, his thick black hair Brylcreemed to the right. He removed his shades to reveal two cobra eyes, watchful in a gaunt, mistrustful face. 'You! No photos, no photos,' he said, waving his rifle at Christy. 'Get out of the car.' The other two soldiers moved forward and stood either side of the front bumper. The three lads leaped out of the car, the camera swinging around Christy's neck. His heart was pounding, his whole body shaking.

'It's OK, no photos. I am journalist. Suhufiyy,' Joey said, all friendly. 'I come to report on the destruction the Palestinian, he do to this area. Here, please, cigarette.' He leaned into the car and grabbed three packs of Marlboro.

The lead soldier smiled and pointed at the unopened cartons of Kent on the back seat, which Joey passed out to him. He then hollered instructions to one of the other soldiers, who pulled a handkerchief out of his pocket and tied it to the aerial on the car roof. An impromptu white flag. Would this somehow, magically, ensure them safe passage? Joey wasn't about to ask; he just smiled a lot, shook each soldier's hand, and called out, 'Ma'assalama', as VW drove off. In the rear-view mirror, Christy could see Mr Brylcreem collecting the cartons from his two underlings for safekeeping, no doubt.

Some time later, they arrived in Jibchit and parked outside a fruit shop in search of some healthy sustenance to treat their raging hangovers. The shopkeeper, a stooped, effete man, laughed derisorily when Joey asked for a kilo of oranges. 'We have nothing,' he explained, pushing his black-framed spectacles over the bony ridge of his hooked nose. 'There is no Lebanese lemon or orange or avocado, no Lebanese fruit. Only Israeli. They want to put us out of business by dumping their fruit on the market at crazy prices.' Earlier they'd driven past an Israeli tank, with a bulldozer shovel attached to its front, tearing down orchard walls; the pretence was that this would prevent guerrillas from taking cover so they could fire on Israeli soldiers, but was it just a happy coincidence that without the protection of the orchard walls, the fruit rotted on the trees from direct exposure to the wind?

The shopkeeper gave Joey directions to VW's connection, Hussein Seyyed, who lived in a large, three-storey villa, accessed directly from the street through a rusting, green iron door. Across the road, an old man knelt on a threadbare prayer mat, bowing in time to the recorded Koranic verses blaring from the loudspeakers of a nearby mosque. A young child opened the creaking door and signalled to follow him into a large courtyard flooded with bright sunlight, its edges smothered in cerise bougainvillaea and blood-red geraniums. A man in his mid-thirties rose from an armchair to greet them, his belly protruding over the waistband of his trousers. Ruddy hair flopped down his neck from under a red keffiyeh. 'Fadal, fadal, ahlan wa sahlan,' he greeted them. 'You had a good journey, Vincent?' Hussein's bushy eyebrows arched quizzically over the searching gaze of his green eyes as he turned to Joey. 'And what are your friends' names?'

'This is Joey and his brother Christy. They're cool, no problem.'

Hussein bowed slightly and brought his hand up to his heart, 'Please, my friends, you are welcome in my house.' After rattling off a series of instructions to the boy, he asked, 'You want cigarette, Joey?'

Red Marlboro, Lebanese-made, naturally. Seemed to be all anyone smoked, the cowboy's cigarette. The usual offering ritual followed: a rapid banging of the soft pack against the palm to extricate a single cigarette, then the flicking open of a Zippo lighter, fuel fumes mingling with the smoke of the first drag. After extended polite enquiries about their journey, Joey asked how life was these days for Shias in southern Lebanon.

'You know, the Israelis thought they would do in Lebanon what they did in the West Bank,' Hussein said, in a BBC World Service accent. 'Their plan was to set up a network of paid informers, arm the collaborators like this evil Haddad to keep the Palestinians quiet, and they would control the whole operation from Tel Aviv. But this is Lebanon, and it doesn't work the same here. The Shias are not like the Palestinians. We are organised, we have weapons, and we have trained fighters who are not afraid to die. Allah's generosity is martyrdom. We will not let these Zionist invaders build their settlements all over our country like they have done in the occupied territories. Instead, we will turn South Lebanon into a death trap for them.'

This seemed like a good time to ask about Hussein's missing arm, which was all the encouragement he needed. 'Before, I worked as a cobbler, repairing all the shoes in my village. One day, a local fighter came to my workshop and demanded that I make him a leather casing for the small bomb he had made. He had some crazy plan to blow up the Israeli military headquarters in Tyre.'

Hussein picked up the sharp knife from the table with his only hand and began stabbing a piece of pitta bread with the tip of the blade, absently cutting it into strips. 'He had smoked too much hashish; his eyes were wild, but I had no choice; he had a rifle pointed at me. I asked him to put the bomb down so I could examine it, but he was clumsy and set the detonator off when he banged it on the table. He was killed instantly, but his body stopped most of the force hitting me. My arm was blown off, and my stomach was shot full of shrapnel.' Hussein patted his ample belly. 'That is why it is so big now. When the stitches came out, all my stomach skin was flabby because the muscles were cut. Alhamdulillah, I survived. But there is no money now working as a cobbler; people just throw out their old shoes and get a cheap new pair instead of repairing them.'

One business crashes, and another booms. Hussein had since moved into the import-export business – trading premium grade local hashish for South American cocaine – and VW had become his prime distribution channel into Europe. Unsurprisingly, VW remained secretive on the specifics of how the arrangement worked and what precise role he played in co-ordinating the network (according to Joey, Hussein was the third major dealer he had met with Weiner), but even a numbnut could figure out this was a pretty large-scale operation.

'Fadal effendi, let us talk,' Hussein said, his crooked smile fixed on VW.

They disappeared inside, arms wrapped around each other, leaving Joey and Christy to play checkers with the young boy. Shortly afterwards, the pair returned, and Hussein called on the boy to drag two large, brown leather suitcases to the car. The boy slid under the Mercedes, dragging the first suitcase behind, then emerged for the second, which he also secreted somewhere under the car boot.

As they drove off, there was no discussion on the just-completed transaction, but the embittered Hussein — years of pain etched deep in his red-bearded face, the frustration of the helpless who cannot take up arms for the cause — cast a long shadow over the two-hour journey back to Beirut. Christy speculated on what the future might hold for Hussein. According to Sam, there were rumours that village imams were using special code words in their sermons, the mention of which was enough to trigger a suicide bomber's mission. Would Hussein one day end up detonating a truck that he had rammed into an Israeli army post?

Death had been ever-present in their eyes and noses and ears as they travelled across southern Lebanon, through those gruesome valleys where steel was pervasive: steel girders exposed in bombed-out buildings, the steely glint in the soldiers' eyes, steel moulded into armour and weaponry, even the steel-grey rocky hillsides that provided the backdrop for much of the devastation. And flowing through the steel valleys, a red river of blood that imbrued all those it touched. Christy was haunted by a rotating collage of faces: men who had challenged them, men they had avoided, and men they had seen lying dead. VW's photos would later show scattered body parts, severed heads, and slit-open torsos, but no picture could capture the putrefying stench of death that hung in the air, the nauseous cocktail of rotting flesh mixed with oozing intestines, bile and faeces boiling under an oppressively hot sun. Nor could they record the noise of the black shroud of swarming flies, buzzing from one corpse to another, dive-bombing open mouths and feasting on seeping flesh wounds. It would take Christy weeks to get that rumbling, carnivorous drone out of his ears.

7.

WHEN SAM ARRIVED AT THE GRENIER RESTAURANT, Joey was already seated at a low table lit by an ornate brass lantern. Before he had even sat down, Joey was into a tirade about the challenge of physically getting his stories onto the presses of the Liban à l'Etranger offices in Paris. 'Man, we are so out of touch with the rest of the world. Just sending a few telexed stories requires this whole big logistics operation.'

By June 1985, it could take six hours to organise a time slot for an international phone call out of Beirut, and even then, the available talking time was rationed, always assuming the electrical power stayed on long enough to perform what was, anywhere else, a routine task. Joey's most reliable communications route was via the Associated Press bureau where Lena worked; during a quiet period, she could surreptitiously interweave his copy with that of the bureau-employed journalists. Earlier that afternoon, she had called him to say the outgoing telex wire was back up and to get his ass over quick so he could dispatch his latest collection of stories from the trip south with Weiner.

'That's the problem with working for a mickey mouse operation.'

'Such a fucking snob, Sammy! We can't all be some big-shot war photographer. Remember where you came from, man.' Joey helped himself to a glass of arak and lit a Marlboro. 'Anyhow, that's it, my final batch of stories. I quit.'

'You're really going through with it then?' Sam said, squinting as if sucking on a lemon. He unwrapped a blue and orange bandana and took off his baseball cap. 'Uggh, smelly,' he said, sniffing his armpit. 'I need a wash real bad.'

'Yep, resignation letter attached as the last page of the telex. I'm gonna move on to pastures new.'

'Which are? You have noticed the lack of pastures, new or otherwise, in this country right now?'

'I know man, but I'm done with war reporting. Khalas. It's not healthy, being around dead bodies every day. You too, man, it's not good. It's fucking with your head.'

'Me, I'm cool dude, don't sweat it.'

'Bollocks. You can't keep playing the cool dude like nothing gets to you. Seriously bro, I mean you hardly get any sleep. And when you do, you're thrashing around like a dervish, screaming and shouting. What's that about?'

'You're better off not knowing.' Sam lit a cigarette and leaned across the table. 'I hear you Joey, but what can I do? That's why I sleep in bursts. I wake myself up soon as the bad shit starts.'

'You need to pack all this in before it's too late. Time to get out of Dodge.'

'No can do man. This is all I know, and it matters to people, they need to see what's going on. Just writing about it doesn't have the same impact. A picture paints a thousand words. Anyhow, what else would I do?'

'I dunno Sammy. I dunno. Let's get some food.' Joey called a waiter over and ordered the house mezze and a bottle of wine.

'Oh, by the way, you seen this yet?' Sam said, handing over a copy of Monday Morning.

'Wow, Sammy, that's got to be one of your best shots,' Joey beamed as he stared at the battle scene on the magazine's front cover. 'I mean, look at this guy. It's like he's just ambled out for a spot of archery and found himself in a spot of bother.' In the centre of the photograph, a young man wearing jeans and trainers paced over a mound of rubble. Behind him, a huge smoke cloud spewed from a bombed building, and a ball of fire flamed between his legs. His curly head was half-turned, a casual smirk back over his shoulder, the fringe covering his left eye. In his hands, he held a loaded bazooka, angled like a guitar, and over his right shoulder peeped the conical heads of three rockets harnessed to his back. To his left, an old man scurried past with three small boys alongside, their short arms raised above their heads. 'Everyday life in Lebanon, eh?'

Joey shifted in his chair and signalled the waiter to bring an ashtray. 'You heard anything more on the Anderson kidnap?'

Terry Anderson was a prominent American journalist and boss of the AP Bureau in Beirut. He had been kidnapped the day before St Patrick's Day, dragged from his car in broad daylight. Kidnappings of Westerners had been going on for some time, but as the hostages were nearly always released shortly afterwards, everyone had grown used to the threat. However, the roll call of kidnap victims (a listing that Lena had been tasked with updating on the AP newsroom wall) had been lengthening at an alarming pace.

'Complete radio silence, nothing since the Islamic Jihad call just after they took him,' Sam replied, a slight shake in his soft voice. The kidnappers' call to Reuters had been recorded and widely reported. What had particularly spooked them both was the part that went: *Assuming the profession of a journalist, merchant, scientist, or religious man will from now on be of no avail to spies staying among us.* Everyone knew how easy it was to get accused of being a spy, let alone a journalist.

The waiter showed up, a large tray balanced on one hand above his shoulder, and soon the table was covered with a collection of small clay dishes: skewered lamb and chicken, stuffed vine leaves, tabouleh, dips, and crispy falafel balls. Sam scooped up some baba ghanoush. 'You've quit your job then. Does that mean you're leaving?'

'I don't know, to be honest.'

'And we like to be honest with each other, don't we?'

'Ha, ha. Funny.' Joey rubbed his bearded cheeks. 'Leaving, that's not the plan. Where would I go and besides, how could I leave Lena? Hey, she's invited me to her brother's wedding. What do you think? Should I go?'

'Hell yes, you should go. Lebanese weddings are supposed to be the dog's bollocks.'

'Yeah, but I don't want to be the only non-Leb there. Let me see if I can get you invited. Might even get you set up with a cute Lebanese bridesmaid. And another thing. I'm going to have to bail out of the Babylon sisters scene.'

'What say?'

'It doesn't feel right, the way things are with Lena now.'

'What's Mariam going to say to you ditching her? She's got a real temper on her.'

'She'll be fine, plenty more fish in the Med for her.'

'But we've always done it as a couple's thing. Two Arab sisters, two Paddy brothers.'

'I know, that was the vibe. But things have changed.' Joey leaned conspiratorially towards Sam. 'The danger of being so absorbed with the search is that you miss the thing you're looking for, sitting right in front of you.'

'You *are* joking me. This is a first. What, now you're a one-woman guy?'

'Seem to have ended up there. Love, they say it happens once, but rarely twice.'

'Newsflash . . . Joey finds the woman of his dreams, settles down and starts a family.' Sam's gold cap sparkled as he grinned.

'Hold on, don't be getting too ahead of yourself. One step at a time. It's hardly paradise, this Lebanon. It's strange. In amongst all the doom and destruction, I seem to have found joy and happiness and love for a woman like no other. Lena's amazing, and I don't just mean at the Sierra-Echo-Xray. Though enthusiastic and adventurous lover is one description I would definitely use.'

'Bastard, spare me the details. She's the one then?'

'The one, man, who knows. What is the one? Can it ever be just one? When do you ever know? All I know is that it has never felt like this with anyone else.'

Joey had been spending a lot of time recently trying to figure out what it was exactly about Lena that had got him so caught up. It was like she somehow completed him, filled in the gaps where he was lacking, a classic case of opposites attracting. She had an extensive family whom she was very close to and saw regularly. She was rooted in one place; besides the odd holiday, she had never left Lebanon and had only ever lived in three houses. She had a stable job and enjoyed socialising without having to get wankered all the time.

'So what? You're going to whisk Lena off? Or . . . you're not thinking of setting up camp here, are you?'

'This madhouse? Loonies are running the asylum, eh? But I'm in love with Lena and want to be with her. She'll never leave, claims she's like a fish, and Lebanon is her pool of water.'

'You've certainly come a long way from the guy who used to share women with Damien and notch each conquest on your bedpost.'

'Yup, a long way from all that. What about you and Joumana?'

'Just friends, nothing more.'

The waiter cleared the table and came back with brandies and Arabic coffees. Most of the tables were now occupied and a raucous noise filled the air as the early evening crowd, now liberated from their Ramadan fast, settled in for an extended jovial night. Fuad from the Commodore Hotel arrived with his family and came over to talk. 'Ah, Mr Joey and Mr Sam, and how is the mezze today?'

Joey slapped palms with Fuad. 'The mezze is good, Fuad, but still, I am looking to find a better hotel than the Commodore.'

'Welcome, Mr Joey. Your beard I no like it,' Fuad said as he gave Joey's chin a friendly tug. 'You have heard about this TWA hijack? Why these people they want to bring more trouble to our country?'

Sam lit a cigarette and blew a cloud of smoke up towards the high wooden-beamed ceiling. 'It's a bad situation, getting worse. Once they killed that American, it was always going to kick off.'

'They say' – Fuad leaned in between Sam and Joey – 'that Nabih Berri is now involved. You know him? The Shia Amal militia leader, his face is everywhere, on posters, souvenirs, tee-shirts, button badges, everything.'

'Isn't he the clown who's trying to shoot the PLO out of the refugee camps?' Joey asked.

'That's the one.' As usual, Sam's finger was right on the pulse. 'Berri's gunmen have secured the release of half the TWA hostages and taken them to the Bourj el-Barajneh refugee camp. Now he wants to use them as pawns negotiating with Israel for the release of Shia prisoners.'

'All these peoples must go' – three rubs of Fuad's palms against each other – 'Khalas. Finish.' Fuad shook his right hand in the air, forefinger and thumb touching. 'We do not need any more problems here.' He placed his palm on Joey's hand and squeezed, the fake Rolex gleaming. 'Okay, I must leave you, my family are hungry. Good appetite.'

Joey swallowed his brandy, then looked around the room, chewing on what was left of his fingernails. 'Beirut feels so . . . like I'm trapped here, with no exit routes, no way to get out of this messed-up country. Airport's closed, with a hijacked TWA plane blocking the runway. The road to Damascus is like the Gumball Rally; who knows what the fuck you'd come across if you went that way.'

'There's the ferry to Cyprus, that's just about running these days. Out of Jounieh, the way you came in.'

'All I can say is the transportation situation better have improved by September. It'll be good to get away from all this crap and see some normal life in Copenhagen.'

'That's still three months away. The airport should be fine by then.'

'You really should come with me, Sammy.'

'No way can I swing the time off. Besides, I'm not sure I could spend a whole weekend with Damien. Not even a druggy weekend.'

'Oh, it won't be so bad. Christy's coming too. They're your brothers, for fucks sake.'

'Maud's letting him escape family life again?'

'She's off back home to Limerick before she has the twins, so Christy's hanging loose in London.'

'Married. Kids. Lawyering. When he should be having fun.'

'I miss everyone. Having Christy visit has stirred it all up for me. Don't you ever miss the family?'

'Not really. I've got you, don't I?'

'Yeah, but that's it, isn't it? You've only got me. I've got Lena. You need people you can talk to man.'

'Hey, chill Joey. Relax. What's brought all this on? Come on. Gimme a hug, then let's go have some fun.'

Cocktail-hour scoops in the Captain's Cabin morphed into late-night drinks in the Mayflower Hotel, then clubbing across the road in the basement of the Napoleon Hotel. It had been a long time since Sam and Joey had spent as much drama-free time together. Despite his concerns for Sam, and stresses of living in Beirut, knowing he was done with journalism felt liberating and Joey had his best night's sleep for months.

PURPLE HAZE

Jimi Hendrix

EUROPE

September to October 1985

8.

THE COPENHAGEN CENTRAL TRAIN STATION BAR WAS EMPTY save for a bunch of bingeing Swedes who'd fled their exorbitant domestic beer prices and journeyed south on a get-pissed mission that had stalled here, their first stop. Outside the open-air bar, down and outs wandered the terminus, scrounging money. At the bar, Joey sat on a stool, his jeans black with dirt. Underneath a beer-stained leather jacket, he wore a ripped tee shirt with the word *Hate* emblazoned graffiti-like across his chest. His grungy beard had bushed out so that only a small, tanned oval of face was visible between his nose and hairline. On his head, he wore a floppy purple hat, below which his hair hung, twisted into long, shaggy dreadlocks.

Getting out of Lebanon had proved as tricky as feared. With Beirut Airport closed again, he had taken a taxi over the mountain and zigzagged in a long, perilous descent through the Bekaa Valley towards the Syrian border. Along the way, he'd passed through a procession of villages, policed by the Syrian army or under the control of rogue militias poised to fight, abduct, or kill anybody they deemed sympathetic to the other side. He finally made it to Damascus in time for his flight to Frankfurt and had caught the morning train to Copenhagen. After a boring day wandering the city, killing time in museums and art galleries (so civilised compared to the mayhem of Beirut), Joey was back in the station, waiting for the other two. Earlier, he had watched a respectable-looking man in a grey suit come into the bar with a goat trailing behind on a string. The man bought two beers, then pulled a bowl from his pocket, placed it on the floor, and poured in one of the beers. Having drunk his fill, the goat dropped an almighty shit, at which point the man led the animal away, leaving the pebbled mess for the busboy to clean up. Totally weird, Joey thought, and I'm not even tripping yet.

Across the concourse, he spotted his brothers, Christy scuffing along like he was carrying bad news, head bent, shoulders stooped, arms swinging tight by his side, Damien out ahead, striding past the crowd around the bar entrance.

'Aha, good to see you, boy,' Damien said. He hugged Joey, long-lost friends reunited, then pulled back. 'You look shit, by the way. What's with the grey hair?'

'Man, that's adorable, good to see you too. And it's silver, not grey. Miracle dye, they call it in Beirut. Got it especially for this trip. Seeing as how I'm unlikely ever to make it to old man hair, thought I'd try it out early.'

Loosening the paisley cravat around his neck, Damien removed his tweed jacket, which he hung over the crook of his arm, clearly suspicious of the bar stool's cleanliness. He surveyed the crowd occupying the train station bar, the disgust obvious on his face.

'Christy, how are ya? It's been . . . what? . . . all of five months. That was mad crack in Lebanon, eh? Did you enjoy it?'

'Mind-bending. Life-changing. Crazy shit. I'm still processing it all, to be honest.'

'And how is the lovely Maud?'

'She's doing good, said to send her love.'

'Everyone's buying baby clothes, you know Damien. You getting into that game?' The mumble disappeared down Joey's throat.

'No way, not me. I've no plans like that. I'm in Rome at the moment, doing some work–'

'Actually, fuck that.' Joey rolled his fisted right hand in the palm of the left and said, 'Let's scull these and move on to the hostel. You know where we're going, right Damien?'

Later that night, their wallets considerably lighter after a pub crawl through central Copenhagen, Damien laid out his plans for the future. 'Nightclubs, gentlemen, that's where you'll find the money in Dublin. I've been running these raves for a while now, got the idea on a trip to London. Christy, you must have been to a rave there?' – Christy's confused look said differently – 'Okay, maybe not. Anyhow, raves are the entry ticket, my gateway drug if you like. What I want to do now is take the rave concept but make it legit and charge for it, of course.'

It all sounded so far from the extravagant careers Joey remembered them fantasising about as kids. As time had gone on, Damien had been squeezed further along the funnel of a conventional life, his options narrowing alarmingly as society's expectations moulded him. No longer did he talk of being a jet-setting diplomat. The plans to become a famous sculptor had been ditched. For certain, he was never going to be an astronaut or win a Wimbledon title. So many interesting possibilities had been filtered out, and now he was left with a sordid scheme to make money from other people's partying. Joey feigned interest in this future, but Damien wasn't really after an audience and kept going with his business plan hose down. 'I'm calling the first club Ecstasy, after our well-known friend' – smug chuckle, theatrical wink – 'it's a warehouse place down the bottom of George's Street. I'm looking at a possible site in Temple Bar for a second one. You should come in with me on this, Joey. It could be big.'

'Not too sure I want to be heading back to the Emerald Isle just yet. I'm happy in Lebanon, gonna keep rolling my stone there for a while.'

'Well, as long as you don't cause too much damage along the way with your stone. You probably want—'

Joey tuned out, and for the rest of the night, he hung around the conversation's perimeter, content with the company of his two adopted brothers, happy for Damien to monopolise the airtime.

They drop the acid at breakfast time the following day. First port of call is Flowery Creations, a hippy gear shop opposite Tivoli Gardens, crammed with the usual hippy, dippy assortment: tie-dye shirts and batik patchwork skirts, psychedelic harem pants and kaftans, vibrant-coloured shawls and ponchos. Rainbow dreamcatchers dangle from the ceiling and the sickly aroma of joss sticks and minty patchouli oil coats Joey's nostrils. The lads descend on a cardboard box of jackets and rootle around. Joey finally decides on a jacket with multiple shades of blue, narrow stripes on a hazy purple background. Damien selects an exuberant orange and red striped combination with six large yellow buttons down the lapel, and Christy opts for a luminous green jacket, offset by a purple and yellow scarf.

Sunlight attacks as they exit onto the busy pavement, just coming up on the acid, senses sharpened and battling the early-phase anxiety. Earlier, they'd asked for directions to Christiania: grab the number eight bus and stay on until all the freaks hop off. Now, confusion over whether to take the bus going east or west. They hop on the first number eight that arrives and scuttle to a seat before any more weirdness kicks in. Passengers, people to deal with. Joey's eyes ache, overstimulated by shifting images, zooming in and out, blurring from sharp focus to wide perspective. Stationary head (he knows because he's holding it rigid in his hands), but it still feels as if his head's pivoting back and forth, the scene in his eyes trailing in a cartoon slide show of still images. Over there, is that . . . an Eskimo girl with a goat on a string? Another one! What the fuck is it with goats on a string in this city? Must be the latest cool thing with Copenhagen vagrants, the scruffy mongrel-on-a-string now passé.

A rowdy gang of Swedes bump against each other and guffaw; a few intrepid souls who had at least made it further than the train station bar, though their mission clearly remained one of blanket intoxication. Joey pipes up and attempts to explain, for anyone inclined to listen, what Christiania was all about. 'People gather from all stations of life there . . . gather together, assemble, you know the sheer mass of them that exist. They get a whole, a sense of community thing, like we're all in this together and there's no reason . . . I believe . . . no reason this same communal thing can't be taken into the outside world.'

Across Joey's roving gaze comes a blonde, scruffy teen hovering in the exit stairwell, mostly hidden by the runaway winner of the "Most Obese in Denmark" competition. Teen whips out his dick and pisses his ample bladder contents onto the bus floor. First, Christy starts up, then all three of them collapse in convulsing laughter, and the effect ripples contagiously to the other passengers. Bus stops, mass exodus. Hurrying from the bus, Christy says, 'Haul ass, lads. Let's put some distance between us and all those weirdos on that bus.'

'Good one, Christy,' Joey says. 'Losing all those weirdos clears the way for all the other freaks that have made it into here.'

Hanging over the entrance, a wooden plank is suspended between tall, forked tree stumps and carved with "Christiania". They emerge into dope alley and walk the gauntlet along a dusty track lined with drug dealers, like street hawkers in a bazaar, hustling and peddling exotically named merchandise: Sinsemilla, Brown Moroccan, Thai Sticks, XXL, Black Kashmiri. Dealers lean against waist-high, round metal tables displaying their wares, a veritable world tour of hashish bricks and weed mounds. 'This must be the filling station.' Joey's grin is wider than the Shannon.

Damien moves in on a hippie-type, long ponytailed hair interlaced with blue flowers. Behind him, a red banner with three yellow discs flaps in the light breeze. Time to make a deal. Mock haggle over the price: How much? 25. How about 20? Fuck off. Okay, 25, then. Panicked search for the cash. Nervous clapping of right back pocket. Nothing. Left back, same. Both front pockets. Shit, where's the wallet? Throws hysterical look to Joey and Christy, both zero use, spaced-out eyes glued to some gorgeous blonde's swaying ass. Smile, smile, all is well. Limited facial muscle control, smile comes out as a twisted scowl. Frantic tapping of jacket pockets, the luminous orange-red jacket, throbbing like a lighthouse beacon: over here, look! Another stoner freaking out. Shit, why is everyone looking at me?

Hippie moves a little closer, restive, eyeing the hashish slab that has somehow made its way into Damien's grasp. Bollocks, never pick up a man's hash! Damien waves, a slow-motion sequence of freeze-framed hands forming a continuous image. Drops slab as if electrified; it hits the table edge and falls to the ground. A loud 'Ehhahhh' from the hippie, the most animated Damien has managed to get him, so far anyhow. There it is! Of course, he'd put the wallet in the inside jacket pocket for safekeeping. Seemed like a sound idea at the time, but when going drugging in a strange city, best to stick with the usual routines (wallet lives in back right trouser pocket) and not get all clever inventing new safe places to stash the cash. Damien peels off the kroner, the hippie hands over his lump of hash, and they're off. Onto the porch of a huge wooden house, some kind of bar. Loudspeakers blow out a mellow sound, a low throbbing drum and bass riff running under a repetitive high-octave keyboard groove. Cool breeze through the open windows. The three lads stand frozen just inside, eyes adjusting from the searing sunlight to the muted darkness. Christy stumbles. 'Over there,' moving on an empty table with four chairs.

Christy starts burning the merchandise as Joey goes for an abstemious cup of coffee. Damien flops and checks out the scene: groups of blonde youths, middle- and older-aged couples, straight-looking and druggie types, friendly and not, hysterical laughers, and worried paranoids. Perspectives lurch: the room rears up then zooms back. Everywhere distorted heads. Christy's face swirls a foot away, then appears to age right in front of him: the lines around his eyes diffuse across a shapeless face, his lips droop as eyelids melt around his red eyeballs. Then Christy smiles, and the whole process reverses; his lined face smoothens and puffs out with baby fat, his tombstone teeth gleam between red lips. Damien's jacket, thrown over the chair, starts flashing, sending out explosive beams of sunball red.

Later, in the after-burn of two joints, the Dublin trio glow and sit wordlessly until Damien says, 'Fancy moving on?'

Joey hears Damien mumbling, after what seems a very long time spent wandering to the outer reaches of his addled brain. 'Eh?' he drawls. The table underneath his saucer is alive, its legs throbbing like beating aortas, and the tabletop wood grain pulses as if powered by a marching bug colony.

'Let's split,' Damien says, this time with more intent.

This is a bad time to be thinking there are two killers in this bar. Two that Joey knows about, anyhow. Who knows, there may well be more. Stumbling to his feet, Joey knocks over the untouched coffee. Every eye in the place turns onto him, focused on the convenient bullseye that he imagines painted on the back of his luminous, vibrating-blue jacket. Scans back to Damien, 'You got the hash, man?'

'No, you rolled, remember?'

'Did I? When?'

'Shit man; you're losing it.'

What's with all the grief? Damien rolled the joint, that I know. I got the coffee, didn't I? Frenzied body frisk, jean pockets pulled out and hanging empty like drained water satchels. 'No dice, man. Christy, you got the hash? Christy?'

Communication breakdown with Christy, who's staring at the wall, clearly flaming. He's fixated on a painting of yellow daisies erupting from a purple ground and gushing a blue fountain over a mountain of bodiless heads. Standing beside him, a shaven-headed stoner, shades resting on his forehead, sniffles out a rolling laugh, head bobbing in time with each heave. Damien grabs Christy and, hands on his shoulders, pushes him towards a door.

'Christy man, you got the hash?' Joey says, overly loud so that, again, every eye in the room swivels to check out the latest asshole to misplace his stash.

'Nah, I . . . did you not have it, Damien?'

'Asshole, I knew you had it. You must have dropped it somewhere.'

All three fall to their knees, asses in the air, and paw the sticky wooden floor, perfectly designed to camouflage a dark slab of hash in a minimally lit room. Miracle of miracles, Christy roars, 'Got it,' and sits back, the hash held aloft in both hands like a priest celebrating the Eucharist, offering the blessed host to the heavens.

'Right, let's put some space between us and all these dipshits,' Damien whispers.

In clumsy single file, now properly paranoid, they stutter towards what looks like the exit, each wobbling footstep powered by a frenzy of communication between brain and limb. The distance seems to lengthen with each step until finally Joey gets his hand on the doorknob and swings it open. Cumbersome bodies squeeze through the now unnaturally narrow door space. They stumble down the few stairs into a huddle, eyes clamped shut from the sunlight boring into their saucered pupils. Like the one-eyed man in the land of the blind, Joey strides off, the long pointed toe of his leather boots showing the way forward, with the other two noodling in his trail.

Along a mazy network of dirt tracks, they pass stray dogs, painted bikes, and all manner of domestic constructions, many whose purpose is hard to deduce from the outside, possibly because their design was inspired by drug-fuelled streams of consciousness. This is a community founded on classic hippie principles, a self-governing society where 'Love and peace, man' is the vibe, and which ironically is built on the site of a former military barracks. Man, look at these buildings: a towering crystal hall, with a patchwork of glass panes, two rooms deep and three storeys high; a glacial pyramid, with a star-shaped wind vane on the apex, immobile in the now still autumn air; concrete constructions adorned with dreamy psychedelic murals and multi-coloured mosaics. An elaborate log cabin, with decking that stretches out into a large pool of water, from which someone cries out, 'Hey you! You Irish?'

Joey scans for the source of the voice and notices a hairy dude standing on the porch, smiling. A worried look jumps from Joey to Damien and onto Christy, a look that screams: How does this vacant know we're from Ireland? Are we draped in a tricolour flag and primed to belt out *The Fields of Athenry* at a moment's notice? A worrying realisation that Joey has no clue where they are, not just the precise neighbourhood they have wandered into, but a more fundamental confusion: what city are they in? The more he thinks on this, the more uncertain he becomes as he attempts a fervent retrace of his recent movements and struggles to remember where it was he had decided to go after Frankfurt. Best keep walking and ignore this guy. But then ignoring him might be the wrong play here. Is that a machete in his hand?

'Ah, yeah, man. We're all Irish . . . just having a look around,' Joey said.

'Sure, man, come in. Good idea.'

Decision time. So much easier to keep moving and achieve the mission objective: put some space between them and weirdoville to enjoy the buzz undisturbed. But not accepting this apparently friendly invitation – okay, from a guy wielding a machete – might not go down so well. Maybe this is how hairy dude spends his days, loitering on the porch, waiting for one of each nationality to pass by so he can notch up another country on his kill chart.

'Ah . . . we're cool, man, just drifting along,' in as casual a we-mean-no-harm tone as Joey can muster.

'Naaah, you must come in; we like the Irish here. Have some tea.'

Some tea! What planet is this guy on? Right now, tea would be towards the bottom of the list of substances he would like to consume. 'Tea, yeah great . . . Damien, Christy, you up for that?'

'Tea? Sure, we could do with some liquid. You got any milk?' Damien asks.

'Sure, we have milk, we have sugar, we have water. Come on in, I'm Kasper.'

'Hey Kasper, good to meet you. I'm Damien.' He pauses. 'You been playing tennis then?'

Joey snickers with relief. A tennis racket, not a machete. Naturally. Exactly what you'd expect in over one hundred acres of parkland in the centre of Copenhagen, inhabited by nearly a thousand people, operating outside of the country's laws and regulations: a stoner sitting on the porch, not picking a bass and singing the blues, but batting tennis balls into the middle of a lake. This is good. This is getting better. This is the best part of the trip.

Sometime later, Christy says, 'Wow, those dudes were strange,' as they fall down the front steps onto the dirt trail. He's glad to be on the move again and to get away from Damien's new best buddies. Chez Kasper, Damien had become Mister Everyone's Friend, gregarious and cheery, shaking hands and hugging, telling them all what a great day it was outside. As if any of Kasper's five waster friends gave a rat's shit for anything outside their smoky den. Christy has seen his fair share of dopers like that, just sit on their asses all day, with their minds expanding and their hands out; they get pissed off if someone tells them what to do but have no idea how to actually do anything unless someone instructs them.

'Yeah, worked out okay. The Friendly Ghost sure likes his orgasmatron,' Christy says.

'Yah, with his' — Damien put on an unconvincing Danish accent — '"You know, maaan, like in the Woody Allen movie, you know Sleeper?" And then they pass round this big rotating globe of purple light to each other, going "Oooh, Oooh." I tell you, those guys are not all there in any way, shape, or form.'

'What was in that tea, though?' Christy exhales through the

concrete blocking his ears and sinus cavities, fighting the fear that those two sips of tea would take him higher than he now wanted to go.

Before Damien can hazard a guess, Joey's onto the next thing. 'Hey, what are those chicks up to?'

'Chicks? Where?'

'There, by the lake.' Christy can make out a short orange hosepipe snaking out of the lakeside ground and stretching to the girl's mouth. The blonde one, who drops the hose, throws her head back and exhales a plume of blue-white smoke.

'Action time.' Joey hastens over to the pair. 'Hello girls, what you got goin' on here?'

'Lake bong,' from the redhead, a blissed smile inviting them with, 'You want some?'

Now, lake bong was not something Christy had tried lately. In fact, he knew for sure that it wasn't something he'd ever tried. 'So how does it work then?'

'You see, we get this hose here and stick it into the pot that's buried down here, in the ground, just at the water level.' As she speaks in her lovely Danish lilt, in Christy's eyes, the girl's rubbery face mutates, her cheeks roll like plasticine balls, and her springy lips stretch open, then snap shut as if tugged by elastic. The technical detail of her elegant bong design flies right over his head . . . 'The pot has lots of small holes in its bottom, so the water flows in and cools the smoke as you suck.'

'Ingenious.' Joey hunkers down at the front of the queue. 'Spark me up.'

Suitably refreshed with none of them know what ('was that a plug of opium?'), they continue walking, the weak autumn sun past its peak. They come across a small rowing boat at the water's edge; towards the rear, a small man balances on a long oar.

'What's with all the Eskimos everywhere?' Damien asks.

'Eskimos?' Joey scoffs. 'Don't let him hear you say that. He's a Greenlander. Greenland's been a Danish colony for two centuries, so the Inuit are free to travel between the two countries. Problem is, just like the Aborigines, they can't handle the booze or the drugs, don't have the constitution for it.'

'Whatever the man's history, he looks like he can handle a boat,' Christy says. 'And a ride with an Eskimo boater — sorry Inuit — seems like a logical next move for a trip as strange as this one has become.'

Their memories of events from that point on remained hazy. Certainly, they'd headed out to the zoo at some point and rode an open-top magical mystery tour bus through the city at dusk. During darkness, they ended up in a movie house, watching a late-night showing of *Altered States*. Sleep came late and consumed them totally so that it was early afternoon when Damien roused Christy.

Joey had already started, primed to go again for another day.

9.

UPSTAIRS IN A NORTH LONDON TERRACED HOUSE, Christy's eyes followed Maud's hands as she massaged toner into her cheeks in wide, circular sweeps. She swapped for the moisturiser and moved onto her forehead, outstretched fingers, the tips laden with cream, tapping the skin in jerky, up-down movements. Prone in the bed, he could feel himself hardening as she reloaded, squished the cream between her palms, and stroked the girth of her neck, from the top of her spine around to the apple pip on her throat. In his mind, he substituted his dick and imagined the sensation as she creamed his throbbing knob-head.

'You still enjoying that?' Maud asked as she put the moisturiser on the dressing table beside the vase of tulips.

'Yeah, it's good,' Christy replied, fluffing his pillow, and hoping she hadn't noticed he'd been five minutes staring at the same page. *The Man Who Mistook His Wife for a Hat* was an impulsive purchase while waiting in the Sainsbury's check-out queue, bought without even reading the blurb on the back. He'd been expecting a tangled tale of a surreal married life or possibly a story about mind-bending drugs that created weird visual illusions of wives turning into hats. Now, it was a question of braving it out, enthusing about these studies of peculiar brain malfunctions and neural defects, all the while trying not to worry that the maladies described in the book were manifesting themselves in their own sleep-deprived, time-poor lives.

Finally, she'd stopped giving him grief about the weekend in Copenhagen, 'Drugging and drinking with those two stoners, for the love of God, don't you know you can't keep up with them.' A whole week since returning, he'd had to listen to how pure useless he was, 'a husk of the man who left her'. All she wanted to hear was how Joey was doing, and how did he look, and was he still stressed, and was he asking after her at all.

'Sounds like they may have gone off,' Maud said, removing the black velvet band that held her flame-coloured hair back.

'Hopefully.'

'Did you lay Áine on her tummy?'

'Ah . . . tummy, yes, think so. Though I don't see the point, she moves all over the place when she's sleeping.'

'Better safe than sorry. All the books say on the tummy is safest. By the way, have you organised the babysitter for Saturday?'

'Me? I thought you were doing it?'

'I am in me hole. Didn't we agree you'd do it this time? But shur, I knew you'd forget so I called to confirm Laura this morning. What time will you be home from your gig?'

'They're playing in the Mean Fiddler so it's usually pretty late shutting up there. I should be home around two.'

'We'll probably go to Dingwalls when the pub closes, so I'll be after you. Can you give Laura the fare home, as well as the babysitting money? Also, make sure you call her a mini-cab from that place near the tube station. They're pretty reliable.'

Maud was excited about her night out with the girls, her first proper social outing since the twins were born. Ahead of her, a night of endless giggling, getting noisily pissed and comparing the joys of married life; all her friends were married, most of them for several years, well past the blush of the honeymoon period. He and Maud got married ridiculously quick, only six months after they first had sex, a decision driven by obligation rather than considered thought. Looking back through the blurry prism of time, Christy couldn't now imagine the alternative, the other life he might have lived. Although it wasn't how she would have planned it (and she'd been working on the details since her tenth birthday), he had now given Maud the life she'd always dreamed of: an uxorious and faithful husband, with a good job and solid career prospects; three gorgeous little girls, and a home all of their own, miles away from that decadent student life (as she liked to moan, 'All those pointless drugs and excessive boozing and rotating one-night stands').

They'd had to leave Dublin, of course – no work there for anyone, not even those that wanted it. Maud was happy out now but initially she'd been against the move to London; all that hustle and bustle, the heaving mass of people everywhere, a jumble of every culture, it was so different from the farm in Limerick where she'd grown up. Christy and his brothers used to visit Uncle Tommy's neighbouring farm for Easter holidays every year and occasionally during summer when his parents were on home leave from the Middle East. Christy was one year younger, but he had always looked out for Maud, and once, he'd even saved her life. A mob of them had gone down to the river for a swim on the first hot summer day after weeks of rain. The river was high and flowing fast. Maud had gone off exploring with Patch, upriver from where the rest of them were swimming. She was throwing sticks for the dog when he was suddenly caught up in a strong current. She tried to grab him from the riverbank, but the dog dragged her in, and her foot got tangled in weeds. When Patch showed up downriver without her, Christy had known something was wrong. He went looking and found her just before she slipped under. Throughout their teen years, they'd kept in sporadic contact, and when Maud decided to move to Dublin for work, she had jumped at the chance to move into St Jude's, as she didn't know a soul in the city. But Christy had never once thought of her in the girlfriend way, and he'd certainly never made any sort of move on her until she did, that night Joey left Dublin, the night she got pregnant.

'Your turn,' Maud announced, it seemed to him almost gleefully.

'Shouldn't we leave her cry for a while, let her tire herself out,' Christy offered as his defence.

'You may think that, but as sure as God made apples, we'll wait ages for her to drop off, which she won't, and then we'll end up going into her anyhow. Besides, I can't bear to hear her crying.'

Christy rose from the bed and padded into the narrow hall, floorboards creaking with age and poor fitting. The housing boom had sucked in boatloads of jack-the-lad-wannabe-property-developers with a beady eye on a quick buck and a blind eye to the quality of building work. And the builder of this house was no different. They'd moved in just after the twins were born, and it still needed a lot of work done to it, but at least the twins' bedroom was finished; they'd had great craic painting the walls and assembling the cots, with the mobiles twinkle-twinkle-twinkle-starring above them. On the way, he went to the toilet, careful to place the toilet-seat down after and to wipe off the floor any piss that had strayed from its intended target. The flush handle was broken again, so he had to lift the cistern lid and pull up the ballcock arm. By the time he made it to the baby's room, she was hysterical, squeezed-shut eyes spurting tears, toothless mouth bawling, and cheeks puce-red from the effort of demanding some kind of attention from her parents. Certainly got the lungs to be a singer, this one.

When he finally got Áine settled and made it back to the bedroom, Maud had turned her light off and rolled onto her side, back facing him. He spooned against her and wrapped his arms so that each palm cupped a swollen breast. She backed into him but pulled away as she felt his swelling prod her. 'Sorry Christy, I'm pure worn out. I need to get some sleep.'

Mind stimulated and body now overtired and twitching, Christy returned to his reading. His brain scrolled through a list of the things he was likely to mistake his wife for if he didn't get some sex soon. Right up until Kathleen was born, they'd had loads of sex; in fact, Maud had never been so horny. But for months after the birth, it had been a sex desert. Then they had just started talking about trying for a second when she'd got langers at his office Christmas party and thought it'd be wild to do it on his desk. Up the spout again at the first attempt and, throughout that pregnancy, Maud had awful problems, carrying twice the load, so she'd had very little interest. And now she was perpetually tired.

Work was a major drag, only two years after finally realising his ambition to become a lawyer, a goal he had set himself aged fifteen. He had hoped to get work as a solicitor in London, but that had proved too difficult, so he'd jumped at the trainee corporate lawyer job when it came up. He hadn't told Maud the half of it, didn't want to worry her unduly, but his boss was a prize asshole, a public-school twit with limited ability and limitless ambition. Julian had seemed likeable enough in the interview; all those questions about Christy's family pedigree in law and how similar it was to his own family, which he had since discovered was bullshit.

Why bother with all this work shite anyhow? Should be having fun, like everyone else. Joey's off doing his gonzo journo gig in Lebanon, with Sam now the famous photographer; who'd have thought? Another postcard from Joey had arrived that morning from Damascus; he'd made it back from Copenhagen. Erratic and unpredictable in their frequency, Joey's postcards glistened like pearls amongst the rest of the dreary post, mostly brown-enveloped bills or junk mail. Even though they could rarely make sense of the garbled, meagre sentence or two, what mattered was that Joey had bothered to write at all, that from across the world, he still thought about them. Pissed off by this train of thought, he cast his mind back to happier times. The college years when he and Joey had spent a lot of time getting stoned. Hash was always his favourite hit, easiest to control, never led to violence or any sort of bolshie behaviour, and no big recovery process the next day. He'd loved it right from the start, that strange first time he had a toke.

Summer of 1978 in Rawalpindi, with Dessie Duffy of Dire Straits, well that's who he thought he was smoking his first hashish with.

Unexpectedly, Pops had been transferred to Pakistan, and

they'd driven the whole way from Jerusalem, all seven of them — the parents and five siblings — and a dog called Bandit packed into a VW Westfalia camper van. A departing Belgian army officer, who was making a hasty return home after having had his leg blown off while on patrol in southern Lebanon, sold the van to Pops for a song (literally: the Belgian was a big fan of Pops' rendition of *Danny Boy*). The ten-day journey took them from Israel up through Lebanon and Syria, into eastern Turkey, and then across Iran and Afghanistan and over the Khyber Pass into Pakistan.

Christy remembered border crossings as tortuously slow, partly just because that was the pace the local customs officers operated at: lots of time was required to fill out the paperwork, stamp the documents, and agree the appropriate fee (including the officers' "tax"). But also because of all the hippies. At the time, the Magic Bus out of Amsterdam had caught the younger generation's imagination, and the roads to India were full of camper vans and buses loaded with groovy types off to find themselves in some eastern mystic's ashram. The border guards figured there was only one cargo on board, particularly with those heading west, so they emptied the vans, then often stripped off the wall panelling, deflated spare tyres, and pulled out seats in their search for hidden contraband.

In Hogan family lore, the Herat to Kandahar route in Afghanistan became legendary for three reasons. The journey was a long series of stops and starts as Sam and Bee – they were the only ones who had an Iranian kebab the night before – alternated puking or diarrhoea pitstops. Along the way, the thermometer on the dashboard in the unairconditioned van blew up when the mercury hit fifty degrees centigrade. Shortly after, at the edge of a village, they stopped for cold refreshments at a roadside shack with a Coca-Cola sign above the door. When the owner started opening the bottles by knocking the caps off a large rock, Ma stopped him and went back to the van to get a bottle opener. The owner stared in wonder at the miracle of this device in action and warily uncapped several bottles himself to ascertain it wasn't just some kind of magic trick. Seeing his delight, Ma donated the bottle opener, and off the shopkeeper went running around the village, showing everyone this incredible piece of modern technology he had been gifted.

By the time they made it to their temporary home in the Kashmir Wala's Hotel in Rawalpindi, Pops was ready to murder a beer. They were met by Kevin Moran (one of his old Garda friends who also joined the UN in the early 1960s) bearing the bad news that there had just been an army coup in Pakistan, martial law had been declared, and the consumption of alcohol in public places was now banned. They spent six weeks in that hotel until Pops found a house to rent that had air conditioning. Bandit the dog, who had completed that epic journey with them, only lasted a week in the new house; one night, he went exploring in the field out back and was discovered the next morning savaged by hyenas. None of the five children ever wanted a pet again.

Daily life comprised a dash from airconditioned home to airconditioned car to cooled hotel swimming pool to airconditioned hotel dining room, then back home. The Hotel Intercontinental was a crossroads where foreigners of all types — diplomats, businessmen, army personnel, mountaineers on their way to climb K2 (Bee was thrilled to get Reinhold Messner's autograph one day) — broke their journey and spent some time relaxing. So, it wasn't really a surprise when a member of Dire Straits called Dessie Duffy showed up poolside one day and got chatting with Damien over a game of table tennis. The band's eponymous debut album had just been released, and *Sultans of Swing* was playing everywhere in Dublin — on the radio, in the Wesley Disco, in the dorms at school — before Christy left for his summer holidays. Soon, Dessie was hanging out with them, and occasionally, he brought his guitar with him. Christy had heard the album a few times in Dublin, and for him, *Six Blade Knife* was the standout track. Dessie could strum that track and had a heap of stories about what the band got up to in Amsterdam, where they recorded the album.

One day, Christy was at the pool by himself, and Dessie asked if he wanted to go on a motorbike ride to meet some of his friends. They set off to a small village on the outskirts of Rawalpindi, to a large, gated mansion surrounded by lush gardens. Dessie left him in a hut on the grounds while he went into the main house, returning twenty minutes later with a big grin on his face, and 'Do you wanna smoke a joint?'

'Ah, I guess so. Do you have anything?'

'Do I have anything? Oh yes, I sure do.'

Dessie took out a cigarette and rolled it between his fingers to empty the tobacco into his palm. He then took a black brick wrapped in cellophane from his back pocket and burned off chunks to mix with the tobacco.

'Here, smell this. Nice, eh?'

Christy took the slab and rubbed it between thumb and forefinger. 'God, it's really sticky.'

Dessie laughed. 'No shit, Sherlock. It's gooey Afghan black.' He fed the tobacco mix back into the cigarette shell, replaced the filter with a cardboard roach, and sparked it up.

On the ride back to the Hotel Intercontinental, Christy was on cloud 9, and from there, his love affair with hash deepened. As the summer wore on, Dessie spent more and more time with the Hogans and tagged along to embassy parties in Islamabad, where the family was a regular guest. Over time, the novelty wore off, and Dessie became a pain in the ass, certainly not cool like you'd expect your rock stars to be. He also started hitting on Bee (who, in fairness, was mature beyond her fifteen years), which was a bad move in the eyes of the four brothers. By the end of the summer, they were all a bit doubtful about Dessie's story. Christy remembered seeing mugshots of the four Dire Straits members on the back of the album cover, but he hadn't taken much notice of the faces, except for the singer Knopfler. First thing he did on return to Dublin was to check it out in a record store; although disappointed, he wasn't really surprised that Dessie's face didn't feature. 'Fucking asshole,' he muttered and soon dismissed all thoughts of Duffy until he got a call from Bee two months later.

'You'll never guess what happened.' Bee said.

'If I won't, why don't you just tell me?'

'I was in English class this morning, and Sister Melanie called me out, to tell me that the police had showed up and wanted to talk to me. The police, as in the drug squad. I'm like, whaaaat? This is mad. Anyhow, they start asking me how I know Dessie Duffy; he had my phone number, and they traced some calls he made to me.'

'Phone calls to you. When? Why has he been phoning you?'

'Oh, he's been kind of pestering me, said he was coming to visit Dublin and could we meet up. I'd forgotten all about it, but seemingly, the cops busted him at the airport and found loads of hash packed into his guitar. You know that shitty acoustic he had in Pindi?'

'You're fucking joking me. A drug dealer. Unreal. Pops was right all along. Took one look at him that first day in the Intercon and said, "I don't like the look of him. Probably a gun runner or a drug dealer". Can you believe we ever believed he was a guitarist in the latest hot band?'

Christy smiled as he lay staring at the bedroom ceiling. It was strange thinking back on those long-ago times; he must have been triggered by all the time spent with Joey recently, two major hookups in the last six months after two years of radio silence. Christy reached under the bed and pulled out the newspaper, folded over on the Classifieds section. In his mind, he rehearsed the conversation with Maud, working through how best to pitch it: *Here's a crazy thing, Maud, I've seen this advert for a job with UNRWA in Gaza; they're looking for people with a Law background.* No, that's a bit direct and sudden; better to lead up to it a bit gentler: *You know how I'm really not happy here in my job or with living in London, darling; it feels like*

life is just passing us by. What about a change? Then maybe go into the bit about the job advert, and what they're looking for, and how he could help: *I'd finally be doing something with real purpose that made a difference to people in need, downtrodden and discarded people that no one is helping.* Probably worth getting in that Joey was talking about UNRWA and the great work they do for Palestinians; Joey's opinion always seems to hold an inordinate influence with Maud. And then, after she'd exclaimed what a fabulous idea it was and how much she'd like to uproot their young, fast-expanding family yet again to move to Gaza, he could laugh and say: *Can you believe it? Amn't I completely mad; I've only gone ahead and already applied for the job.* Comforted somewhat by this happy, if unrealistic, scenario, Christy set aside the newspaper, took off his glasses, and pulled the quilt tight around him as he turned to face out from the bed.

STRANGE PARADISE

Beach House

LEBANON

October 1985 to May 1987

10.

THE DAY AFTER JOEY RETURNED FROM COPENHAGEN, he sheared his hair and beard, and booked a dentist appointment to sort out the tooth that Sam had chipped. New look, new Joey. No more mind-bending drugs; he didn't want to end up an acid casualty. A bit of dope was harmless, but that's it. It was a big decision, but his recent past was littered with an accumulation of bad decisions, and it was time to start making some better ones.

Decisions weren't Joey's strong suit. His normal MO was to go with the flow and make the call on the hoof. Movement was often a substitute for thinking. Momentous decisions, routine decisions, superficial decisions, they all got the same treatment. And so it was with this latest life-changing decision, a flashing realisation inspired by an ambiguous Talking Heads lyric about heaven being a place where nothing ever happened. Now he understood that he could happily live free of the ceaseless pressure to do something new, without needing to constantly move onto the next thing. There was no mystery to it. It had become clear what he must do, or more accurately, what he must not do. He needed to stop chasing that green light across the bay, tempting him towards some new experience. He needed to stop running, never sure whether he was running away from something bad or towards something good. He needed to just be, to embrace the life he had fortuitously fallen into.

Outside the barbershop, Joey flagged down a taxi to take him across the Green Line to Ashrafiyah in East Beirut, where Lena's parents lived. The demarcation line was like a deep scar that sliced through the city, dividing Beirut with Christians in the East and

Muslims in the West. Crossing during the day was generally safe if you were out and back before dark; like clockwork every sundown, the fighting kicked off and continued until dawn. The taxi driver turned his radio down and sniffed, 'The man who has just got out' – jerking his head backwards – 'he was Muslim' – curling his upper lip and wrinkling his nose – 'he smells bad' – pulling at skin on his forearm – 'Skin, bad smell, yah?'

Joey shifted squeakily in the passenger seat, its leather polished to a shiny glaze by thousands of arses. 'Got it,' he said, then rolled down the window, ignoring the familiar Beirut background aroma of sewage. None of the convenient crossing points were open, so the taxi driver took him south, in a loop around the airport. As they passed the end of the overgrown, potholed boulevard that led to the terminal, Joey could see numerous travellers passing in and out of the shell-damaged building. An MEA 707 sat on the runway, the familiar cedar tree logo on its tail, thick green chevron branches balanced on a brown tree trunk. Two barefooted children stumbled along the dusty roadside, a stick straddling their shoulders to transport plastic jerry cans sloshing with water. Further along, as the traffic jammed at a busy crossroads, a group of kids were collecting large pieces of jagged shrapnel and bullet casings, much like boys back home would collect conkers or ripe apples.

Shrapnel was the reason Lena had moved in with her parents. Out shopping in the local supermarket, her mother was caught in the crossfire of an argument between a group of Kurds. A stray piece of shrapnel tore a chunk out of her left thigh and severed a major artery. The doctors were unable to save her leg, and it had fallen to Lena, as the only daughter, to care for Halina until they figured out a longer-term plan.

Joey was greeted like the prodigal son and drilled on the news from Europe. His new hairstyle was universally popular, as were the Danish biscuits he'd brought back with him. Halina sat in a wheelchair, her elegant face pale beneath short, hennaed hair. Nobody mentioned her accident; all the talk was of the upcoming wedding: Lena's oldest brother, Antun, was marrying his childhood sweetheart, Jamila. It was the first time Joey had been exposed up close to a wedding planning process, and he was amazed at the level of consideration given to every small detail.

After dinner, Joey and Lena's father moved into the lounge for their customary game of chess. Over time, Michel had warmed to this interloper in his camp, although he remained wary of Joey's intentions towards his cherished daughter. Currying favour with a parent was an unfamiliar situation for Joey, but any discomfort was moderated by the fact that he really liked Michel and found they had a lot of common, despite their vastly different backgrounds. And chess was an ideal way to get to know each other better, without the intensity of a front-on conversation.

Michel was an accomplished player but rarely got the better of Joey. 'I think it's my turn as white, no?' Michel said as he uncorked the bottle of Chivas Regal that Joey had brought for him. His black hair, streaked with grey, was combed back, forming three rolling waves along his head. In profile, his patrician nose and high forehead conveyed a sense of authority in keeping with his station in life. The Sarkis family were Christian Maronites, and although Joey couldn't get a fix on specifics, Michel was clearly an influential player with fingers in many political and business pies. As he handed Joey a glass of brandy he said, 'You know, the Irish and Lebanese, we have very similar situations. Your war is simpler, with just Catholics and Protestants fighting. Here, we have a complex mix of militias and foreign armies.'

'It's not really a religious war, though, is it?'

'No, it's not about religion, of course not. God, whoever he may be to different religious groups, is too often used as the banner for men to fight under.' Michel lit a thick cigar and puffed a smoke cloud, obscuring his sallow, moustachioed face. 'But what the Israelis did in Palestine was very similar to what the British did in Ireland, no? The big difference is that the Irish weren't squeezed into crowded patches of land, like the Israelis have done on the West Bank and in Gaza. What an uproar that would have caused! And then imagine all the displaced Irish fleeing to France, or Spain, everywhere across Europe, to live in refugee camps that soon become their permanent home. The Western world would never stand for it, and yet when it happens in the Middle East, poof, nobody cares.'

'It's strange, I've never thought of it like that. There's nowhere else in the world where something like that has happened, not over such a long period of time at least.'

'C'est ça. Of course, there's no nation quite as ruthless and obstinate as the Israelis with their so-called righteous cause. With the Americans at their back, pushing them along. All the other major Western powers, the British, the French, none of them will go up against Big Sam.' Michel leaned over the chessboard to make his opening move. 'It is the great failing of the Palestinians. You must have powerful friends, it's essential. They ended up with the weaker superpower and now Russia has too many of its own problems. The Arab states tried to reclaim the land that was taken from them in '48, but they lost the war in just six days. Again, at Yom Kippur in 1973 Egypt and Syria attacked, but the same result. And now Egypt has made peace with Israel, they have washed their hands of getting back land for the Palestinians.'

As Michel took one of Joey's pawns, Antun came in with a tray of biscuits and pastries and cardamom flavoured coffee. 'Please, try this baklava Joey, it's Halina's speciality.'

'Nice one, thanks.' Joey looked back at Michel and said, 'But what about your duty to the Arab brotherhood? Don't you have —'

'Pah! The Maronites don't consider themselves Arabs. We are more French than Arab. We Maronites are opposed to anyone dominating Lebanon. Instead, we want a sovereign Lebanon free of all foreign influence. You know, Lebanon is very different from its Arab neighbours' – Michel wagged a fatherly finger in Joey's face – 'and there is a danger that news articles like your treasure trove story, with the Palestinian keys, send the wrong messages.'

Surprised that Michel even knew about his article, Joey was momentarily stumped. 'But don't you have a duty to help the

Palestinians?'

'These Palestinians, they show no respect for our country,' Michel said as he tossed his hand in the air, the cigar tip passing close to Joey's face. 'Instead of behaving like our guests, they behave like invaders, just like all the other invaders we have suffered under. If we are not careful, they will take over the entire country. Me, I cheered when the PLO and that clown Arafat were finally thrown out.'

Joey directed his attention to the chessboard, moved his queen forward, and said, 'Check,' ending the conversation while the combatants considered their next moves.

Antun filled the conversation vacuum. 'We are a unique nation, Joey. Once they called Beirut the Paris of the Middle East.' He smiled, the same dark, warm eyes as Michel. 'I remember when they first came, different Palestinian factions would fight each other on the streets around the camps. We would say, "But your enemy is Israel. You are brothers. Why are you fighting each other?" Lebanon is not their country. They do not respect it.'

Michel looked up as he moved his king to safety behind two pawns. 'Believe me, I support the Palestinian right to fight the Israelis. I am not a supporter of Israel, but I don't like what the Palestinians have done since they came to Lebanon.

'You know, Joey, after the Israelis left in 1982, we had a big chance to end this war,' Antun continued. 'There were presidential elections, and Bashir Gemeyel had finally managed to get the support of all the Maronite factions. He was also winning over those with suspicions, especially the Muslims. We all wanted an end to the war and could see that Bashir was the only person strong enough to hold Lebanon together. In the end, he was the only candidate; no one dared run against him.'

'But someone dared to kill him,' Joey said.

'Yes, and only a few days before he was due to be sworn in as president,' Antun said. 'He was assassinated like all the Arab leaders who have dared to deal openly with Israel. The same happened to King Abdullah of Jordan and Anwar Sadat in Egypt.'

'There were many dark days after Gemeyel,' Michel said. 'Palestinians were blamed for the assassination, but in fact, it was a Syrian plot. In retaliation, the Phalangists massacred thousands of Palestinian refugees in the Sabra and Shatila camps. God forgive their stupidity. Since that barbarous act, the Phalangists have steadily lost importance and have split into many rival factions.'

'With Bashir's death, the Christians joined the Muslims and Palestinians in the loser's circle. And now, all these years later, none of us are running the country. It has been taken out of our hands by foreign powers.'

'Yanni, you men. Politics, politics all the time,' Lena said, emerging from the kitchen and wiping her hands on an apron. 'Poor Joey, he has no interest in all this. Finish your game, then I'm taking him to The Laser bar for a drink.'

Joey laughed and threw his hands up in a what-can-I-do expression. He was quite happy talking politics with Michel, something Lena had said only happened with his closest friends.

The streets were busy as Joey and Lena walked, arms wrapped around each other, the chill October air a shock after the warmth of the Sarkis apartment. Joey marvelled at the contrast to nightlife in West Beirut, where most evenings he and Sam sat out on the balcony drinking and watching the sunset across the sea. Day and night were about the only things that cooperated reliably in West Beirut. Curfews were common, making it too dangerous even to make the short journey around the block to their favourite hangout, Your Father's Moustache, where Joey occasionally moonlighted as guest DJ. Only last month, they had moved their mattresses back into the bedroom, after a fortnight sleeping in the apartment corridor for fear of an errant sniper bullet penetrating the windows. Inside the apartment, they were reliant on battery-powered gadgets, as the electricity was almost always off. Candles lined the sitting room floor along each wall, with a candle in a hollowed-out watermelon glowing red in each corner. Packs of water bottles were stacked two deep in the dining area, and on top were two layers of tinned vegetables and meat; the water supply remained sporadic, and now even food was becoming scarce.

Here in the East, cafés overflowed onto the pavements, and the restaurants were packed with couples and families. Shops were open late and doing brisk business. They passed a tin beater's workshop where hand-carved metal spoons, brass jugs, and aluminium oil cans hung on strings below the ceiling. Shisha pipes and collections of enamelled saucepans filled any available ground space. The crackling sizzle of chicken-on-the-spit mingled with the smell of charcoaled corn-on-the-cob and exhaust fumes. This was where he needed to spend his time, away from the temptations and hedonistic lifestyle of the journos and other foreigners in West Beirut. That intoxicated life was in his past; going forward, he was keeping on the straight and narrow, and saving his brain from any further damage, if it wasn't already too late.

The Laser was heaving, with a mostly young, trendy crowd that the lovers pushed through to get to the bar. When they were seated with their drinks, Joey asked, 'Are you still thinking of quitting the AP Bureau?'

'Yanni, I think it's time. If they can take Terry Anderson for no reason, then none of us are safe. There aren't many journalists like Terry who are both popular with the locals and respected by their peers.'

'But what would you do?'

'Papa wants me to work in his clothing business. But I am not so sure I want to. And we must see how things go with Mama.' Lena leaned over and rubbed her palm along Joey's head. 'I love the feel of your short hair; it's spiky like a baby hedgehog.'

'Listen, Lena, I've been thinking. Workwise, we need to do something completely different, something that we both enjoy.'

'I don't think we can make money out of that,' Lena said, a seductive ripple in her voice. The aquamarine lapis glistened on the chain around her neck.

'No, not that, my love. Dancing. We both like dancing. I've been thinking about nightclubs.'

'Nightclubs?'

'Yes, let's open a seventies-style nightclub; rotating disco balls, flashing dance floors, mirrors everywhere. Remind people of better times, the fun times when Beirut truly was the Paris of the Orient, as Antun was saying. We should call it something like Paris Disco. Or Parisian Heaven.'

'But what do we know about nightclubs?'

'We can learn. There's not much to it; we just need a venue with a bar and a loud music system. Beirutis like to have fun. I mean, soon as the shelling stops, everyone's out and about looking to —'

'There is that club in Gemmayzeh that closed recently. I think Papa knows the owner.'

'Imagine what this city would be like if the war ever stopped.' That was something Joey found his mind turning to more and more, as he became more embedded in the Lebanese way of life and dreamed of a future here when the madness finally ended.

Jumping aboard Damien's nightclub business in Dublin may not have appealed to Joey, but there was nothing wrong with the concept in a city that partied like Beirut. Ever since Copenhagen, he'd been thinking it through and had decided they could maybe make it work. He was pretty sure that Michel would get behind it; he was happy to support whatever enterprise his precious Lena wanted to pursue, and he was already doing what he could to help Joey out with work. When that fuss with the English essays blew up, Joey's whole life had changed like a flicked switch. He used to think that it had sent him down a bad track, but he'd changed his mind. If it weren't for dropping out of university, he would never have come to Lebanon, would never have met Lena and her welcoming family, and this whole new future would never have opened up to him.

11.

AS LENA PARKED her white Mercedes sports convertible outside the bride-to-be's family home, pandemonium broke out. A group of older women were greeting people with, 'Ah Weeeee-ha, Ah Weeeee-ha,' a long, wavering, high-pitched screech that penetrated deep into the eardrums. Everyone was dancing, an unruly mass of bodies swaying in time to throbbing Arabic music. Two men banged out a rhythm on goat skin drums strapped around their shoulders. In front of them, a group of flamboyantly dressed men blew into short double-barrelled flutes. The crowd joined in a bout of improvised singing and shouting.

'This is what we call the *zaffe*,' Lena explained, 'where the arrival of the groom's family is greeted with music, dancing, and singing. Lebanese weddings mean a lot of parties. Today is the third day; we already had the party in our house, and yesterday there was a party in the groom's own house, where they will live when they are married. Let's wait here a minute.'

The wedding was taking place in Jamila's hometown of Sofar, a little higher up the mountain from Aley, where the Sarkis family used to live. The area was popular with wealthy Arabs from across the Middle East, who visited in the summer to escape the baking heat of their own countries. Today, the February air was cooled by low cloud cover and a sharp breeze that carried a sweet, pine-tinged fragrance from the forest further up the hill. As the crowd dispersed into the house, Joey leaned over and kissed Lena fully on the mouth. Wiping lipstick off his lips, he beamed at her. 'I'm going to find Sammy. Fancy coming with me, my lovely Lebanese lover?' Joey asked, caressing her bum as he grabbed her in a hug.

'Stop that, Joey,' she whispered. 'You go on, and I will find you later.'

'Love you, Lena,' Joey called out as he made his way through the crowd.

The musicians circulated, their numbers swelled by a cluster of women dressed in matching Santa Claus-like outfits, long red robes with red bobble hats fringed with white wool. In their wake, they pulled a snakelike procession of weaving dancers. As the troupe made their way into the house, a chain of dancing girls erupted from the basement, dressed in matching pink skirts and skimpy tops, their bellies bare and bronzed. All had black, shoulder-length hair tucked under pink bandanas. The dancers strode forward, waving white lace scarves above their heads, as around them, everyone clapped, banged an instrument, made a shrieking noise, or just shouted if they had no more melodic contribution to make.

Across the room, Joey spotted Sam, busy snapping a curvaceous belly dancer who was playing up for his camera. He sidled over and said, 'Tell you what, the Irish may do funerals best, but the Lebs have weddings nailed. And don't forget, Sammy boy, today's your day off. No need for photos. How are you getting on with the cute blonde?'

'Yeah, not too bad. She doesn't seem that interested,' Sam said as he produced a joint. 'Barely said a word to me on the drive up.'

'Shit man, you can't light up in here.'

'I'm in fucking agony again.' Sam rolled his shoulders and stretched his neck. 'Body's all tense and there's a shooting pain down my spine. Same shit every time I have a bad night. This is the only thing that helps, loosens the muscles a bit.'

'You really need to sort out your sleeping problem. Go on over there, blow it off the garden.'

Joey wandered into what Lena called the formal lounge, a huge room with opulent Persian carpets scattered on marble floors and obviously expensive artwork adorning the walls. Massive flower arrangements occupied every spare surface; Antun's vase of fifty red roses was in prime position alongside the bride, so they appeared in every photo. Jamila's black corkscrew curls bushed out under her veil as she stood in a traditional white wedding dress and smiled for the endless round of photographs. Lena came over, ankle bracelet jingling, and nudged him. 'Come on, Joey, duty calls. We must have our photo taken with the bride.'

After their smiling-with-the-bride photo, they moved back onto the balcony to join the rest of Jamila's family. 'Ah, eventually, some booze,' Joey said, grabbing two glasses of champagne.

'Remember now, Joey,' Lena said, 'take it easy today. I don't want you getting drunk.'

'As if I would, my love.' Joey leaned in to kiss her luscious lips and smirked. 'Gotta make sure I can perform later.' Lena play-punched Joey and blushed demurely.

Soon after, Jamila emerged from the photo shoot, her face frozen in a perma-smile, and everyone piled into their cars. Cue a cacophony of blaring car horns, which continued all the way to the church in Ain Dara. As Joey and Sam crammed into Lena's car, she said, 'It will be a traditional Christian Maronite ceremony, though you will notice we don't do the "You may kiss the bride" thing, like you Irish.'

At the end of the lane leading to the church, Antun waited, shuffling nervously beside his best man, younger brother Butros. Both wore dark blue suits, white shirts, and red ties, the designated uniform for all the family's menfolk. *Will definitely lose the red ties when I'm doing this*, and then, concerned he had vocalised the thought, Joey dismissed it from his mind. Once the congregation was seated, the wedding party entered with the bride's father and Halina in her wheelchair out front, followed by the bride's mother and Michel, then the bridesmaid and Butros, with Antun and Jamila bringing up the rear. An hour later, the order was reversed and as the newlyweds exited the church, they were showered with rice and rose petals to the joyous cries of ululating women.

The wedding party moved onto the Chateau Bernina Hotel in Sofar. Festivities were down poolside, where the zaffe troupe of dancers and Santa-attired musicians had fired up again in anticipation of the wedded couple's entrance. People formed a line, holding hands, swinging arms, and kicking legs. Others approached, clapped their hands, and then joined by grabbing the hand of the person at the end. Soon after, everyone was directed into a huge dining room for a five-course meal, starting with the most enormous mezze Joey had ever seen: salads, dips, nuts, raw vegetables, and dozens of small fish and chicken dishes. Between courses three and four, Antun and Jamila started the dancing on the improvised poolside dance floor with a smoochy *Sweet Caroline*, accompanied by stage smoke and fireworks flaring high into the cloudy evening sky.

'For once, exploding fireworks don't have to mean take cover,' Joey quipped to Sam. Then he turned serious, and with an intense stare, asked, 'Do you sometimes hear a voice in your head?'

'A voice?' Sam looked back with droopy, hooded eyes. 'Not really. Sometimes, if I concentrate on my thoughts, it can seem like I'm listening to my own voice.'

'No, it's not that, it's like hearing another person. I'm starting to hear voices, chattering away to each other in my head.'

'Shit, bro, I'm out of my depth there. Are you sure it's not in your imagination?'

In fairness, Sammy couldn't really be expected to understand what was going on. It was all fine and dandy for him to pass it off with, 'Well, what do you expect if you take all those drugs?' Joey knew better; the voices were real, they were messing with his mind, and they were becoming more forceful. He tried not to worry about it, but it was getting harder to fool himself that everything was okay, that this was somehow normal. He needed to talk to someone about it, maybe some expert who could figure out how to stop them. Lena would be totally panicked if he said anything to her.

As the blue of the day faded into night, the party moved up a gear. Jamila's lively eighteen-year-old cousin poured a bottle of bubbly over herself and a friend on the dance floor, then both promptly jumped into the swimming pool. A huge circle of dancers formed, and someone pushed the garter catcher into the centre. She placed the garter on the leg of the bouquet catcher to a backdrop of loud whistling and lewd shouting. A man dressed in an ancient warrior outfit appeared, swinging a long, curved sword from side to side, and cut the five-tiered wedding cake into bite-sized pieces, which were distributed to the tables topped with mini fireworks. Then, a woman appeared with a jug on her head and belly-danced until the jug was knocked off by a low-hanging tree branch and smashed on the stone floor. Another woman appeared with a new jug on her head; Joey figured it was some sort of competition to see who could keep it going the longest. Not to be outdone, the men took over the floor and performed a traditional sword dance involving lots of swirling ribbons.

Towards dawn, Joey and Lena decided to crash and went to say good night to the happy couple. As she leaned in to kiss goodnight, Jamila accidentally stood on Lena's toes. Both women looked at each other, laughed, and hugged each other tightly.

'What was that all about, with Jamila?' Joey asked as they fell into bed.

Lena hesitated. 'Okay. The final Lebanese wedding tradition for you, but it's just a myth. It is said that if the bride steps on a single girl's foot, it will bring the girl good luck, and she will marry soon.'

Joey cuddled into Lena and whispered, 'Well, these myths do sometimes come true.'

12.

NO SOCIAL EVENT GALVANISES THE EXPAT COMMUNITY in a warzone quite like Paddy's Day. Back in Ireland, Sam and Joey never bothered doing anything on the day, but in Beirut, they were keen to celebrate; as children, they had been to many lively United Nations and Irish embassy parties across the Middle East and, given the universal popularity of the Irish peacekeepers in Lebanon, the festivities were guaranteed to draw an enthusiastic crowd. Sam wasn't keen on taking the girls along, but Joey insisted.

Nimer drove them, as usual whenever Lena went out at night. He worked for Michel and was renowned for his skill at navigating the treacherous night-time streets of Beirut, where the balance of power continually shifted between the various rogue militias and occupying armies. At night, Nimer would often drive with the headlights off, relying on his intimate knowledge of the local topography to avoid trouble. There were checkpoints all over Beirut, and everybody knew that the checkpoints were where the militias kidnapped people. Tonight, four bottles of Jameson rolled around the passenger's foot well where Joey sat, offerings for hostile checkpoint guards on this most Irish of nights.

In the six months since returning from Copenhagen, Joey had managed to cut his drug intake, but booze had flooded into the void and from an earlier hour each day. They argued about it all the time, but Joey was in no mood to listen. He batted away Sam's concerns, raging that he didn't need his brother turning into some kind of minder, he was well able to look after himself. Things weren't helped by his move into the smuggling business; Michel had introduced him to one of his black-market connections, and Joey had found a rising tide market flogging hard liquor to desperate Westerners, whose easy access to duty-free supplies had long ago dried up. Signs of overindulgence called out from Joey's flushed face: his eyes were bloodshot, he had turned jowly, and thread veins bulged on his nose. Five days of sustained drinking may have clouded Joey's brain, but his tongue was as loose as ever. The words of some disjointed story slurred from his mouth in a jumbled torrent until he succumbed to a violent attack of hiccups, then suddenly said, 'Pull over, Nimer, quick.'

A tense silence filled the car as they watched Joey bend over and heave the contents of his stomach onto a pile of broken bottles by the roadside. 'Leave him, Lena,' Sam said, placing a restraining hand on her arm. The evening was shaping up much as Sam had feared, and he was close to bailing out with Lena and Joumana. Joey wasn't the only one who had shit to deal with.

On virtually a daily basis, Sam came across and photographed some kind of bloody scene — a car bomb, the aftermath of a shoot-out, dead bodies in a shelled building — and for the most part he had become immune to the shock of it. But then occasionally a particularly horrific event broke through his shell of coolness and left him with a new set of images to play on his mind as he lay in bed at night, waiting for sleep to come. Just last week, he had seen his good buddy killed right in front of him. The scene was sprayed onto his mind's eye: Eddie jumping from the Jeep, cameras swinging, then creeping up the road, towards the gunfire, documenting the casualties of war. Boot to metal and then a white flash. Eddie spun through the air, thumped to the ground five yards from his ripped-off leg, and rattled his last choking breath. Sam had been ten paces behind.

'Joey's got some stuff going on in his head he needs to work through, Lena,' Sam continued. 'It's a big decision for him, committing to you. Joey's never done commitment. He doesn't like ties, anything that might stop him moving free as the breeze.'

Sam was pissed off with constantly making excuses, having to explain Joey's irrational behaviour, one moment all over Lena, the next disinterested and up his own arse. They'd talked it over and Joey had opened up about his 'internal battle against my better nature', as he called it. It was hard not to be sceptical; countless times before he'd heard how smitten Joey was with some girl or other, but this time certainly seemed different. He'd never been this close before, this willing to even consider settling down properly, like a normal person.

Lena fumed beside him, eyes blazing. 'What do you mean? He's so afraid of getting stuck with me that he must drink all the time?'

'It's the only way he knows,' Sam said, searching for a better explanation and coming up blank. 'He avoids the issue by escaping down the neck of a bottle. But he is *madly* in love with you.'

They watched Joey stand up and wipe a sleeve across his dribbling mouth. Flashing an idiotic grin, he winked at Lena as he slid back into the passenger seat.

'You are a total asshole when you're drunk, Joey,' Lena called from the back.

'Oh, but what about the rest of the time,' Joey scoffed. 'Go, Nimer, all is well.'

'Dear God, Lena,' Sam said, 'don't tell me Joey's been polluting your lovely English with his foul language.'

'Fuck that, Sammy, she nicked that asshole quip off you. Heard you saying it often enough recently, that's for sure.'

'What does being Irish mean to you, Joey?' Lena asked, her voice gruff. 'Is it just about getting drunk and playing the fool and singing rebel songs?'

Joey's hand cupped his face as he planted a cigarette in his mouth and sucked. Lit by the cigarette tip, his red chipmunk cheeks glowed in the dark car interior. 'Being Irish means . . . if you're Oirish, you've got the best passport in the world for travelling in troubled areas. Everyone loves the Irish and waves them through, welcoming them as friends.'

Sam asked Nimer to turn up the volume on the car stereo and looked out the window. Recently, Joey's behaviour had become even stranger than normal; all this talk of voices in his head was mental.

'Look! Up there' — Joey bent forward, pointing through the widescreen — 'God, I wanna shine like a great big star.'

The voice that came out of Lena was cut with a steely edge. 'First, you'll need to dig yourself out of your deep black hole.'

'Dark seeks dark,' was Joey's reply.

Having held her tongue all night, Joumana chose this moment to break her silence. 'Hey, Joey, how come you're such a dumb ass when you're drunk?'

Joey turned grinning to face her, then tossed his head back in a rolling laugh. Soon, they all cracked up, as much from the release of tension as at the strangeness of hearing that Irishism come out of Joumana's refined mouth.

'Here we are,' Nimer said with relief, as he parked outside the Irish embassy.

Inside, the function room was packed with dignitaries and hangers-on, whose nights were bookended by G&Ts around sunset and Bloody Marys to chase away the morning-after DTs. Sam led Lena and Joumana to the buffet. Joey grabbed a glass of punch and wandered off, interrupting complete strangers' conversations with, 'Hello there, excuse me' — a polite smirk to mask his slur — 'I'm looking for Fergus; have you seen Fergus?'

A story was doing the rounds about an Irish military observer, Fergus Keenan, who had been kidnapped as he walked home from the vegetable market the previous Sunday evening. Fergus was well known as a *big* talker – never one to say in ten words what could be said in twenty-five – and notorious for dominating conversations with anecdotes of limited interest. Word was that within a couple of days, his kidnappers had been bored into submission by his monotonous, interminable stories and, concluding that his value as a ransomable pawn was nil, released him as a bad mistake.

Circulating through the crowd, Joey spied the ambassador and lurched forward to shake hands. As Sam watched his brother stumble and fall towards the table of freshly made Irish coffees, all he could think was: where the hell did they get the fresh whipping cream? He raced over and heaved Joey off the ground, apologising for the damage with the limp excuse that he had had some bad news (a good friend's death back home) and had been drowning his sorrows ever since. With an arm wrapped under Joey's armpit, Sam guided him out of the embassy into the cold night air.

Moments later, Lena came out, raging as Sam had never seen her before. 'This is what you do. You keep drinking and drinking until other people are forced to stop you.' Lena's jewellery jangled as her hands flailed like fighting birds. 'It's always us that must set the boundaries, never your responsibility. Well, fuck this, I've had enough. Fuck you and your shit attitude, Joey.'

The sound of a fuming Lena — a first for Sam — had a sobering effect on Joey. 'Baby, I'm sorry. I'm just going through a bad patch,' his voice choking, close to tears. He backed up against the wall and slid down to a cross-legged position on the ground, head drooping forward, with Lena, Sam, and now Joumana standing over him.

'What bad patch?' Lena said, hands locked to her hips.

'Everything's so fucked up,' Joey said, scrunching his knuckles into his eyeballs. 'I thought I was going to be seeing . . .' The words trailed off as Joey tipped his head back to the wall. 'Not only can my only friends . . . besides you Sammy . . . not only can they not visit me, but now we can't even get out of this rat-trap to meet them in London.' Having hit his stride, Joey's disappointment erupted in a waterfall of words. 'Christy and Maud were so looking forward to finally meeting you, Lena; even Damien was going to come over. Now the fucking airport is closed again, and we're marooned here. And to top it all, even Sammy's talking about leaving me.'

'That's bollocks, bro, and you know it.' Sam glanced across at Lena and saw the confused look on her face. 'You know Fred, the Tribune correspondent I work with. Well, he's being moved on to Angola, and my boss wanted me to go too' — Lena's eyelids parted wide — 'they reckon it's getting too dangerous here.'

There was no disputing that conclusion. Most western journalists had left Beirut, fearful of kidnap or worse; soon, the correspondents still based in Beirut would be outnumbered by those held hostage.

'Are you leaving, Sam?' Joumana's voice came out as a surprised croak.

'No, I'm not. As I've already told Joey. I refused the move. I'm not going anywhere.'

'Oh, Sam,' Lena exclaimed and threw her arms around his neck.

From below them, Joey lifted his eyelids with effort and whispered, 'Hey, you guys, what about me? I'm feeling all alone, down here by my lonesome.'

'You'll be alright, habibi,' Lena said. 'You always are.'

'I am now that I've found you, Lena. You're the only reason I stay here.'

Lena stooped down, stroked his face, and said, 'Oh Joey, you're impossible. Come on, get up.'

By the time Nimer deposited them at the ILMAC offices, hostilities between Lena and Joey had ceased. ILMAC was the umbrella name for the United Nations peacekeepers, many of whom were Irish and well known for the quality and length of their parties. Joey led them up the stairs, past green banners and tricolours stuck on the walls, towards the din on the second floor. Entering between two ghoulish, child-sized teddy bears dressed in leprechaun outfits, they headed for the bar. Crates of stubby Heineken bottles were stacked on a table, and bottles of Irish whiskey and Baileys lined the bar counter. Sam grabbed a beer for each of them, and they slalomed through the crowd who were whooping along to a Dubliners compilation tape.

Sam and Joumana found themselves in the company of two middle-aged women, listening to their competing tales of woe. 'Of course, I'm an old hand at this evacuation business,' said the bee-hived, jewellery-laden one. 'Over the last twelve years, we've been evacuated four times from Beirut, twice to Cyprus, once to Damascus, and once home for a month.'

'Where is—'

'County Cork. But nothing will keep us away. We love it here.'

Sam smiled across the room at Joey, who was batting away the flirtatious advances of an inebriated UN wife and trying to steer Lena onto the dance floor. Beside him, the tall Scandinavian one was saying, '. . . lucky to have been evacuated. Thor and I were stuck here with the kids during the 1982 Israeli aerial bombardment. My God, we-'

'Why didn't ye leave when ye had the chance?' the bee-hive said.

'Four days we spent stuck in the basement of our apartment,' the blonde continued forcefully. 'We lived down near the Phoenicia Hotel. There were twenty other families, with only one toilet between us—'

'Ugh, disgusting,' bee-hive butted in.

'—which didn't flush. There was hardly any drinking water. And the only food we had was bowls of rice with tinned vegetables. Every morning, when the militias rested after their night's shooting, we raced up to the apartment and cooked the tins on a paraffin stove.'

The bee-hive placed her hand on Sam's shoulder, closely watched by Joumana, and screeched in her sing-song voice, 'You'll never guess what's going on in the apartment block opposite us. Some militia group has taken over the entire third floor. They spend the night shooting out the windows, but during the day, they prance around in Colonel Minotti's uniforms '— you know him, Inga, the Italian officer who had to race home suddenly when his wife went a bit peculiar. Well, now all these *gorillas* have moved into his apartment and are smoking his cigars and drinking his whiskey. There were five of them the other day, all beautifully dressed in the colonel's shirts with matching ties. By night, they're fighters, and by day, they assume the life of an Italian army officer.'

'It sure is a crazy place,' Sam said, placing his arm around Joumana's back. 'We'd better go rescue our friend. Anyone want a drink?'

Towards daybreak, a mellower mood settled over this well-practiced partying crowd. A burly army officer with a handlebar moustache launched into *The Four Green Fields*. Before long, the predictable singsong rippled around the room as the baton passed from one eager singer to the next, with plenty of prompters available for those who struggled for the words after the first chorus. For a while, Joey joined in but soon drifted off. Of late, he could only handle instrumental music; songs with lyrics just set off too many thoughts in his head. He'd been fine with Pink Floyd — even when their songs had lyrics, it didn't require much mental energy to figure them out — but then just yesterday, listening to the start of *The Great Gig in the sky*, there was that guy's voice taunting him, *Why be frightened of dying?*

Whereas previously Joey lived by a specialise-in-having-fun credo, all that had now changed, utterly changed. New voices were directing operations. Guilt, and its cruel cousin, paranoia, had broken into his mind and settled in with troubling ease.

13.

CHRISTMAS DAY DAWNED CALM after a thunderous night of storms and intense street fighting. Plumes of black smoke spewed from the upper floors of the Holiday Inn; its elevated, strategic location had again become the focal point for sniper activity. A weak sun was burning through the drizzling rain as Beirutis stirred into life, tentatively hoping that the promise of a festive ceasefire would hold so that those who wanted to celebrate the holy birth in peace could get on with it. And everyone else could get off the rollercoaster, for one day at least.

Festive preparations had started early in the Sarkis household, and Joey had done his bit by sourcing the wine. He and Lena had driven up the mountain to a vineyard in Chtoura, run by a Muslim called Walid, although everyone knew him as Ironside, after the 1970s wheelchaired TV detective. The war had taken its toll on business, and the winery had clearly seen better times, but Ironside was effusive in his welcome. 'Come, my friends, let us sample some wine,' he said, rolling down the ramp to the underground cellar. Afterwards, when the car boot was stocked, Ironside invited them into his house for a sobering coffee before the drive home.

His small, dingy living room was lit by a single bulb hanging from the ceiling. Red and white damask sofas and armchairs lined the walls. An ancient, bulky TV atop a heavy wooden cabinet filled the space at the far end of the room, and a low, tilting coffee table stood in the centre of the stone floor. Christmas was a lonely time for Ironside. 'My family has suffered greatly in this war. Five years ago, my wife was killed by the same bomb that took my legs away. And both my sons have been kidnapped at Syrian checkpoints.'

Although the Syrians had been greeted as saviours when they first arrived in 1976, with promises to end the civil war, they had long since outstayed their welcome. Theirs was a devious game involving regular switches in loyalty to whichever side was winning so that, over time, they formed alliances with virtually every party to the Lebanese conflict. Ironside continued, 'I found my first son soon after he was taken. They were keeping him in a prison near the Syrian border. Two guards had to carry him out to see me. He could not walk because his feet were so swollen; they had tortured him by beating his soles. They said he was fighting in a militia against Syria, but it was just talk. My son is a peaceful boy. He was a student at the AUB. I have never managed to find my other son. Allah-u-Akbar, I have given money to so many people, people who say they can get me information about him, but always they find nothing. The Syrian soldiers, they say, "We have seen your son; if you want him back, you must give us ten thousand lira, and we will bring you news of him." Or they tell me, "Give me twenty thousand lira, and I will find your son in a week." I know it's all lies, but yanni, what I can do? Maybe they can find something out. Finally, I said to this man, you must tell me something about my son that only I would know, some real proof that you have been in contact with him. I never saw that snake again. Now . . . Khalas, I give them nothing; it is a big . . . how you say, scam?'

'I am so sorry to hear that, Walid.' Wouldn't Pops do the same for him or Sam? Kidnappings ruptured a family apart, yet how disjointed was his own family, scattered across the globe. In truth, they may as well have been kidnapped for all the involvement they had with the Hogan family these days. Occasionally he exchanged a couple of jokey postcards with Bee, and Pops never forgot his birthday, but there was no real participation in any of the other's lives. It was just him and Sam. Relations were better there now that Joey had his drinking under control and the voices had calmed down a bit. Sam reckoned he was a transformed character since the low point of Paddy's day, when it all went to shit and he was staring down the barrel of losing Lena. That was the shock to the system he needed.

Thoughts of family filled Joey's mind that Christmas morning as he drove across the Green Line to Ashrafiyah where the extended Sarkis family were gathering to feast together: parents and grandparents, brothers and sisters, aunts, uncles, and cousins. Joey parked his Peugeot opposite their house and gathered up his collection of presents. As he crossed the road, three armed youths appeared ahead of him, and banged on the Sarkis' front door. The one closest to Joey – black helmet-shaped hair, a thick moustache, and an unlit cigarette dangling from his mouth – turned to check him out, a Kalashnikov under his muscular right armpit, pointing downwards. A bulging ammo belt hung over his tight trousers, and a pack of Marlboro was tucked into his tee-shirt sleeve. Beside him, another man, shirt unbuttoned to show off the medallion shining against his hairy chest, was pretending to smoke a pen while waving his rifle one-handed. A third camp-looking guy with fair hair, white trousers, and a dark vest stood a way off, holding a gun behind his back. Feeling overdressed in his suit and tie and groomed hair but too far advanced to turn back, Joey just smiled and wished them a happy Christmas. One of Lena's cousins opened the door, and helmet-head asked for Butros. Joey looked on as the guy with the pen smiled and blew imaginary smoke rings at him.

'Ahlen,' Butros called as he came through the door. 'Go in, Joey, I will see you later.'

Lena appeared in the doorway and hugged Joey, then kissed him full on the mouth. 'Merry Christmas, habibi.'

'Who are those guys?' Joey asked as he scuttled in and closed the door behind them.

'They are thugs that Butros is friendly with. Many of these disaffected young men are taking things into their own hands. Don't say anything to Michel, it will upset him.'

Most of the family had already arrived and were gathered in the spacious sitting room, drinking coffee and eating sugared almonds. An enormous Christmas tree, covered in sparkling decorations interspersed with orange peels cut into traditional Yuletide shapes, filled the window facing onto the street. Joey went over to Halina, bent over her wheelchair, and kissed her right cheek, left and right again. He then made his way around the room, repeating the greeting with the women and shaking hands with the men, handing everyone a cracker as he went. Having failed to source genuine Christmas crackers, Joey had mined his Blue Peter memories and made some himself using wrapping paper twisted around a toilet roll. Each cracker contained a party hat and popper, a token gift, and a Joey-crafted Paddy-the-Irishman joke, which kept the bemused family entertained until Butros returned and dinner was called.

When they'd finished eating, and coffee and liqueurs had been served, Joey looked nervously across at Lena. Buoyed by her encouraging smile, he wiped his clammy hands down his trouser legs, stood, and rattled his spoon against a wine glass. 'Your attention please, everybody . . .' he said, mouth sticky. 'Yesterday, I asked Michel for his blessing, and I am delighted to say that the one and only true love of my life, Lena, has agreed to marry me.'

Until very recently, if you'd asked Joey about the chances of him marrying at the age of twenty-five, he would have marched you off to an asylum. Maud always said that every girl was a one-night stand with Joey, and there weren't many nights when Joey didn't have a stand. Now, he was looking at a September wedding date. 'In Lena, I have found a woman like no other one. Before I came to Lebanon, I'd never known real love, not like I feel for Lena' — Halina was smiling through her tears — 'and I have a very disjointed family life, with everyone scattered all over the place. But look at me now. I've got all you lot, and there's lots more of you that aren't even here.' Everyone liked that joke. 'I have no roots anywhere. I've spent my life wandering like a Bedouin, but now, for the first time, I've found somewhere I want to stay, where I can settle down for good, with a good woman by my side.'

Everyone clapped and hollered around the table as Michel stood to say, 'Joey, we are delighted to welcome you to our family, and I wish you and my angel Lena a very happy and prosperous life. For me, I am particularly happy. Now, I am assured of a regular chess game, and maybe one day I will even be the victor.'

The celebratory mood continued for the rest of the day. Joey fought to contain his emotions and the swelling hope that he had finally conquered his demons, slain and banished them from the kingdom to leave him carefree again. Everything was falling into place. There was just the nagging concern that once you call some place paradise, you may as well kiss it goodbye.

14.

SARKIS CLOTHING IMPORTS occupied the ground and first floors of a modest building on a side street off rue Hamra. After the nightclub idea crashed and burned – it transpired that the required level of militia protection money was prohibitive – the young lovers turned their attention to importing clothes, fashionable French and Italian lines, which appealed to the strata of Lebanese society trying to maintain appearances despite the war's best efforts. Michel had started the business in the late seventies but had handed over the reins when Lena quit her job with the Associated Press. Lena ran the shop on the ground floor, where she showcased their better-selling lines, although most people bought off the catalogue; carrying stock in wartime Beirut was a risky business. Upstairs, Joey took care of procurement and dealing with the fallout from the plummeting Lebanese pound; the currency that had proved amazingly resilient throughout the war had been plunging south since the turn of the year. Slouched on the table, phone to his ear, Joey yawned as he talked prices with their Italian supplier.

Lena came into the office, coffee cups in each hand, and sat at the desk, waiting for him to hang up. 'Habibi, you are good at this negotiation business. Better than you realise.'

'Hello baby, how are things below?'

'Yanni, the shop is empty. There are no customers. So far today, I had one person who wanted two shirts at half price. Cheapskate, you say?' Joey laughed and leaned over the desk to kiss her. 'It's not funny, Joey. People can no longer afford to buy at these prices.'

'It's not only our customers who are struggling,' Joey said. 'Enrico's basically saying it's not his problem if it's costing us double what it did last year to buy his shirts; he still needs to make the same money. He's refusing to send the next shipment unless we pay up-front.'

'Maybe we should have stuck with the nightclub idea,' Lena said, an unfamiliar note of gloom in her croaky voice.

'Bugger this. Let's go shopping for rings,' Joey said as he took her hand in his and stroked her long fingers. Some retail therapy was required, a favourite Lena pastime. Two months previously, after moving into their apartment on rue Gouraud, they'd gone on a weekend trip to Damascus and returned laden with rugs, camel stools, leather poufs and all kinds of brass: lamps, coffee tables, ornaments, ashtrays, Joey never realised how many uses brass could be put to. After three chaotic years living in Sam's minimalist apartment, he was ready for some clean, well-furnished, safer living, on the east side of the city. And Lena needed to move closer to her family in Ashrafiyah now that her mother spent most of her days in bed, depressed.

Since moving east, Joey had gone native, most visibly in the way he dressed: smart chinos, wide collared silk shirts and expensive Italian leather shoes. His Arabic was near fluent, and Michel's wide network helped with his assimilation into Lebanese high society. Besides Sam, he had minimal contact with other Westerners and couldn't remember the last time he'd had a mad night out. It felt like he had finally gotten his act together.

They locked up the shop and wandered down the back streets towards rue Clemenceau, holding hands, Joey loose-limbed, whistling the bass line to *Love Cats*. Earlier, the stifling May heat had sent most of the population scampering indoors but as the sun fell, they began to emerge onto the streets. A brown-suited man with a burgundy fez shuffled past, two small girls in colourful dresses by his side. The eyes beneath the fez regarded Joey with suspicion as the man hurried along, pulling the girls closer to him. Westerners on Beirut's streets were an even rarer sight since January, when Terry Waite was kidnapped on his latest attempt to secure the release of some hostages, including Lena's old AP boss

Terry Anderson.

After checking out a couple of jewellers, they sauntered down the hill to the Corniche, a seafront promenade popular with street vendors and strollers seeking exercise, or just out to be seen. As they turned a corner, a pack of emaciated cats scattered from the pile of chicken heads they were devouring. Lively waves swelled against the sea wall but further out the water was a sheet of turquoise glass, sparkling beneath the setting sun. A group of fishermen stood silhouetted on the mossy rocks, their long rods arching into the water. Nearby, four men grappled with a fishing net, each holding a corner and pulling to unravel the tangle. At least this lot were going with traditional fishing methods, Joey thought; often when he used to come this way on his early morning run, he would hear the muffled boom of dynamite exploding underwater and watch as piles of stunned fish were blown to the surface and scooped into a dragnet behind a boat.

Joey veered Lena towards a stall with neatly arranged, sloping boxes overflowing with all sorts of nuts. 'Marhaba, Ahmed.'

'Ahlan wa sahlan, Joey.' Ahmed grinned two rows of stained, crooked teeth. 'You want sunflower seeds?'

'Not today. Today lawza, shukran.'

Ahmed thrust the curved steel shovel into the pile of almonds, tipped it backwards to pour the nuts into the gusseted paper bag and placed it on the scales. Joey laughed. A hundred grams exactly, not a nut less. 'Shukran, Ahmed.'

They moved on and sat awhile on a stone bench under the meagre shelter of a palm tree, chewing nuts and people-watching.

'The ideal woman for an Arab man,' Lena said, pointing at a broad-hipped, buxom woman.

'Voluptuous, I would say. Definitely not fat.' Joey turned sideways and kissed Lena, her face reflected golden in the fading light. 'Look at those two guys.' Two tall student-types had met up, embraced, and kissed on the cheeks. 'I still can't get used to all these straight guys kissing each other.'

Lena chuckled. 'At least they're not holding hands, like you see in many Arab countries.'

'Real men, that's what I'm after. Look over there, those are proper workers.' A hunched old man passed in front of them, a hessian sack slung over his back, followed by a tottering young man with a tray of flatbreads balancing on his head. 'You won't see those men doing any of that namby-pamby kissing.' Joey swatted at the flies buzzing around his head and looked out to sea. A shimmering trail of light gilded the trembling sea surface, all the way to the flaming ball on the horizon.

Off to the left, the crowd parted to make way for a group of soldiers marching with rifles pointing skywards. Out front, the leader stopped hollering into his walkie-talkie, halted abruptly, and wiped the remains of his lunchtime hummus from his drooping moustache. Beside him, a mean-looking bearded soldier, wearing sunglasses and a backwards-facing baseball cap, pointed his rifle in the direction of the American University, and off they went.

Lena and Joey talked of the future, of their life together, of making Irish/ Lebanese babies, of Michel finally meeting Pops. September twentieth had been set as their wedding date, and they were due to meet Christy, Maud, Bee and Damien in Rome the month before for an early celebration. It was still way too dangerous for the gang to visit Beirut; Michel's connections at the airport could only do so much. Crossing from one side of the city to the other remained a treacherous undertaking. The previous week, Nimer had been killed by a lone sniper's bullet as he led a trail of cars across the Green Line. Nimer's bona fides may have been powerful on the ground, where his ready supply of gifts for checkpoint guards generally ensured safe passage, but he couldn't cater for those shooting from on high.

Just as they were thinking of moving on, some of Lena's friends walked by. 'Look at you lovebirds,' Ibrahim called out as they came over.

'Come join us; we are going to my apartment for a meal,' Mahmoud said.

The lovers set off with the group, Joey's yellow-stained fingertips interlaced with Lena's pink polished, squared-off fingernails. On a bench, a man dressed in a white suit and with a white sailor's cap on his head slowly fed a string of worry beads through his fingers. A mob of young boys dived off boulders and grappled to sit in an inflated car tyre bobbing in the water. Spray blew from the waves crashing against the rocky shoreline, and Joey wiped the sea's salty spit off his face.

Lena wrapped her arm around his waist. 'Maybe instead we should go back to our apartment and start making those babies.'

'Later, habibti, let's not disappoint your friends.'

The party of seven headed back towards Hamra, detouring via the Idriss supermarket to pick up booze and food to barbeque. Out towards the horizon, a bank of clouds caught the sinking sun and wrapped it up so that only an orange winking eye remained visible. An airplane passed along the coast before dog-legging east towards the airport just as the clouds extinguished the remaining speck of sun.

PAINT IT BLACK

The Rolling Stones

LEBANON

June 1987 to October 1988

15.

SUNRISE STREAMED THROUGH THE BATHROOM WINDOW and bounced off the shaving mirror, blinding Joey. From the kitchen, he could hear *Lovely Day* purring on the radio. Lena had phoned the previous afternoon, but there was still no news of Butros. He was last seen in a village in the Shouf Mountains called Moukhtara, where she had now gone to search for him, fearful that he may have been kidnapped.

As Joey was forming a loose plan to head down to the Bain Militaire for a spot of sunbathing and a day of doing nothing at all but doing it well, the apartment door burst open, and Sam raced in. 'Let's haul ass, Joey. We need to hit the road. There's been another massive bomb.'

'Another bomb, great! Why do we care about this one?'

'Just get ready; I'll tell you on the way.'

'Nah, man, I just want to chill today. No shelling, no bombs, no death, no any of that shit. I was thinking of heading down to the sea for a swim.' Joey noticed Sam's face, reflected in the mirror, chalk white, eyeballs popping. 'Hey man, lighten–'

'Listen, Joey, the bomb went off in the Shouf Mountains. It might be nothing, but I think we should check it out.'

The blood drained from Joey's face, and his legs wobbled. He grabbed hold of the sink. From the street below came the growl of a chainsaw. Someone was attempting to restrain Mother Nature as she advanced remorselessly on downtown Beirut; left untended for so long, grass patches bushed into mini jungles, shrubs burgeoned into trees, and tree roots ruptured paving stones as they thrust upwards.

Despite the early hour, all roads out of Beirut were clogged as the masses sought respite from the scorching June heat. Joey rocked like a metronome in the passenger seat, his tanned face spotted with shadows cast by the bug-spattered windscreen. Finally, they shook off the city traffic and climbed into the Shouf mountain range. On the way, Sam filled Joey in on what he knew about the bombing. At twilight the previous day, a red-bearded man rode a donkey into the centre of Moukhtara, stopped outside an apartment block, yelled out a supplication of some sort, and then detonated the three hundred kilos of explosives he had packed into saddlebags on the animal's flanks. Across the road from the building, there was an ammunition dump; the munitions cached there exploded in a chain reaction, causing devastating collateral damage.

As they arrived in the village, Sam said, 'Lena could have been miles from the scene; let's not jump to hasty conclusions.' Half a kilometre on, the bomb had blown a colossal crater in the road, blocking any further progress. Sam parked Joey's red Peugeot on the roadside. 'We'll have to walk from here.'

'I've . . . I've got . . . got a real bad feeling about this,' Joey wailed. 'I don't think I can do this.'

'C'mon, we're here now. Let's find her. Move man, let's go.'

'How the fuck do you know? You have no idea what's happened. And please, leave that fucking camera behind. You're not seriously thinking of snapping away while I'm racing around trying to find Lena.'

Chaos was now running the village. People scattered in all directions like frightened hens from a chasing fox. Emerging from the doorway of a gutted villa, two men carried a stretcher, a blackened foot dangling from one end of a blood-soaked blanket and a scarred head from the other. An old woman stooped over a child's body on the pavement and screamed a bawling lamentation. Beside her, a casually dressed, younger woman tried to comfort the old woman, oblivious to the extensive burns seared on her own face and the large black weal across her forehead. Straddling the road, a shelled and still smouldering truck blocked their way. In the driver's seat, a glass-eyed soldier gazed vacantly into the distance and muttered as if in prayer. Beside him, another soldier was toppled against the windscreen with a gaping head wound oozing a white liquid spiked with dark blood. A group of five soldiers showed up, pushing two blindfolded men ahead of them at gunpoint. From what Sam could make out, these two were accused of collaborating with the Israelis and planting the bomb. Ignoring their pleas for mercy, the militia leader raised his pistol to each man's temple and pulled the trigger. Joey turned away, horror etched on his face, as he flashed back to that photo of the Vietcong prisoner on Sam's teenage bedroom wall.

Passing a row of skeletal trees, they plunged into the carnage. The bottom three floors of a five-storey block had compressed onto each other like a concertina, crushing all inhabitants under an enormous heap of masonry. The apartment walls on the remaining floors had sheared off to expose tables, chairs, beds, and cabinets, all scattered across the open space. A sofa was balanced precariously, half in, half out of the building; behind it, a row of perfectly aligned pictures still hung on the wall, illuminated by an elaborate chandelier whose bulbs continued to glow, powered by a deviant electricity source that the explosions had failed to obliterate. Dozens of sweating men and women scrambled through the wreckage, scooping bricks and concrete with their raw hands, in a valiant but ultimately futile rescue mission.

'Oh my God . . . Oh FUCK . . . Oh fuck, fuck, fucckkk.'

'Calm down, Joey. Hang on, take a deep breath,' Sam said. 'That's it, calm down.'

'Maybe we should help these guys,' Joey said. 'She could be under that pile.'

He rushed towards the dusty ruins, Sam close behind calling, 'Hold up . . . hang on Joey. This is just wasting time. Let's go ask if anybody has seen her.'

Some Red Crescent medics confirmed that they no longer expected to find people alive and that this was now effectively a body recovery exercise. They suggested trying the hospital half a kilometre away for any news of the wounded. They went back to the car and Sam took a side alley to circle around the crater, but progress was tortuously slow. The road was cluttered with villagers searching for loved ones and strewn with wreckage from blown-up vehicles. Sam eased the car past what remained of a pickup truck, its roof blown off and its axles melted into the road. Joey roared warnings out the car window for people to get out of their way. Soldiers directed traffic and barked contradictory orders, generating confusion rather than restoring calm. Sam diverted Joey's attention from an incinerated Renault on the right, where a detached hand was stuck on the steering wheel, but there was no sign of the rest of the driver.

'There it is! Oh no, man, oh man . . .' Joey wailed, pointing to the crossroads ahead. And there on the left side of the road was a burnt-out white convertible, the numbers 539 492, in silver on a rectangular black licence plate. 'I knew it. A funeral pyre, that's–'

'Okay, shut up, Joey, just shut up. You're of no help if you get all hysterical. Get a grip; we'll go check out things in the hospital.'

The hospital turned out to be a three-storey residential building, which had been converted into a stopgap medical facility-come-morgue. The initial influx of casualties had abated but everywhere was cluttered with the wounded and dying. Out back, corpses were laid out in lines across the yard, covered in claret-stained blankets. Joey clamoured his way through the crowd towards the reception area. A medic was triaging a hysterical soldier on the floor, staunching the blood pumping from his head with swathes of bandages. Two colleagues pinioned the soldier's body as he thrashed around in a delirium.

'Please, please. I'm looking for someone. Lena Sarkis, is she here?' Joey screamed at the harassed receptionist. Streaks of gritty sweat poured down his face, and his blackened yellow shirt stuck to his back like a layer of skin.

'Let me check, sir . . . Sarkis . . . Sarkis,' the receptionist said as she scanned down the list of names on her clipboard. Behind her, the clock on the wall showed five to one. 'Sarkis, yes . . . Ramid Sarkis. Faisal Sarkis. No, I don't have a Lena Sarkis. But we don't have everyone's name yet. There are so many. And many are hard to identify.'

'No Lena Sarkis? You're sure?' Sam said. 'She was driving a white Mercedes.'

The woman looked up, shifting from Sam to Joey and back again. 'A white Mercedes . . . was it a sports car?'

'Sort of—'

'Why? Why do you ask that?' Joey wailed.

'There was a woman . . . A man . . . he would know. Wait, let me check,' as she ran down her list again. 'You need to go to Ward C, on the first floor, the big room on the right. Ask there for Kamal Halawi.'

With a sense of hope tinged by panic, they ran down the first-floor corridor. Kamal Halawi peered through slitted eyes as Joey and Sam sprinted towards his bed. Both his arms were bandaged from shoulder to wrist, and his hands were slathered in cream, under which the skin glowed a dark crimson. The heat in the room was oppressive, unperturbed by the powerless ceiling fan. Sam put his hand on Joey's shoulder to hold him back, and said in Arabic, 'Hello, Mr Halawi, sorry to trouble you. We were told you may know a woman called Lena?'

'Lena. Yes. I know her. My sister. Is she all right?'

'Your sister?' Sam said, exchanging a confused glance with Joey, whose bulging eyes looked ready to pop. 'Lena . . . Lena Sarkis.'

'No, no, Lena Halawi, she is my sister; she is just fifteen.'

Joey exhaled deeply and smiled as Sam said, 'Ah, okay, a different person. The woman at reception said you would know about Lena Sarkis. The woman in the white Mercedes.'

The soldier's burn-scarred face squirmed with pain as he closed his eyes. Slowly he began to speak. 'Yes, I know . . . that car . . . I saw that poor woman. God have mercy.'

Kamal had been shopping for vegetables when the bomb went off and immediately ran to see if he could help. He saw a screaming woman in a white Mercedes struggling to free herself from behind the steering wheel. Flying rubble had wedged the driver's door and crushed her legs against the gearbox. Smoke was rising from the rear of the car as Kamal clawed at the jammed passenger door. Scorching heat spread along the metal frame and seared his hands, forcing him to let go just as the car was engulfed in flames and exploded in a fireball when the petrol tank ignited.

Joey retched and sobbed hysterically, the howl of a hundred Trojan women mourning their dead. Sam hugged him close. 'Okay, okay, Joey. Hang in there … Thank you Kamal, thank you for trying,' Sam said. He wrapped his arm around Joey's shoulder and directed him out of the ward. From the back of the house, where two men were loading the claret-sheeted corpses onto a truck, came the sound of a generator stuttering into life. The fluorescent lights in Ward C flickered on as the resurgent power circulated through the walls, invigorating appliances throughout this newly-purposed house.

Outside, Sam squinted as his eyes adjusted to the sudden brightness. Beside him Joey stared unseeing into the distance, eyelids prised apart to reveal lifeless black holes in red-streaked eyeballs. Sam had heard of the thousand-yard stare but had never seen it for himself until that day when it came to occupy Joey's face, after which it stuck around for a long while.

16.

AT STREET LEVEL, life in Beirut remained as hazardous as ever. One dusky evening a month later, as Joey drove home from the souk, a Mercedes appeared in his rear-view mirror, flashing headlights on full beam. He slowed down, and as they overtook him, a bearded, wild-haired man waved an AK-47 rifle out of his window and gestured to pull over. The Mercedes moved in front of Joey's car and stopped up ahead. Dark curtains obscured his view through the back window, but he had seen enough to understand that this wasn't just another Lebanese driver in a hurry to the next coffee shop.

Joey drew his Peugeot up alongside, then suddenly swerved to the left and floored the accelerator as he fishtailed down towards the coast road. The streets were deserted, and Joey, driving like a manic Nelson Piquet, managed to put some distance between himself and his would-be kidnappers. One hand shaking on the steering wheel and the other rammed on the car horn, Joey kept his eyes fixed on the mirror. Two gunmen hung out of the Mercedes, waving rifles, though mercifully not yet firing them. As he rounded the bend at the top of the Corniche, Joey was blinded by the reflection of his pursuers' headlights, and the Peugeot veered right, scraping the sides of two parked cars. His front bumper got stuck and peeled off as he sped down the hill. Salty sweat trickled off his forehead and stung his swivelling eyeballs. Five hundred metres ahead, he could make out the white neon sign on the top of The Riviera Hotel; behind him, the stalking Mercedes was gaining all the time. In one continuous movement, Joey slammed on the brakes outside the hotel, hopped out, and raced through the revolving door just as the Mercedes went screaming by, four rifles firing indiscriminately into the dark night sky.

Much later — after steadying his nerves with half a bottle of Johnnie Walker in the hotel bar whilst simultaneously agitating them with the dregs of the speed he'd retrieved from the Peugeot's glove box — Joey took a taxi to the Commodore Hotel, where the usual crowd gathered around the bar. Only the crazy ones remained in Beirut; anyone with half a brain had escaped long ago. Really, he should also run from this hellhole to a safer place. But what was the point? Clearly, his life was cursed, and death was hot on his trail. That track he'd been on since Dublin, the one which brought him to Lena and an illusory contentment, had taken a violent turn, and he was now dangerously lost.

'Good evening, Mr Joey,' Fuad said, a crescent smile hanging on his moon face.

'Bring me a bottle of Tequila, with salt and lemon.' Joey was in no mood for company. He parked himself beside Coco and spent the rest of his night hacking at walnuts with a nutcracker and trying to get the ever-obliging parrot to say, 'Fuck Lebanon'.

Hunched over Sam's coffee table, Joey fiddled with the radio. 'I've turned into Pops,' he declared to the empty room, recalling a childhood dominated by his father's daily ritual of tuning into BBC World Service news bulletins. After Lena's death, Joey had moved back in with Sam, and since his near-kidnap he rarely ventured out. His whole being was numb, her loss too horrific to process, but as his new reality became more apparent, as he grew accustomed to the entirely different, empty future stretching out ahead of him, he retreated inwards. Her funeral had been like no other. There was barely enough of her remains to fill the urn sitting on the table in front of the altar, let alone a coffin. Joey didn't speak a word for weeks before or after the service. One time, he'd gone back to their apartment on rue Gouraud with Michel, but even five minutes with Lena's ghost was too much. Most days, he lay spread-eagled on the sofa, munching sunflower seeds and olives and watching threadbare videotapes or Arabic TV programmes. Aside from Sam and occasionally Michel, Joey's only contact was with the stray cats and dogs that he fed through the iron gate entrance to the apartment block. Sam put a stop to that routine when he came home one day to find Joey tossing steaks to a ten-strong pack of dogs who were growling at each other and attracting militia interest.

Joey switched to the LW band and twirled the radio knob past the station markers into the zones of static. A splurge of interference burst from the radio, and he paused, ear pressed to the speaker. As his understanding of their master plan grew, he came to realise that this had been going on for years. Like father, like son, spies both of them, helping the CIA with clandestine intelligence operations. For reasons unknown to Joey (classified, eyes-only reasons), he had been planted on the ground here in Beirut to gather intel for the Americans. Even now, weeks later, he wasn't sure exactly how it all worked, except that the information exchange only operated on certain radio frequencies, in the gaps between stations, where interference swamped the transmitted signal. Once he tuned the dial to the right wavelength, the bi-directional communication commenced: through the radio static, his handlers tunnelled into his mind and injected instructions for a new mission; simultaneously, they extracted from his head the intel he had been unknowingly gathering, for transmission back to Langley.

It had all started so innocuously. The radio had been buzzing in the background, Joey barely listening. Constantly bombarded by noise — the TV, a slammed door, the honk of a car horn from the street below — he found it difficult to filter the sounds; everything was given equal weight so that he couldn't determine what was important or what he needed to concentrate on. In a rare moment of quiet, he had zoned in on the radio programme, something about broken families, when suddenly the woman presenter said that she needed to talk to the young man who had recently lost his fiancée. Her voice swirled around his head, reverberating insistently, emphasising how critical it was that he make contact. As he moved closer, the presenter called out to him, *Turn the dial clockwise until you can hear only static, and then you will be issued with your first instructions.* Since then, they had established a firmer schedule. Check-in time was on the hour, every daylight hour, just in case they needed to get in touch.

With practiced precision, Joey twisted the dial towards 200 kHz and landed on the station just as Big Ben was ringing: bong-bong-bong-boonng, repeated four times, and then: 'This is the BBC World Service in London, the time is eleven a.m. Greenwich Mean Time.' Speaking in code that only Joey could pick up — he figured perhaps in the echoes between their words — the newsreaders acted as the go-between. The voice on the radio crackled, *Welcome to the machine; you've done good, Joey. Let's find out where you've been, shall we?*

August melted into September and brought with it a hostile heat. Every time the electric power came back on, Joey got into an ice-making frenzy. He would throw the ice into the bath, top up with tap water, and lay submerged for hours, pulling Heineken bottles from the ice around him. His behaviour became increasingly capricious. Convinced that there were coded messages in the *Hotel California* album, he did the lyrics to death until the tape wore out, packed in like his hopes and dreams. He lived caged in his twisted mind, a tinderbox ready to explode. The spark came following yet another bout of street fighting closed all east-west crossover points for ten days. Shelling continued almost non-stop, day and night. People piled sandbags against windows and doors, blocked flights of stairs, and holed up with their food rations. From the relative safety of their apartment, Sam and Joey watched the final battle for control of Ras Beirut play out on the streets below.

Crouched behind a wall of sandbags, Kalashnikovs poking through gaps in their barricade, two men and a ponytailed woman sprayed everything in front of them. At the far end of the road, three cornered men made a run for it, hunched over and shooting blind. A man in flared trousers peered cautiously around the corner then signalled, and four men, red keffiyehs flapping on their heads, jumped out and gunned down the fleeing three. Moments later, another man joined the keffiyeh gang, positioned himself in the middle of the road, one knee bent, the other resting on the ground, and raised a rocket launcher to his shoulder to discharge his deadly cargo. And suddenly, all was quiet.

Victorious gunmen ran from buildings on both sides of the road and discharged their weapons into the air. Residents emerged cautiously to a scene of total carnage. Along the street, cars were in flames, belching acrid, black smoke. A woman with a blood-spattered blouse stumbled on the glass shards strewn across the road and screamed at the inhumanity of this close-quarter fighting. Behind her, a man in white trousers and a yellow shirt raced out; his arms spread in a cruciform, his face angry as he demanded an explanation for the devastation of his neighbourhood. An ambulance siren grew louder as it neared the scene. Three civil defence volunteers hopped out with stretchers and hurried into the building opposite. Joey waved at them, then returned to his ice bath as Sam gathered up his cameras and bolted down the stairs.

Next morning, after a sleep-free night, Joey found himself on the balcony, sitting naked on the outside of the balcony railings. His brain was fizzing with rage. There was a telephone exchange in his head. He was monitoring many different conversations, three maybe four distorted voices, some playing in fast forward, others slowed down and whining. All tormenting and criticising him: *Go on now. Jump! You're worthless now that the fighting's over. Nobody wants you around. Stop thinking; just do it.*

Cutting through the maelstrom in his head, he heard a familiar voice, 'Hey bro . . . Joey . . . JOEY, what the hell are you up to?'

Joey shifted his bare ass and gripped the railings loosely, facing outwards, a four-storey drop below his dangling feet. 'Stay away, leave me alone.'

'Come on, Joey, this is dangerous. You could —'

'The Eagles, man, they get it. They know what it's like when your baby's gone, leaves you all alone. And —' The rest was lost in loud humming and slurred, mumbled words.

Sam moved to Joey's right and positioned himself against the railings at the other end of the balcony. An elderly couple in the street below pointed, attracting attention to the scene above.

Feet wrapped behind the railing, Joey rocked, tipping his head skywards on the backward roll. 'Had me fooled there for a while, this place. Gonna kiss it goodbye now.' Joey puckered his lips and stretched forward to roar into the still air. 'Help me . . . M'aider . . . Mayday.'

'Here, Joey,' Sam said, his voice forcefully calm. 'Take a hold of me.' He held out a shaking, pleading hand.

Joey's tragic eyes looked at him. 'You know what day it is today?'

'Ah . . . Sunday?'

'It's September twentieth. This was going to be my wedding day.'

'Oh, shit. Okay, Joey, I know. Listen, come inside, and let's talk about this.'

'Nothing to talk about anymore. It's all over now. Stay back —'

'Okay, okay. I'm just going to stand here.'

Joey stood and angled his body forward, arms stretched behind him with fingers wrapped around the thin railing. The pebbles of his knobbly spine protruded down his tanned, emaciated back. In his boggling mind, the never-ending stream of voices provided a running commentary, like subtitles flashing along the bottom of a TV screen. 'Can you hear that voice: *Don't ever try and love again, you'll never love again.* The sneering fucker, over and over, warning me. Well, he got me good now. I–'

'Jesus, Joey, sit down, will you? You're going to fall.'

He could hear Lena now, her voice calling to him like that time in her family home in Aley, imploring him to get her out of there. 'I didn't just lose Lena; I've lost my crack at a proper family, a future with some kind of purpose. What's the point now? Lena was like no other; she can't be replaced.'

'Don't talk like that, bro.'

'Why a bomb? A fucking donkey bomb, why such a horrific way to go?' Joey wailed. More people had joined the couple in the street, a crowd of faces upturned in horror.

'I dunno, Joey. I have no answers.'

'It should have been me. I should have been with her.'

'You mustn't go over all that again.'

'Just fuck off and leave me alone. I want to end it now.'

'Okay, fine, you do that, Joey.' Sam moved back from the edge of the balcony and turned to go in. 'Jumping's probably a good way to go. Although it'd be better if you had a bit of a stone on. Why not have a last spliff with me, then you can jump?'

Joey didn't go for it at first, but Sam persisted and finally managed to coax him back inside, then locked all the doors. Reluctant to leave his brother alone, Sam buzzed the concierge to get word to Fuad in the Commodore that he needed to find Michel quick. When he showed up, Michel stayed only ten minutes, then returned an hour later with a psychiatrist friend who sedated Joey, insisting that he needed to be hospitalised. 'I believe Joey is very sick. To me, it looks like he is having some sort of nervous breakdown.'

17.

ALTHOUGH STAFF AT THE AUB HOSPITAL were proficient in dealing with the flood of physical casualties of war, they had little to offer the mentally scarred. Besides medication, confining the patients was their principal treatment method. Located in a secluded area on the top floor of the main building, the psychiatric ward comprised fifteen small, doorless rooms – each with a bed, locker, and small wardrobe – and one large communal area, where patients watched TV and gathered to smoke. Movement in and out of the ward was controlled by an armed guard permanently stationed on the door.

Lying rigid in bed, naked except for a pair of shorts, Joey watched the ceiling press down on him, forcing compressed hot air across his exposed skin. Shadows crept along the wall and hopped up to the ceiling, scurrying and whispering. Footsteps echoed down the corridor, and ahead of them, the funnel of light widened as Florence Nightingale walked her rounds, swinging a sputtering oil lamp like he's ended up in a fucking Crimean War hospital. From the next room along, the Groaner ramped up, killing any chance of sleep. The racket built to a scream then dropped back to a steady pulsing moan. If the asshole would just keep the noise at the same level, Joey could get used to it, maybe tune it out of his brittle mind. But the babble undulates, forcing him to listen, a dripping-tap kind of torture. Joey leaped from his bed, palms clamped tight to his ears. The blood throbbed beneath his sweating skin, carrying the voices' messages in a circuit around his body and downwards to his feet. Galvanised into action, Joey pursued the nurse with the lantern, begging for something to knock him into sleep.

Sam visited the hospital whenever he could, but for the first week, Joey had been doped up and non-responsive. Once the medication levelled out and he became more coherent, the incessant badgering began. 'This place is crazy, Sammy' – the sound of the word, the shape of it on Joey's lips, scared Sam – 'I don't belong here. You've got to get me out.'

'I will, Joey. Soon. But they're still not sure what's wrong with you.'

'Wrong with me? There's nothing wrong with me.' Joey spat the words out. 'I was just a bit depressed, is all.' In the corner, the kerosene heater flickered and spat out a smoky plume. 'Now the guy in the room next door, he's fucked up. Spends every night roaring and screaming, he's cuffed to his bed frame. Wrists and ankles chained to stop him running.'

'They're not going to do that to you.'

'How the fuck do *you* know?' Joey rocked his upper body and rubbed his hands feverishly along his thighs. 'Night-time's a freak show here, I can tell you. Continuous howling and wailing, fuck knows what's going on in these guys' heads. The docs' only solution is to chain us up and fill us full of drugs, not the fun type, of course.'

'Joumana said she'd keep an eye on you.'

'A fucking eye, I don't need an eye on me. I need to get out of here.' Joey scratched his head vigorously, then tugged on his earlobe.

'In time, Joey. You need to get better first.'

'That's all I need, another nurse sticking her oar in.' He tugged on the other earlobe. 'Get Joumana to give me something to block out the sound of all these nutters.'

'Nurses don't have it easy either, Joey; they work sixteen-hour shifts, if they can even get into work. And constantly–'

'Do you hear that fucking intercom system?' Joey jumped up, fingers plugging his ears. 'They're always making announcements.

It freaks me out. Every time, that irritating voice gets into my head, warning me there's an evacuation or a militia attack.'

'That was actually a good news announcement. Today, they've got a treat. Everyone's having a shower.'

'Every silvery lining has a cloud.'

Following the cessation of fighting in Ras Beirut, things were returning to some kind of normal, and the water supply had finally been restored. Across the city, water was so scarce that it had become more expensive than whiskey. Although the AUB Hospital had its own well, electricity was needed to pump the water out, and that utility was even more erratic; militias, chasing a quick buck, frequently tapped into the hospital's electricity and re-routed it for domestic usage at a fee. A nurse came in and ushered Joey towards the shower room for a much-needed wash in the freshly flowing, rusty water.

After six weeks, it became clear to Sam that Joey wasn't getting any better. If anything, he was getting worse. The medication wasn't working, unsurprisingly, given that the doctors seemed to have little idea what was wrong with Joey. Nobody now believed he was having a nervous breakdown. A breakdown would have been fine; just fix up the broken parts and set him on his way right as rain. Something more fundamental had fractured in Joey's head, and nobody seemed to know how to stick the broken pieces back together.

Not a day went by without a mention of Lena and a tortuous reliving of the inenarrable horror of the scene in Moukhtara. 'Why did she have to die in a bomb, Sammy?' – deep suck on his cigarette – 'Why so brutal? – curled knuckles scrubbing his eyes – 'I can smell her skin burning . . . I see her bones melting in my head.' Each vision was delivered in a bawling scream. His deluded guilt tumbled out in an avalanche of words. 'I should have gone with her, I should have been there, but no, I wanted to enjoy myself, thought I'd chill out that day. I was chicken about leaving Beirut, if

I'm honest, certainly had no interest in chasing around the country after that waste of space Butros brother of hers. He was a bad apple, part of some fucking militia himself. I should have died with her; maybe I could have saved her if I'd been there.'

Using cartons of cigarettes, Sam bribed the guard into relaxing the total patient lock-down on Joey's ward, and the pair took to wandering the hospital corridors. Most areas were crammed with beds as the injured and maimed flowed in and out of wards; some insisted on moving their beds into the corridors — far away from the windows, fearful of injury from stray bullets — while others, more afraid of danger outside the security of the ward, vowed never to leave their room.

Sanitary conditions throughout the hospital were appalling. Buckets of wastewater were scattered in convenient locations on every floor, readily available for flushing toilets and mopping floors. Mosquitos and flies, breeding in the piles of uncollected garbage on the streets, buzzed into the hospital and circulated unimpeded. Bedding and hospital wear remained dirty after sporadic, ineffective washing. Cooking in the patients' rooms was commonplace; whole families would gather around their loved one's beds, frying vegetables in bedpans or boiling meat in the hospital's metal flower vases. Outside, the hospital grounds had become the frontline of General Aoun's so-called war of liberation. Syrian tanks occupied the parking lots, a convenient vantage point for launching shells at their erstwhile Christian allies in East Beirut. Joey had become convinced this was the reason he had ended up in hospital. 'It's the CIA, man; they organised for me to get in here, so I can feed them intel on the layout of the university and where the Syrian tanks are located.'

'No, Joey, that's not you. They say that it's some AUB students, loyal to Aoun . . . they're the ones passing on the information.' Lack of access to a radio had stopped Joey's nonsense about tuning into the spy network and decoding messages filtered through the static, but the secret agent fantasy still thrived in his splintered mind.

'You have no idea how it works, Sammy. I've tried to explain before how they use me. It's because of the intel reports I send that the Lebanese army can pick off Syrian tanks, one by one.'

In addition to concerns about Joey's deteriorating mental health, Sam grew increasingly worried about his physical safety. Hospital-wide, security had been stepped up as staff – caught in a treacherous bind treating the wounded from multiple warring factions – struggled to cope with the flood of demands raining down on them. Hospitals were the one place where fighters from all sides converged, each demanding care for their fallen colleagues, with all the attendant risks of dangerous flashpoints. One day, a militiaman showed up waving a gun and forced an intern to give him a lab coat. Disguised as a doctor, he wandered from ward to ward until he found and promptly shot the enemy he was looking for. Another time, two gunmen showed up waving hand grenades, demanding four doctors follow them to a nearby cinema bombsite, where their fighters lay dying on the ground. In response to these threats, hospital guards were issued with weapons and walkie-talkies and instructed to patrol the corridors and main entrance points. But these initiatives were largely cosmetic; part-time security guards were no match for lawless, armed militias.

Sam's mind was made up for him one cold March morning as he walked towards the hospital reception. Without warning, a huge explosion rocked the main building, plunging it into darkness and scattering glass and debris into the courtyard. It transpired that a woman wearing Western clothes, and with a box of chocolates tucked under her arm had passed through the main hospital entrance and sat on a bench in the grounds outside the cashier's office. At the time, the area was milling with people waiting to pay their bills. The woman stood and walked off, leaving the chocolate box behind, and within minutes, the bomb exploded, killing seven and wounding many more. The blast carved out a huge hole in the car park and destroyed three ambulances, parked nearby and ready to retrieve the wounded and dead during lulls in the fighting. One week later, everything was back to normal. Windows had been replaced, doors fixed, walls rebuilt, and the electricity restored. All that was missing was the bench; in its place stood a large terracotta plant on a newly concreted slab below a Red Cross flag.

By the time the repair work was completed, Michel had managed to source a supply of Joey's prescribed medication from a doctor in Cyprus. Sam moved Joey out of hospital and back in with him on condition that he stick to a self-medicating regime. Overjoyed at his liberation, Joey was buoyant, although he never left the apartment, preferring instead to read or just watch TV, so for company, Sam bought him a white poodle called Snowy from a departing diplomat.

As Joey lolled in Sam's armchair, the door buzzer broke his reverie. He ignored it for a second and a third time. Cowering on the chair, knees pulled up to his chest, the thumping on the door sounded like a battering ram. Finally, he heard footsteps padding down the corridor and the elevator door open. The walls closed in, corralling him in the centre of the room. He focussed on the wall painting of the ghostly man, silhouetted against a dark mountain, with a pale bird flapping above his head, its beak skywards, unleashing a piercing cry. The bird's haunting notes burrowed along Joey's ear canals and drilled deep into his brain. Snowy, camouflaged against the white floor tiles and muslin curtains, looked anxious. He stared at Joey and yelped a rolling bark that exposed his teeth, sharp as pine needles. Joey spread his arms and shooed him towards the kitchen. The dog scampered ahead, stealing confused and frightened looks over his shoulder. The barking cranked up when Snowy realised Joey had locked the kitchen door. To block out the dog's noise, Joey turned the music up loud. He thought it would be better with the window shutters closed. It wasn't. He wrapped his arms around his head, forcing his mind to ride the helter-skelter, waiting for the lunacy to recede.

On the radio, the jokey Radio Caroline weather forecaster was saying, 'There's just no stopping the weekend weather' — thunder cracked outside and echoed around the apartment — 'September storms are set to continue, but our boat will keep rocking out here on the Med.' A bright yellow streak flared across the sky. When Joey looked back at the radio, the voice had changed and was talking to him with a mocking sternness,

Do you hear that, you worthless shit. What you gonna do about it? You have to stop the rain. Another voice, French accent, joined in. *Are you just gonna sit around with your stupid mouth open? Do something! They're coming for you, you know that, don't you?* The forecaster again . . . *This is entirely your fault. You're stupid. You should get out of here. Walk away from it.* The French woman . . . *Something's wrong. Did you forget to take your medication?*

Joey stepped onto the balcony and sucked in the dry morning air. Sudden vertigo forced him to step back into the dark sitting room. He moved sideways along the walls, pawing for the door with mounting panic. From the kitchen, each Snowy bark was a hammer blow to the back of his head. Eventually, he found the apartment door, dragged the latch open, and fell into the floodlit corridor. The huge black pools in his eyes shrivelled under assault from the bright strip light. Thinking they probably had cameras in the elevator, he took the stairs, two at a time, then three, as the sound of whoever he thought was following grew closer. Out on the street, he stumbled into a beggar lying near the doorway. Two mangy cats meowed aggressively and ran after him, hopeful of scraps. Shuffling along the back streets, head swivelling to check the progress of the unseen chasing party, Joey came out onto the Corniche. The right move hit him with a clarity that his troubled mind had lacked all day. Cold water enveloped him as he broke the surface of the sea, and then nothing.

Until he woke up in an AUB Hospital bed, back in the psychiatric ward, his hand in Sam's and his mind more disturbed than ever. The time had come for decisive action. With Christy's help, Sam tracked down Pops and he showed up a week later.

'We'll get a UN Jeep down to Naqoura, and from there, we

can grab a lift with the mail run down to Nahariya in Israel,' Pops said. 'Donal O'Connor is based there, and he'll be able to arrange transport on to Jerusalem.'

'Are you . . . can you stay with me in Jerusalem?' Joey said weakly.

'I'll stay until you're settled in, Joseph. I've pulled some strings and arranged a bed for you in the Hadassah Hospital in West Jerusalem. It's a world-renowned hospital. They did the first coronary bypass and transplant in Israel; they were the first to have a child conceived using IVF. They performed the world's first hip replacement. They also have a great psychiatric department. Hopefully, they can figure out what's happening with you.'

'But I . . . I.' Joey's moist eyes stared unseeing. 'I don't want to go to Jerusalem.'

'Christy's there, and Maud. They can look out for you until you get better, and then we'll see what to do from there.'

'Is Christy coming to Beirut?'

'No,' Pops said, crossing his arms. 'He wanted to, but it's still too dangerous.'

In the corridor, a dishevelled youth shuffled past, swinging a bell. Pops looked puzzled. 'That's one of Joey's neighbours,' Sam whispered through narrow lips. 'He's always at that, calling people to prayer.'

Pops went to open the window. 'Things are going well for you, Sam. I'm forever coming across your photos in the papers.'

'It was money well spent, Pops, all that help you gave him, funding those photography courses.'

'You were right all along, Joseph. You always said Sam had talent.'

'Joey's the one we should be praising,' Sam said, his lips curling. 'He may be crazy, but he's one in a million.' Sam clenched his fists and the nails bit into his palms.

Joey smiled at Sam and pointed a reprimanding finger, 'How many times do I have to tell you? I'm not crazy. I just can't control my mind right now.'

'Ma sends her love, Joseph. She'll meet us in Jerusalem,' Pops said, scraping a hand through his thick, black hair. 'Bee was asking after you. And Damien, of course.'

'I miss them all so much, but I don't want them seeing me in this state.'

'Things will be better in a proper hospital like the Hadassah. They'll soon sort you out.'

'For sure,' Sam said, though he wasn't so sure. This didn't look like a quick fix situation.

'Right, well, I'd better be moving on. We've an early start tomorrow. I'll meet you here, Sam, at seven a.m. sharp.' Pops grabbed hold of Joey and hugged him. 'We'll get through this, don't you worry. We're Hogans, after all,' he called out, leaving with a timid wave and fighting to hold back the tears.

Sam sat in the chair beside Joey and a long, comfortable silence swelled between them. Thunder clapped in a steel grey sky, pregnant with rain and shortly due to break its waters. Although desperate to speak the torrent of conflicting thoughts flooding his brain — fear that Joey may never recover from this, remorse that he hadn't acted sooner, dread at his impending loneliness — Sam was struck dumb by sadness. Joey may have found some temporary peace of mind in civil war-torn Lebanon, but he had truly lost it now. The great adventure was over, and Joey was leaving like a refugee, with a haunted look and a lunatic in his head.

CALL ME THE BREEZE

J.J. CALE

ISRAEL

July to October 1990

18.

JOEY WAS DOING FINE. As far as Maud knew, he was taking his meds having agreed to play the game by their rules. They now had a label for his illness – something called schizophrenia – and if he didn't take his meds, the loony upstairs started looking for trouble. Doctor Shapiro hadn't minced his words when Maud and Christy visited Joey in Jerusalem's Hadassah Hospital, where he was confined on arrival from Lebanon nearly two years ago. Shapiro was a short, officious man with dull eyes, magnified by tractor-headlight spectacles. Through barely moving lips, he had told them, 'Joey is a very sick young man. We believe he is suffering from schizophrenia, which may have developed some time ago.' Years of trauma condensed into one loaded word.

'Schizophrenia? What does that mean?' Maud asked, her emerald eyes on stalks.

'It means that Joey's mind is very broken. Schizophrenia is an illness of the brain; they used to call it the fragmented mind. It occurs when the body's biology goes wrong. Joey is–'

'But how did he get it?' Christy said. 'What causes psycho . . . whatever it's called.'

'Schiz-o-phrenia. The simple answer is that we don't know. It's not like someone with a broken leg, where the diagnosis is obvious, and the remedy is self-suggesting. Someone with a mental disorder earns a diagnosis based on the checklist of symptoms they present with, as best we can uncover them. They are put on anti-psychotic medications to control those symptoms.'

Joey sat across from them, hands pinned beneath his thighs,

a dull expression on his face, antsy at the way this doctor spoke about him like he wasn't there, listening.

'Is it something you can inherit, like a genetic disease?' Maud asked.

'For the reasons I've been telling you, we don't refer to mental illness as a disease.' Shapiro explained, all doctory. 'A disease has a specific etiology, which means a set of known causes, which we don't have here. Instead, we talk about a mental disorder. For this disorder, there can be many contributing factors. One in every hundred of the general population develops schizophrenia. Certainly, a predisposition due to genetics is not uncommon. Is there any history of mental illness in Joey's family?'

Maud's immediate reaction was that, 'Shur, of course, there wasn't; they were all very bright and clever in his family . . . Although there was Joey's paternal grandfather, it was never really talked about; he was a bit of an omadhaun. Could he maybe have had this illness?'

Christy's eyebrows arched. 'I'm not sure. I'll have to check with Pops.'

'That would be good,' Shapiro said. 'Anything you can provide to fill in the background would be helpful.'

Maud glanced across at Joey, then back to the doctor. 'Can it be caused by . . . I'm sorry, Joey, I have to ask . . . by excessive drug use, by taking hallucinogenic drugs?' She remembered there had been a period when he got really into acid, read all the books – Wolfe, Leary, Go Ask Alice, Huxley – and spent nearly a whole year tripping practically every week.

Shapiro turned to Joey. 'Clearly illegal drugs don't help. While we don't believe they can cause the illness by themselves, drugs can lead to a psychotic episode that triggers the illness. It may have been lying dormant for some time.'

'They're going to give me the gold medal for tragedy,' Joey piped up.

Shapiro batted aside the interruption. 'Joey hears what he believes are voices in his head. What he is hearing are misdirections of inner speech, a collection of unexpressed thoughts and imaginary conversations that become all too real for him. He cannot tell the difference between reality and what's going on in his mind. Noises become indistinguishable from thoughts. Often sufferers hear voices for a long time before the illness itself develops fully.'

'Oh, my God, that must have been awful for you, Joey,' Maud said.

'Shit happens. I guess that's why they invented the expression, so we'd have something to describe situations like this.'

'From what Joey has told us, he has been having delusions for some time, without realising it,' Shapiro continued. 'Typically, people suffering from schizophrenia see the world through a strange distorting mirror. They have vivid hallucinations that become their reality. All their senses are heightened, and the quality of those sensations changes. Sound and light become more intense. With this constant sensory overload, schizophrenics have difficulty screening out what's relevant or important and what inputs can be ignored. Naturally they often become suspicious and distrustful.'

'Maybe Joey just needs some rest and quiet time,' Christy said.

The doctor cast Christy a look of disdain and continued without even honouring this suggested treatment plan with a reply. 'People with schizophrenia can imagine they see ghosts and witches, all sorts of demons. With Joey, it is complicated by the terrible things he has experienced. It seems he has had a very distressing recent life in Lebanon. Traumatic events can trigger the condition.'

Maud and Christy's eyes locked, unsure how much Shapiro knew. God only knows the impact of the horrendous things he'd experienced, living side by side with death for over four years. He rarely talked about it, and never in any detail, except for that time he was nearly kidnapped; he liked to joke about how he'd outrun his pursuers in his small Peugeot, using racing driver skills he never knew he had. And Sam, well Sam never said much about anything, but he was also totally messed up. Living with a constant threat to your life, not safe in your own home, exposed daily to the awful things that humans can do to each other, of course that's going to destroy your mind. Especially as you become immune to the horror and learn to shrug off things that normal people would find insufferable. It took Christy weeks to recover from his visit there; the stories of his trip across southern Lebanon still sent shivers down her spine. And to cap it all, to lose your fiancée, blown up in a donkey bomb of all things, that wasn't something you got over easily. Even Maud had nightmares about that, and she hadn't even been there. To cap it all, he was ages suffering with this schizophrenia before anyone figured out what was wrong with him. She couldn't bear to hear Sam talk about that hospital in Beirut, Joey perpetually paranoid and neglected, suffering with a mental illness that no one has time to deal with because they're rushed off their feet fixing the war wounded.

'What's the outlook here?' Christy said. 'How long before Joey recovers?'

'That is a very difficult question to answer at this point. It is still very early. The illness can be treated. But you must know, there is no cure. Statistically, we expect around a third of people with schizophrenia to recover with limited further problems once they continue taking their medication. Another third may have further psychotic episodes, but over time, they learn to live with the illness. And a final third never get better.' Shapiro scanned the three faces and continued in a more reassuring tone, 'Try not to worry. Joey is in good hands here, the very best. The Department of Psychiatry at the Hadassah is a leading centre internationally for treatment and research; we have the world's specialists in many areas of mental health.' And with that, Shapiro had stomped off, called to some other disturbed patient requiring his medical counsel.

So yes, Maud, Joey's being a good boy. He's taking his meds. There was no need for her to ask *every single time* they met. It was one of the reasons he rarely came to their house. He'd been through the locked-up phase — in the cuckoo's nest at the AUB Hospital in Beirut, and then nearly a year in the Hadassah's psych ward — and he was never going back to that again.

When you're out of circulation for that long, a lot of things happen in your absence but what tortured him the most was missing Ma's funeral. He'd only been in the Hadassah a few months when she died suddenly from pancreatic cancer, aged only fifty-seven. Shapiro was adamant that Joey was in no condition to leave hospital, especially for yet another traumatic occasion. Her death had devastated him; the pain of losing her gentle guiding hand and friendly ear was compounded by the agony of losing a mother for the second time. It was Ma who had encouraged him to do an English degree, when all his numeracy skills argued for Engineering. That she hadn't given birth to him made not a bit of difference; even before they'd adopted him, she was always there for him, his biggest cheerleader. In her eyes, he could do no wrong. Joey struggled to shake the guilt that all these people dying, his very nearest and dearest, was somehow down to him. As soon as he was finally discharged, the first thing he did was fly home to lay flowers on her grave.

Entering the Hogans' Jerusalem house, Maud's infectious laugh boomed above the raucous party noise. Joey and Moshe twisted through the mob in the hall and headed for the kitchen, where Maud stood skewering chicken kebabs. Her flaming red hair was cut into a short bob, and as Joey grabbed her in a hug, he complimented her on the new hairstyle. Even after four kids, she still had a great body. Pushing him playfully away from her, Maud said, 'And this must be Moshe? You're very welcome.'

'Thank you for inviting me, Maud,' Moshe said as Maud shook his hand. Moshe was Joey's new, old friend; they'd gone to school together in Jerusalem for Joey's last two primary school years and had remained pen pals for years before losing contact. Shortly after getting out of the Hadassah, Joey tracked him down again, and the pair hit it off immediately, helped by their shared Irish parentage

(Moshe's Irish mother had moved to Israel from Dublin after the 1967 war) and their shared appetite for drugs.

'You've a big crowd in,' Joey said, looking into the sitting room adjoining the kitchen. Tucked into an alcove, the television flickered with the volume down, primed for the big event: Ireland were playing the hosts in the quarter-finals of the Italia '90 World Cup, the furthest any Irish team had got in any football competition. The table was laid with a green tablecloth, and the cutlery was rolled in green napkins. "Up Ireland" banners straddled the walls of every room.

'Shur, we've got to do our bit to support Jack's lads.'

'Is Sammy here yet?'

'I think he's out in the garden with Christy. Maybe you could help him get the barbeque going. He always buys that cheap charcoal.'

It was five years since Christy had seen that UNWRA advert looking for legal staff to work on behalf of the Palestinians in Israel. As it turned out, Maud was mad keen on the idea and jumped at it as a wonderful opportunity to escape the drudgery of her life in London, where she was totally absorbed rearing three young children and where she 'never met anyone interesting'. Within a month of securing the job, they'd packed up their London life and moved into this stone-blocked, semi-detached house in Beth Hanina, an Arab neighbourhood in East Jerusalem. The house was in a small complex nicknamed "Peyton Place" (after the sixties American TV show), which had always been popular with United Nations families. Back in the mid-1970s, the Hogans lived there and were famous for having the best parties, with singsongs lasting until the early hours, the highlight being Pops' party piece: *Let it Be* in an Elvis voice. Wherever they were based, the Hogan household was a welcome haven for loners and stragglers, particularly around Christmas when they invariably had some army guy or a visiting dignitary in attendance. Ma loved to tell the story of the French general who announced at the end of his Christmas dinner, 'Thank you for that dinner, Maeve, I am completely fed up.'

In those days, Beth Hanina was surrounded by open rocky fields where the children played freely, and goats grazed on the meagre pickings; now, the village was ringed by Israeli settlements, concrete cookie-cutter apartment blocks creeping their way up the hillside. Since the early 1980s, across the country, the number of settlements had mushroomed as Israel expropriated more and more land from Palestinian owners, forcibly displacing them and demolishing their homes under the guise of security concerns, and on religious or historical grounds. The settler movement had started innocently when, after the 1967 War, a small group of religious Jews rented rooms for Passover at the Park Hotel in Hebron. No Israeli had lived in the West Bank since the creation of the state of Israel two decades prior, but this group soon established a small settlement in the area, and within twenty years, hundreds of thousands of Israeli Jews resided in the disputed territory. While initially these settlements were small encampments, many grew into large subdivisions, in some cases sizeable cities, with populations in the tens of thousands. Often, they were supported by governmental financial incentives that encouraged Jews to settle in remote, isolated areas to solidify Israel's hold on the territory. In the process, Palestinian localities fragmented as the settlements split communities apart, and businesses, particularly the critical olive farming, were forced to shut down due to restrictions on Palestinians moving around. Numerous United Nations resolutions condemning Israel's construction of settlements were blatantly ignored; the settler movement is a powerful political force, and no Israeli Prime Minister wanted to risk the collapse of their government by fronting up to it.

By now, clusters of people filled the small patch of withered grass out back that Maud had called the garden, faces glowing red in the baking afternoon sun. A group was gathered around the shirtless, tubby Christy, encouraging him as he fanned a bin lid in front of the smouldering barbeque. Sam stood nearby in black jeans and a Black Sabbath tee shirt. Two speakers, with wires trailing back through the sitting room window, guarded either side of the gravel path, blasting out *Put 'Em Under Pressure* on a loop, Horslips tearing through the fiddles and guitars, building to the frenzy of the *Ole Ole* chorus.

Joey shoved through the crowd and slobbered a kiss on Sam's cheek as they hugged. 'Moshe, meet Sammy, my other brother. He's got me into and out of a lotta shit and saved my life more than once in Lebanon.'

'You are living in Jerusalem now, Sam?' Moshe asked.

'Absolutely no way. I'm not one for normal city life. Just having a short holiday, seeing this crowd of wasters, before I head out to the Gulf.'

'The Gulf?'

'Yeah, ole Sade-ham Husni has moved shedloads of troops near the Kuwait border. Looks like things are about ready to blow up there.'

'Different location, same shitty mess,' Joey said, and they all laughed heartily. 'Moshe's a journalist also.'

'It's true. When I was drafted into the Israeli army, I didn't want to do any fighting, so I got a job as a reporter for Israel Army Radio. Then, after my conscription service, I started writing for Haaretz, a left-wing daily newspaper. At the time, I was so innocent about what was going on in the West Bank and Gaza. I thought it was just one individual settler who was intimidating Palestinians or cutting down their olive trees. Or that it was only a rogue soldier mistreating Palestinian women at a checkpoint. I told myself these were exceptions, one-off incidents, but as I saw more and more of these things happening, I understood that this was, in fact, government policy. The way Palestinians were being treated in the disputed territories made me ashamed to be Israeli.'

'That's good to hear, man,' Sam said. 'Must be difficult as not many of your lot think that way.'

'Now, it is my mission to write honestly about these things so that no Israeli can later say, "Oh, but we didn't know what was going on." Can you imagine? That expression has already cursed Jewish history, you know what I mean?'

'Surely, no Israeli can claim they don't know what's going on now?'

'Most people know a little, but often not the details, they avoid that. You know, our mainstream media is just a cheerleader for the government. They brainwash people with scare stories that incite fear and hatred of the Palestinians. Also, taking the other side can be dangerous. Some prominent dissenters have faced calls to be put on trial for treason. Many of those who oppose the Palestinian policy are cautious about voicing their views openly. This is why opinion polls regularly show overwhelming support for the military operations when the reality is different.'

Christy cast the bin lid aside, sprayed more lighting fluid liberally over the smoking charcoals, then flicked a match at it. The flames whooshed up, forcing him backwards, laughing nervously. He joined the group, ignoring jibes about the nasty sunburn on his back and shoulders. 'Ah, Moshe, giving everyone your views on the one-state versus two-state solution?

'Not at all, Christy. Thank you for inviting me.'

'Nothing to do with me, mate, you've Maud to thank for that. Tell me, how do you like the view up the mountain, all those gleaming settlements?'

Moshe's smile faded, and he glanced at Joey. 'There are many more buildings since the last time I was in Beit Hanina.'

Christy wiped the sweat off his glasses with his tee shirt 'You do realise that Palestinians are now being forced to live in ghettos? Why don't you write about that for your newspaper?'

'Ah listen, Christy.' Joey held up his palm and grinned. 'Enough already.'

'It's fine, Joey. In fact, we do often write about the settlements and make the case for restraint.'

Christy sneered. 'And of course, the settlements control all the utility supplies, some of them even try to make a dirty shekel by reselling water on to their Palestinian neighbours. We know what the plan is. Nobody's blind to the agenda. With all these Jewish settlers embedded in land stolen from Palestinians, there's no way Israel will ever agree to evacuate. A viable Palestinian state, forget about it.'

'Christy, pipe down, will you?' Joey pushed him on the shoulder. 'You're making a show of yourself.'

Just then, Maud wandered over, waving a football scarf above her head. 'Lads, enough of the politics. We're all Irish today, c'mon ye boys in green,' she roared. 'The game starts in ten minutes.'

Beside Christy was an UNWRA colleague called Mikey with a forever twitching body that unsettled Joey: the constant chin rubbing, bollocks scratching, back flicking his greasy fringe, blowing his nose. And blinking, all the blinking time. Joey was pretty sure that Mikey was trying to communicate covertly with him, that with each blink, he was sending coded messages, but he couldn't for the life of him decipher the meaning.

'Trying to keep body and soul together,' Joey said to no one in particular. 'And my mind, of course, gotta keep my mind together. Don't want to end up back in the crazy farm. Years ago, I didn't have this mental problem. I don't know why I have it now, but it's pretty . . . no, I'd say terribly, inconvenient. I take these anti-psychotic drugs to help me decide what's real and what's not. I don't have to obey everything they say.'

The flashbacks, both the acid-induced and the Lebanon-inspired ones, had now receded in intensity and diminished in number, although one could be triggered at any time by a harmless event and quickly morph into a full-blown re-enactment of some past trauma. Just last week, looking out the window of a bus on Saladin Street, he'd seen a black-haired woman, a Lena doppelganger, driving a white Mercedes sports convertible.

Within seconds, he was back on that mountain, the smoke swirling and biting his throat. Even though there was no war as such in Jerusalem, a tense atmosphere pervaded as everyone knew a suicide bomber or a rogue gunman could shatter the fragile peace in a flash. The Israeli army was everywhere, rifles hanging on their shoulders. Lately, Joey had become progressively less convinced that he was being watched. That middle-aged guy in the grey felt hat and sports jacket hadn't been around for weeks, although yesterday, he was pretty sure that he'd passed one of those two Mossad spies, pretending she was out walking her dog. Maud had grown exasperated with all this talk of skulduggery, demanding he come up with a reason why anyone would be interested in trailing a harmless Irish lad around Jerusalem. But there were many things Maud didn't know. For now, best to continue taking evasive action and stay dark until he could find out some more.

Christy glanced timorously across at Sam and pulled Mikey off to meet some other people. Joey leaned over and whispered, 'Hey, Sammy, fancy doing an E?'

A few days later, Joey was back in the Hogans' house for Sam's farewell dinner. As usual, he had made his way on foot. Jerusalem was so much more spread out than Beirut, and he felt somehow more connected to what was going on if he experienced it up close, powered by his own feet. Besides, he didn't trust wheeled transport and got overwhelmed by all the attendant noises – humming fans, rattling carriages, squealing brakes, bus drivers mumbling over buzzing speakers – which resounded in his ears, distorted like speech underwater. Now, the noise in his head was screaming kids chasing each other and twisting around his legs.

'So how old are you now, Kathleen?' Joey asked.

'Ahh . . . ahh . . . six and a half,' Kathleen said and then hid behind Christy's legs.

'That's right, pet,' Christy said, ruffling her long, brown curls. 'They've been playing up in King Hussein's palace all afternoon.'

'Hussein's palace, no way. I remember us playing there as kids. How weird! It's not still there, is it?'

'It sure is. A relic of the past. It'll stay like that, I reckon. There's too much potential for a flare up if the Israelis were ever to demolish it or even worse, build on it.'

The skeletal, cement shell of the so-called palace, overlooking Beit Hanina from the hill behind Christy's house, was originally intended to be a summer residence for King Hussein of Jordan, a grandiose structure over three levels, interconnected with arches plated with Jerusalem stone. Construction started in the mid-1960s but was halted when Israel captured the area during the 1967 War. Ever since, it had remained empty. Instead of hosting world leaders and dignitaries, it now served as a playground for local kids – Arabs and foreigners alike, including two generations of Hogans – who could run up staircases that led nowhere, play hide-and-seek behind lines of pillars, and explore dungeons festooned with spider webs.

'You know Kathleen, as a kid, I used to play up there with your daddy,' Joey said.

'Will you come play with us tomorrow, Uncle Joey?' Kathleen said as she rubbed her eyes and yawned.

'Maud insisted on keeping her up well past her bedtime so she could see you, and now of course she's over-tired.'

'No, I'm not, Daddy.'

'Let's get the twins sorted. Say good night to Uncle Joey,' Christy said as he scooped Kathleen into his arms.

Joey wandered into the kitchen to see if he could help Maud with the cooking.

'No, I'm grand, thanks; it's all under control. Fill up our wine glasses if you want something to do.' Maud was an enthusiastic cook – schooled by her mother from an early age in the tradition of a Delia or Mary Berry – and was relishing the rare opportunity to cook a proper meal for adults.

'Roger that.'

'Is Charlie still quiet?' Maud said, flicking a strand of red hair from her eyes. She hadn't wanted to call her fourth child, and only boy, Charlie (Garrett was so much nicer), but Christy had insisted he'd had enough of all these Irish names and wanted his boy (*his boy,* the cheek of it!) to have a cool name: Joey really could do without Maud sharing these intimacies with him.

Just then, the doorbell rang, and Joey went to let Sam in. Maud's worthy attempt at Tandoori Chicken Masala was soon ready, and they gathered around the kitchen table to tuck in. Over dinner, the conversation turned to the Dublin scene and their left-behind family. 'How's Damien?' Maud asked Joey. 'Have you heard anything from him?'

Joey gulped down some water and flapped his hand as he exhaled in short puffs before saying, 'Nah, nothing much. He wanted me to go over for the opening night of his club, but I'm never going back to Dublin.'

'Oh, I'm sorry, Joey. It's the first time I did this recipe. Is it too spicy?' Maud said as she scooped up some curry with a hunk of naan bread.

'He's opening another nightclub? How many is that now?'

'No, it's lovely, very tasty. Just need to get used to it,' Joey said, fixing his burning lips into a smile.

'I hear Damien was with Babs for a while. Remember her?' Maud said. 'She's a strap of a wan. Short, quite fat, hair tied back in a ponytail. Anyhow, he seems to have copped himself on and dumped her. I hear that he's raking it in with his nightclubs.'

'You don't want to believe everything you hear, Maud,' Christy said, struggling to keep the condescending note out of his voice.

'He's certainly going for it. Where is he getting the money for all this?' Sam asked.

'He started out running those raves after he left college,' Joey said. 'He opened the first club around the time we were in

Copenhagen. Remember Christy?'

'Man, Copenhagen. That was a fun weekend,' Christy said in a mournful tone that hinted at limited fun since.

'Running a nightclub, I can easily picture it,' Joey said. 'Just the sort of high profile, ostentatious thing that would appeal to Damien.' After a pause, he continued, 'I gave him the pox once, you know.'

'No way,' Maud giggled. 'You're a fright to God, Joey. How did you do that?'

'Oh, it was way back, the summer of 1982, when we spent a couple of months in Germany. One night, I ended up screwing this Turkish chick, the only one left in the bar at closing time. About a week later, I was at home pissing, with Frank Zappa's *Why does it hurt when I pee?* playing in the background, and for the first time, I zoned in on the lyrics. Now, I certainly couldn't claim that I'd got it from the toilet seat, but it had definitely started to hurt when I peed.'

'Yerra Joey! Spare us the details,' Maud said, desperate to hear more and tugging on the crucifix around her neck.

'Before I found out I had the pox, the night after being with Miss Turkey, I was with this Hungarian lady. And then Damien was with the same Hungarian two nights after me. Funnily enough, Damien soon had the same issues peeing. No stress, though, the clinic was typically German efficient: fill in a form, no accusations or fire-and-brimstone warnings, just take these pills twice a day, and within ten days, the problem had been eradicated.'

'Well, at least you only gave it to him indirectly, if you get me?' Christy said.

Maud shot him a dismissive look. 'He'd wear you out, so he would.' She refilled the glasses from a freshly opened bottle of Rioja.

'Funny to think Charlie was born in Jerusalem, like his uncle Damien before him.' Sam looked over at Christy. 'It must be strange being back in these places where we grew up. I get that it's fun in a way, but it must be very different from how we remember it.'

'Do you remember that family of boys that used to live on the track up to Hussein's place . . . what were they called?' Joey asked.

'Ah, you mean the Murphys, wasn't it?' Sam said.

'Yes, that's them. Remember that time—' Joey said.

'They were the ones who got—' Christy interrupted.

'Listen to this, Maud,' Joey raced to get the words out. 'There were three of these Murphy boys, oldest one was called Sean, he was about eight or nine at the time. They were playing in the fields around their house, just up the road from here, and suddenly Sean starts screaming. His brother comes running over, lifts the stone beside Sean, then he starts screaming. Then the youngest Murphy comes over and lifts the same stone again and gets bitten by the same scorpion!'

'No way,' Maud exclaimed. 'All three of them. Were they okay? Can you not die from scorpions?'

'Only some scorpions kill you. Not the ones you get around here. Even their mother could see the funny side, went around telling everyone the story of how one scorpion got her three boys,' Joey said.

'Really, all the parents were very slack in those days,' Sam said. 'They used to let us run wild, climbing around empty palaces, getting into stone fights with the Arab kids, nicking sweets from Freij's shop. From the age of about ten, we used to get the bus into the Old City from the top of the road. I mean, anything could have happened to us.'

'Changing subjects,' Christy said as he lit a cigarette. 'I was reading at the weekend that there's still no news on the Terry Waite kidnap in Beirut. It's been more than three years now. Bet you're glad to be out of there.'

Over the years, as an envoy for the Church of England, Terry Waite had been involved in several hostage negotiations in

Lebanon and had even managed to secure some releases. However, his association with the Irangate scandal damaged his credibility and instead of providing safe conduct to meet with the hostages, his hosts had grabbed him on his last visit, and no word had been heard since.

'Yeah . . . kinda . . . you know, lot of memories.' Joey scratched a scab on his arm with chewed fingernails. 'Sometimes it does my head in.' As if to remove the load, he scraped the hair back off his forehead with both hands.

'Shit, sorry, Joey, didn't mean anything . . . to remind you.'

Maud threw another daggered glance at Christy and moved the conversation on. 'How's the Lebanon book coming along? Have you got a title for it yet?'

'I think so. I'm fixed on calling it *Adolf & Other Tales from Lebanon's Streets*. Adolf was this street bum in Beirut that Sammy and I knew, well thought we knew —'

'We had him pegged as a nutter, a homeless guy living in a roadside shack.'

'It turns out he was a Mossad spy all along. Playing the bum was the perfect cover, planted in the centre of Beirut, picking up the word on the street and relaying the intelligence to the military planners back home. No one could ever figure out how the Israeli air raids on Beirut were so accurate.' Joey sipped his wine and looked at the three smiling faces around the table. 'In a way, the writing's kind of therapeutic, going back over all the old stories I wrote, my notebooks, memorabilia, all that . . .' The words faded as the memories surfaced in Joey's mind.

In fact, the twenty-seven-year-old version of Joey was struggling to reproduce the discipline of focused writing that had been second nature to his eighteen-year-old self. His work with the Jerusalem Post helped and occasionally he could detect some lingering echo of that ability, but it had grown faint, and he could find no way to amplify it.

'Well, here's to getting out alive to tell the tale. Let's celebrate,' Christy said and went to crack open a bottle of bubbly.

'What are we celebrating?'

'Good times. Us four, being back together again.'

'And Pops' retirement. Praise Buddha; he finally packed in the UN life,' Joey said as they raised four fizzing glasses. They'd all been back to Dublin in March for the retirement party. He'd planned to keep working another few years but of late he'd been complaining that his memory was going and, ever the professional, was worried about dropping the ball should he forget something major.

'Mustn't forget dear Ma. God, I miss her,' Christy said, as he looked up and raised his glass to the ceiling. The others followed suit, with a chorus of, 'Love you, Ma.'

'And, while we're at it, congratulations to Bee on winning her first proper women's boxing competition,' Sam said. 'I have to say, it was very exciting to see her fight live, in front of a huge crowd, in Sweden of all places.'

Sam took out his wallet and showed them a photo, Bee standing facing backwards beside a joyful Pops, "Female Rebel" in green stitching across the top of her orange boxing robe, below it, "This one's for cool Bob" which she'd added just for this bout.

'Ha, brilliant, good old Government House Bob McCool, her first proper coach,' Christy said. 'After me, of course; it was me donating my boxing gloves that really set Bee on her trail to European Women's champion. Who'd have thought?'

'Hear, hear, well done, Bee. And best wishes to Sam, too, on his next adventure,' Maud said as they clinked their glasses a final time.

'Sammy's a guy who's got his nirvana trinity sorted.'

'Oh God, not the holy trinity thing again,' Christy said.

'What's this? What's the holy trinity?' Maud said, sounding

irritated at being left out of this previous conversation.

'I have this theory,' Joey leaned back in his chair, hands wrapped behind his head, 'that when you boil it down, everyone is looking for a sense of purpose, a work-life balance where three fundamental conditions overlap: working at something they like doing, which they're good at, and they can make money from it. For instance, lots of artists and creative types have got the first two sorted, but they'll never make any real money. Christy, by contrast, is good at law, and I expect used to make good money in London, but he didn't like the work. Now he likes what he's doing, but the money's not great.' Joey leaned forward and put a hand on Maud's shoulder. 'You Maud, with your life as a mother, I guess you're in with the artists: like it, good at it but not money-making. I've got no overlapping circles in my Venn diagram, but Sammy's got all three.'

'I'm not too sure about that,' Sam said. 'It's not all fun and games.'

Joey marvelled at the change in his insecure and socially awkward brother. Since leaving Lebanon, Sam found himself in the enviable position of picking and choosing who to work for. His photos appeared regularly in the international press, and he had won numerous photography prizes. As his fame spread with each magazine cover shot, Sam's confidence grew, and he became more comfortable with the fact that he made his living from the misery suffered by the innocents of war. He still suffered from insomnia, although he was supposedly sleeping better than he had in years. The back pain had worsened, in fact all his joints seemed to be acting up. It was hard to escape the conclusion that the untreated mental damage was manifesting itself throughout his body.

'Did you ever think about other types of photography?' Christy asked, with a sneaky glance over at Maud. 'You know, men's magazine stuff.'

'Christy!' Maud said. 'Keep your mind out of the gutter.'

The lads all laughed. 'No, is the answer, Christy.'

'Is there any more of this wine?' Joey said, tipping his glass to drain the last drops.

Even the distraction of the twins waking and the ensuing argument over whose turn it was (Maud yielded in the end, claiming it would take Christy too long to settle them and would ruin the night), didn't detract from the fun. Until in no time at all, it was well after midnight, and Sam had to leave to get some sleep before his red-eye to Kuwait.

Christy went to refill their Jamesons while Joey rolled a spliff. Maud had crashed out on the sofa, refusing to go to bed until Joey left.

'Good man, me old mucker. Cheers,' Joey said as he accepted the whiskey from Christy. 'Speaking of sex, how's it working for you these days then?'

'Sex, huh. Is that a pig I see cruising across the sky?' Christy said, looking out the window with dry, bloodshot eyes.

'What? She's no interest?'

'Always too tired. After Kathleen was born, Maud was completely caught up with all the baby stuff, and I was pushed to second in line, literally in the case of access to the tit,' Christy said with an ironic twist of his mouth. 'Then, when she was pregnant with the twins, she had awful morning sickness for the first seven months. And now Charlie's, what? Just over a year old. I'm down to fifth in line for Maud's attention, and by the time she gets to me, she's too exhausted to care.'

'Bummer, man,' Joey said, passing the billowing joint. Maud slumbered nearby, occasionally snoring.

'You know, you talk about that nirvana trinity,' Christy said. 'But with Maud, I think she's down to just one of those dimensions: good at it. She's always complaining that this child-rearing business is one long, hard slog and not at all what she'd expected. She misses having a full-time job to go to, not only for the diversion it would provide but also the cash. Maud wants her family living in a nice house and wants to be able to afford the odd little luxury, as she calls it, without constantly having to worry about the next brown envelope through the letterbox.'

'And what about you, man? Do you miss work in London at all?'

Christy exhaled a cloud of grey smoke. 'Not a bit of it, to be honest. My boss was a prize asshole, public school twit; Julian, don't you know? During the job interview, he gave me this bullshit about how the Hogan pedigree in law was so like his own family. I discovered later that the closest Julian's family ever came to involvement with the law was when his father was charged with insider dealing, and they put him away for five years.'

Once they started giggling, neither of them could stop, egging each other on until their eyes watered. Christy wiped his tears and held his hand up. 'No, wait, there's more . . . Ah, gee . . . Yeah, so when I started working there, Julian is all talk about the huge mansion he lived in, which it turns out is a Victorian terraced house at the top of Archway Road, much closer to seedy East Finchley than the grandeur of Highgate.'

'And what about the work in UNWRA? How's that going?'

'It's grand, I'm happy to be involved, but reviewing tenders and contract documentation out of a portacabin in Jerusalem? That's not what I signed up for. Too much bureaucracy and I'm way too far from the action. But I'm excited about a new position that's coming up as head of Legal in Gaza. That would be ideal.'

'Right. But you'd be based in Gaza?'

'Yeah, there's some details I need to work through. By the way, don't say anything to Maud about all this for now. I don't want to worry her unduly.'

As if on cue, Maud stirred on the sofa, reared up, stretched out a long yawn, then said in a tired voice, 'What have yous been talking about?'

'Oh, late night chitter-chatter, Maud, just passing the time. I better go, actually; let you good folks get to bed.'

Morning was breaking as Joey rose to leave. They opened the front door to a melodious chorus of birdsong and a moon hanging like a tilted smile in the lavender-pink sky. After a group hug, Christy and Maud stood on the doorstep and watched Joey swagger off, hands raised above his head, free as the breeze blowing down the road.

19.

JOEY SAT ON A BENCH BESIDE A RUSTED RELIC OF A TANK in the Ammunition Hill Heritage Site, brown hair curling down his neck and bushy sideburns stretching to his jawline. That morning, 13th October 1990, the long-awaited news had come through: the war in Lebanon was over. The final solution had reverted to effectively the same political configuration Lebanon had at the start of the war, with Syria and an assortment of its buddy militias back in control of the country. One of the most tragic chapters in the Middle East's perpetual story of conflict and, after fifteen years of bloody civil war, all the combatants had achieved was to turn the Paris of the Middle East into the Beirut of the Middle East; the city name was now synonymous with horrific atrocities, bombed-out buildings, and a fractured, traumatised population. More than 120,000 people had been killed, nearly a million displaced, and several billion dollars worth of damage done to property and infrastructure.

Meeting up in Ammunition Hill somehow felt auspicious. A strategic location for anyone wanting to control access to Jerusalem, it was a key battle site during the Six-Day war. Now, young children ran around those curving stone-wall trenches, play shooting each other where, in 1967, a brutal conflict played out. The Israelis had since turned the area into a memorial site, replete with the burnt-out remains of military ordnance scattered like artefacts throughout the park.

The morning was frostbite cold, and the breeze cut through Joey's clothes. Across the park, he saw them approaching, Kathleen swinging Maud's hand, revelling the quality mummy-time away from the twins and baby Charlie. She tumbled giggling into his arms, then ran off to play as Maud sat next to Joey on the bench. Maud had a conventionally pretty face, which today had a ruddy glow despite the layer of make-up. When Joey complemented her outfit, she moaned, 'It took me most of the morning to find something to wear. It's fierce depressing how shabby all my clothes are and how few of them still fit me.'

'Well, I think you look lovely.'

'Thank you for saying that. How are tricks? Any gossip?'

'Did you hear they finally caught that motorcycle bank robber? He's supposed to have robbed twenty-two banks over the last two years, but he's become a bit of a folk hero, especially with young Israelis. He's named after the red and black motorbike he used for his getaways.'

'Never heard of him. What's the big deal?'

'I guess it's one in the eye for the authorities. There's a lot of resentment knocking about, you know, among young Israelis. Just talk to Moshe. Although it turns out this robber guy isn't so anti-establishment. He comes from a very wealthy family but he ran up debts of more than a million dollars building himself a luxury home. The police found letters to his family apologising for his crimes when they searched his home. He'd only managed to rob 150K.'

They followed Kathleen's progress as she shimmied along the length of a decaying tank barrel. 'She's a great kid, Maud. You must be very proud of her.'

'She is, isn't she? She loves you too, of course.'

Two women passed by arm-in-arm and tapping white sticks on the path, 'Literally, the blind leading the blind.' When they'd stopped cackling, Joey said, 'How are the bridge lessons going?'

'Err . . . sort of OK, there's so many bloody rules. And there's some real bitches playing. I tell you this one French wagon, she's . . .' And she was off, in that meandering way Maud had of making a short story long, with detours to expand on irrelevant details, stressing and underlining her words as she built to a punchline that often failed to deliver. Joey had drifted off, half following her tale of the yummy mummies' difficulties with card games, when he noticed Maud had turned all serious, demanding his attention with, 'Do you ever wonder why you have such a fabulous connection with Kathleen?'

'Do I? I didn't realise I did. She never seems that interested in me after she's said hello.'

Maud held Joey's dark pools of brown in a steady gaze. 'Have you ever looked closely at her? Really looked.'

Joey turned his attention to Kathleen as she scuttled over the stony ground, her tumbling heap of brown curls blowing across her face. She looked up and waved, chestnut eyes gleaming in her heart-shaped face, then disappeared into one of the tens of bunkers where once the Jordanians had fought so hard to defend this barren hill.

'Who do you think she looks like?' Maud said, her cheeks flushed and her eyes ablaze.

'I dunno . . . I'm not very good at this business of seeing a likeness between people. The way people go, oh, he looks the spit of his uncle Paddy, or that long nose is just like her mother's. Funnily enough, she looks a bit like me.'

'She does, doesn't she? Have you ever wondered why that might be?'

'Have I ever wondered why that might be? Well, no, I've never even given it any thought until just now.'

'I need to tell you something,' Maud said as she crossed her right leg over the left and smoothed down her red linen skirt. 'Christy will have told you all about how he married me when he made me pregnant. The problem with that story is that Kathleen wasn't his baby. I know for a fact because I kept my cap in when I first started sleeping with him.'

'Not his baby? Whose baby is it then?' Joey scratched his ear.

'She's yours, Joey. Kathleen is yours. I named her after your mother. I know I shouldn't have done it, but that last night we had together, we —'

'What last night? When was that? What the hell do you mean, mine?' Her words washed through his ears and sloshed around in his head as he tried to think back to having sex with Maud.

'I knew you wouldn't remember. We were together the night before I first slept with Christy. You knew I was mad into you in those days, Mr Cool Rockstar University Student. I would have happily made love with you every day, but I wasn't going to be taken for granted; you were only ever interested when you'd no other options . . . So, I restricted myself; I wasn't going to behave like a floozie. But you had gone very queer; you were so upset about getting caught writing those essays for other students. I remember you were worried about what Pops would say.' Maud took hold of Joey's hand and ploughed on despite his incredulous look.

'I thought you needed some comforting. Plus, I was afraid it might be my last night with you. You were about to leave Dublin, and I got this pure mad idea that . . . I was afraid I might never see you again. I didn't know where you were going or what you were going to do . . . Before you left, didn't I decide that I wanted to have a little bit of you to keep for myself? I took my cap out just before we made love; you probably don't remember how wonderful the love we made was that night. I didn't really think it through; just thought if I got pregnant, maybe you'd come back to me if we were having a child. If not, at least I'd done my best.'

An anguished silence smothered any further words. Joey's mouth hung open as he tilted his head. Aged seventeen, Maud had lost her virginity to Joey on that same riverbank in Limerick where Christy had saved her from drowning. When he was at university, Joey had sex with her on and off, but it had never meant anything, a meaningless convenience, two old friends sharing a passing intimacy. He stood and paced off a short distance, then turned back as Maud called, 'No, wait, Joey, you need to hear this.'

Joey wandered back and sat at the far end of the bench, eyes lowered to the ground, hands pocketed in his overcoat, as Maud continued, 'Then the following night, your very last night, you were supposed to come back to St Jude's, but you never did, as I was afraid would happen. I was . . . I wanted one last time with you . . . I was gutted and went for a little chat in Christy's room, brought him a cup of tea. Musha, didn't we both get carried away? It was all the emotion of you leaving Dublin so suddenly. We ended up in bed together. Silly, really, Christy meant nothing to me back then. I suppose I figured if you were going to stay in touch with anyone after you left, it would be him. Next thing we started going out together. Then I discovered I was up the duff. We were both out one night and I got langers. I'd decided it would be my last night of drinking before having the baby, and I ended up telling Christy I was pregnant, and he assumed it was his. In the moment, it was easier to say it was, and then before I knew what was happening, we were getting married.' Maud's voice fled down her throat.

'Shit, Maud, I can't believe you never told me.' Joey puffed out his cheeks and exhaled. A long pause. Maud's words reverberated in his head, the loud rumble of consequences that might flow from this revelation rather than the voice itself.

'I wanted to tell you, of course I did, for years I wanted you to know. But you were off in Lebanon, and then after that you were sick, and I didn't want to worry you with yet another problem. I wasn't sure how you'd react or what you'd want to do. It's only now that you're so much better that I thought you could handle hearing about it.'

'Handle it?' Joey sneered. 'Hmm, handle it . . . I dunno. Does Christy know?'

'Yerra, of course, he doesn't. And he mustn't, Joey, you can't tell him. Promise me you won't; it would break his heart.' A room in their marriage locked to hide an inconvenient truth, to which she had now given him the key.

When Maud turned around, Kathleen was making her way out of the bunker and walking along the top of a stone wall, calling out, 'Ice cream, please, Mummy.' They headed up over the other side of the hill, Kathleen racing ahead, Joey submerged in his thoughts and gazing at his feet as he kicked a stone along the sandy path.

'I love you, Joey, you know that. I always have and always will. But I'm not looking for anything from you. I don't expect you to get involved with Kathleen's life. I know you're not interested in settling down, and besides . . . I'm happy with Christy now.' Joey stopped and looked at Maud, struck by the lack of enthusiasm in that statement.

'That's good to hear because the last thing I need now is to start playing happy families. I'm perfectly happy that I've got nobody, and I ain't looking for anybody. I am glad you told me, though Maud, I really am. I'm just . . .' Joey let the thought trail away, distracted by a flash memory of Lena's smile, her in the crook of his arm as they walked along the Corniche at sunset, that day he'd bought the engagement ring.

FROST & FIRE

Everything But The Girl

ISRAEL

January to July 1991

20.

CHRISTY'S WHITE RENAULT 5, with Joey in the passenger seat and Bee in the back, crossed into the Gaza Strip with only a short delay. It was Bee's first visit to Israel since Christy abandoned his promising law career in London to join UNWRA and do his bit for the Palestinian cause. It had taken a while to find his groove, but ever since he'd got the job in Gaza, he'd been walking around with a puff in his chest and a hop in his step. An inconvenient downside was that he had to commute down from Jerusalem every Monday morning, leaving Maud and the kids behind for the week.

In the opposite direction, heading into Israel, a long line of cars and pedestrians waited to have their exit permits checked by the border guards; these were only issued to market traders and workers in businesses inside Israel or patients requiring medical treatment outside of Gaza. The besieged coastal enclave was where most of the Palestinian refugees, whose homes were taken in the 1948 War, still called home. Pushed far out of the way, down into the southwest corner of Israel, one million people were packed into a strip of land twenty-five miles long by five wide. With their backs to the sea and severe restrictions on their movement in and out by land, the refugees lived in extreme hardship and were dependent on UNWRA assistance for all aspects of life. In the absence of an official Palestinian state, the UN agency acted as a quasi-state body for the refugees, providing education, health care, and a wide range of other support services to a people who, at one time, were prosperous and independent.

Once through the border checkpoint, the tarmac road turned into a slushy mud trail, saturated after the recent two-day downpour. Car tyres had gouged deep trenches into the squelchy ground, and a stream of what smelled like sewage trickled diagonally across the road. Christy beeped the horn to clear a bunch of kids jumping in puddles by the roadside, their trouser legs pulled above their knees. Further on, two men, ankle-deep in the swampy mud were pushing a battered Renault and shouting at a boy of about ten behind the steering wheel.

'What a fucking mess,' Christy said, sounding apologetic. 'It's a bit overwhelming sometimes. Health, education, all the infrastructure, houses, roads, and bridges, all of it only happens with UNRWA support. Generations of Palestine refugees have grown up dependent on us.'

'So many young people hanging about,' Bee observed, 'I guess they've nothing to do.'

'Nothing to do but plot revenge,' Christy said. 'When you box people in like this, forcibly confine them to a crowded space, like cornered rats they're going to strike back. It's bound to blow up some day, they're left with no other choice.'

'That's exactly right,' Joey said. 'All the Israelis are doing with their Gaza policy, and of course on the West Bank, is breeding the next generation of terrorists.'

'The tragedy for the Palestinians is that they got hooked up with the wrong superpower. You ever hear of an influential Palestinian in America?'

'Look at the shit show since the fall of the Berlin wall. Whatever power Russia once had on the world stage, that's all over now.' Joey craned out the car window and shouted, 'Hang on, what's that over there? Christy, pull over so we can take a look.'

On a wall pockmarked with bullet holes, a faded mural of PLO leader Yasser Arafat in his trademark black and white keffiyeh looked down on two old men (themselves wearing matching keffiyehs) who were sitting on stools and puffing on a shisha pipe. Beside them, a teenaged boy was carving shapes out of watermelons.

'Look, look, that's what I thought,' Joey called back into the car. 'He's cutting watermelons into the shape of Palestine. That's genius! You see the colours, same as the Palestinian flag.' To the boy, Joey shouted in Arabic, 'Please, effendi, give me three pieces.'

As they drove off, Joey said, between bites of watermelon, 'This reminds me, in the bad times in Beirut, we made lights out of watermelons. The electricity was on and off all the time, so along the floor, we set up a row of carved-out watermelons and stuck candles in them to light up the dark nights. All Halloween like.'

'How funny,' Bee said. 'I remember a time in Beirut when you were both back in boarding school; the shooting was so bad we had to sleep in the corridors.'

'Ha, Sam and I did that for a while, too.'

'There was this one time, I must have been about eight or so,' Bee continued, 'and I was really into ballet. We were in the parents' bedroom, and I was doing a ballet routine, showing off my moves because I wanted them to buy me a tutu. There I was twirling around on their bed when suddenly a stray bullet came flying through the window and missed me by inches.'

'No way,' Christy called from the front as he swerved to avoid a pair of scrawny dogs running alongside the car, wild and barking. 'Why have I never heard about this?'

'Go on, dare I ask?' Joey grinned as he turned to face Bee.

'Yes, you may, and no, I never did get that tutu.'

Just then, a gang of boys chased after the car, slipping and sliding in the mud, as they called out, 'Baksheesh mister, Baksheesh.' From nowhere, two older boys appeared, both with smaller kids propped on their hips. 'No, no, not today, please,' Christy called out, then to Bee said, 'Don't encourage them, or we'll be mobbed.'

'Ma was always a sucker for people begging, do you remember?' Joey said as Christy floored the accelerator. 'She could never resist, and next thing she'd be swarmed.'

'I feel so sorry for them.' Bee waved at a woman peeling vegetables cross-legged on the ground in front of a makeshift house with corrugated roofing held down with rocks. 'The housing's still terribly basic, isn't it? What's with these corrugated iron shacks?'

'There's a mixture,' Christy said. 'Some people have houses with blockwork walls, but many still have corrugated roofing.'

'I'd say that makes quite a racket when you've got heavy rain pounding down on it,' Joey said.

'All the camps are ridiculously overcrowded, so people build houses right beside each other. As families expand, they often add an extra floor to fit more people in, but it's usually poorly built, and often they collapse.'

Driving the familiar route, Christy saw his workplace afresh through his visitors' eyes. The jostling press of vehicles and donkeys pulling laden carts, splashing through puddles of brown rainwater. People sweeping water out of their houses back onto the road, and over there, a young boy bailing out a flooded house with a plastic container. Three teenaged boys astride the husk of a burnt-out car laughing as a man carrying a bed base slipped in the gloopy mud and banged into his child, who had a cot mattress balanced on his back.

'I can't get over the change since we were last here,' Bee said. 'Remember, we used to come down to the Beach Club all the time.'

When the Hogans last lived in Israel, in the 1970s, at weekends, the UN peacekeepers' families decamped to a beach club in Gaza. By day, the mothers drank coffee and gossiped as their children splashed on Johnson's baby oil and lay on loungers worshipping the sun king. They raced in packs down to the sea and body-surfed the predictably large waves, watched over by Husseini, the lifeguard. They played table tennis in the clubhouse and volleyball on the beach. They went for saunas, interspersed with cold showers and bottles of Tuborg. And they behaved like horny teenagers, hot from the sun and the hormones, flirting in bulging Speedos and skimpy bikinis. By night, there were barbeques and

G&Ts and happy hour cocktails and, every so often, classic movies on a rickety old projector. For a few, romances that had started at a young age with, 'Show me yours and I'll show you mine', behind the shed in the Anglican School progressed to, 'Let's go to third base' (and sometimes further), in a quiet corner of the Gaza Beach Club. Meanwhile, the parents unwound by drinking and singing and playing bridge, occasionally casting a watchful eye on the goings-on with the younger folk.

'I know, a different world altogether. In fairness, that's nearly twenty years ago,' Christy said. 'The last four years, with this Intifada, has been a disaster for Gaza.'

'What's the Inti . . . what?'

'The Intifada. It started back in 1987, from nothing really, when an Israeli army truck rammed into a car in Gaza and killed four people. That spark galvanised a collective Palestinian frustration with Israel's military occupation which by then had been going on for twenty-years. Anti-Israeli protests, boycotts, all sort of acts of civil disobedience broke out across the country and they've been virtually a permanent feature of life since, no matter how aggressively the Israeli army try to suppress it.'

Reminiscing about the freedoms of their childhood and the relaxed nature of parenting in those days, Christy wondered aloud whether he and Maud were getting it right. Everything seemed so much more controlled nowadays. Parents were so much stricter with their kids and involved in every aspect of their lives. Maybe they should be taking a page out of the UN parenting book. 'I mean, we all turned out fine, didn't we?' he said.

'Depends on who you're asking,' Joey snorted. 'Not all would agree with that conclusion, my man.'

Bee laughed. 'One day, I overheard one of the mothers talking about Declan Clancy, remember him, with the blonde hair and the dreamy blue eyes, and one of them said, "I saw him making eyes at so and so girl", and his mum Bernadette quick as a flash says, "Well, I suppose we should be grateful that he's a normal healthy boy who's into girls". Can you imagine? Parents were so unpolitically correct back then, especially out here in the UN, isolated from any conventions or trends that were happening back home.'

'Remember Ma used to spend her days roaring at us to be careful in the sea,' Christy said as he lit a cigarette. 'She and Nuala Dempsey used to stand on the shoreline, waving us back in, saying that it was too dangerous. Neither of them could swim, of course, which didn't help.'

'Did you ever hear the reason why they didn't swim?' Bee asked.

'I just presumed they never learnt.'

'Ah, sort of. Ma told me all about it.' Bee was animated and having fun. It had been way too long since Christy had spent time with her, and he'd forgotten what good company she was. Spiky, platinum blonde hair and tie-dye tee-shirt, with a cheeky smile, Bee brought a lot of colour to this drab Gaza morning as she continued, 'Seemingly Barney Nolan, remember him, the tall, muscular guy with a bald head? He was very sporty. This one time, they're all out at Abu Ghosh pool, Ma, Nuala, and Eithne Maguire, and Nolan decides he's going to teach them how to swim. None of the ladies had ever been in the water before. He lines them up along the side of the pool, starts giving a little spiel on what he's going to show them, and then, without any warning, walks along behind, pushing each of them in.'

'You're fecking joking,' Christy guffawed. 'What a hero.'

'For real, I'm telling you. He'd read in National Geographic about how babies instinctively swim if you throw them into water as an infant. Well, it turns out that doesn't work for grown women, with their fully developed danger radar on red alert. None of those three women ever got into the water again.' For a moment, they were lost in their own thoughts until Bee continued, 'It's weird being back here. Plus ça change. Seeing all this, Jerusalem too obviously, it stirs up lots of memories. Ma in her prime, always laughing, making people feel good, that's what I remember most.'

'She was so encouraging of all of us, always—'

'It was kind of embarrassing sometimes, in a lovely way though, how she'd go on about some success or other one of us was having. So sweet of her.'

Joey turned to face Bee and said, 'You're right though, Bee, everything's the same as it used to be, yet it's all so different now. I find that too. When we were kids, we used to drive through Gaza City and pass right by Beach refugee camp; back then I didn't even know it was called that, wasn't even aware there was a refugee camp there.'

'It's scary how insulated we were from what was going on,' Christy said. 'Basically Israel, or wherever we were living, Egypt, Lebanon, Syria, we just existed in a cocoon with all the other UN families.'

'I guess it was the parents doing that on purpose, to protect us, keeping us away from any of the nasties,' Bee said.

'You know, before the Nakba, when they were thrown off their land, the Palestinians were skilled labourers, they had jobs, they were self-sufficient,' Christy said. 'But now unemployment is out of control — we have the highest unemployment rate in the world — and very few families can provide for themselves. You'll see for yourself. I just want to pop into the office, and then we'll go out to Jabalia camp.'

Entry to Christy's office compound was via a large, blue metal gate, emblazoned in white with "UNRWA HQ Gaza" beside the UN globe and olive leaves emblem. As they approached, a security guard came out, shook Christy's hand then signalled to have the gate opened. They drove through and parked in front of a white stone, three-storey building that curved around a grassy courtyard. Christy gave them a quick orientation, and they continued talking as they walked along the corridor and up the stairs.

'I guess Maud has no interest in moving down to Gaza with

you?' Bee asked.

'Nah, you can see living conditions are pretty shitty here for a family, and besides, the kids are all set up in school in Jerusalem.' And Maud's already struggling enough with life in Israel, he could have added. Nor did he elaborate with details of yesterday's rant, in front of Kathleen, about how boring and pointless her life had become. Or his concerns about the amount of time she was spending with Eithne Mulcahy and her bottles of gin. Instead, he went with, 'And, of course, all Maud's friends are in Jerusalem.'

'Again, so weird,' Bee said. 'The kids are back at the Anglican School, just like their daddy and his brothers and sister before them.'

'I know, it's quite nice, actually, going back there. They're very happy in the school. Kathleen is in second class, and the twins just started last September.'

'Remember we used to have Mrs McAndrew, Orla's mum, teaching us,' Joey said.

'I loved that school.' Christy sometimes wondered if Maud found it difficult adjusting to life in Israel because she hadn't grown up as a UN kid like he had. But plenty of their friends had never been anywhere near the Middle East before they moved here, so it's not like prior experience was a prerequisite for satisfaction.

'When you look back at those school class photos now, it's hilarious. There's every country represented,' Bee said. 'The photo from my last year in the Anglican, I counted up, and there were eighteen of us in the class and sixteen different nationalities.'

'Actually, the quality of education was surprisingly good,' Joey said. 'Both of us were there for the two years before we were sent back to boarding school. I was worried we were going to be behind the other lads, but we had no problem keeping up, and in some subjects, we probably knew more.'

'Here we are,' Christy said as he pushed open a door into a cluttered office with two desks facing each other.

'Guys, meet Sadie Sorenson. Sadie's from Sweden. This is my brother, Joey, and my sister Bee.'

Sadie had straight, shoulder-length blonde hair and glowing blue eyes. She smiled broadly and nodded as she shook hands and said in a lilting voice, 'Hello, Joey. And your name is Bee? Like the buzzing thing?'

Joey exchanged a glance with Christy, a glance confirming that men could resist anything but temptation, and expressing concern that Maud was living seventy-five kilometres away.

'That's it, Bee, as in B-E-E,' Christy replied. 'When she was five years old, Bee announced to all of us that Bridget was a stoopid name, and she didn't want to be called that anymore—'

'Stoopid name,' Bee echoed.

'—and that people should henceforth call her Bee. This was before she got seriously into boxing, although at the time, she had fixated on Muhammad Ali.'

'Boxing, for a girl. That's unusual,' Sadie said.

'Yeah, well, that's Bee for you. European Women's Boxing champ, I'll have you know. She can tell you all about it while I grab that paperwork about the new health centre in Nuseirat camp. Then I'm going to take them to Jabalia.'

Sadie was all ears as Bee explained that by 1973, when Pops was reassigned from Amman to Jerusalem as UN Head of Security, she'd had enough of always being in her brothers' shadows sports-wise and demanded that, if the boys had their football, then she wanted to have her own sport too. 'In fairness,' Bee laughed, 'I could play football as good as any of them — the brothers and their friends — and these were a sporty gang of boys; two of them went on to play rugby for Ireland, and another made it to the Irish athletics Olympic team.' At the time, sporting options for ten-year-old girls in Jerusalem were limited, but one of Pops' colleagues, Captain Robert McCool (everyone knew him as cool Bob), had just started giving boxing lessons in Government House, the United

Nations HQ. Bee had spent years jousting with her older brothers and, by then, could hold her own in play fights. The previous Christmas, Santa had brought boxing gloves for Christy, but Bee had commandeered them, and she soon had a matching punch bag hanging in her bedroom. When she got wind of cool Bob's classes, she wanted in. Bob had some boxing pedigree (he had won numerous competitions with the Canadian army) and was delighted to have Bee as his first coaching protégée.

Joey interjected. 'Of course, Bee has always been a maverick; it's hardly a surprise that she uses the "Female Rebel" as her boxing nickname. Check out her tattoos.'

Bee leaned forward and twisted her neck to show the butterfly tattooed just below her ear. 'And a bee on the other side, I like it,' Sadie said, grinning.

'You know, women have been boxing for as long as there's been boxing,' Bee continued, her cheeks flushed and her lively eyes fixed on Sadie, 'but actual fights between women that people could pay to watch were outlawed everywhere until very recently. Even though, right back in 1904, women's boxing appeared as a demonstration sport in the Olympic Games. After that, all the naysayers piled in, worried that women boxers were unladylike, that they would be gratifying a perverse crowd of vulgar men or some nonsense like that. But things are changing, there's growing pressure. A number of states in America and, more recently, Sweden, your place, Sadie, have issued licenses to women boxers. That's where I won my championship title.'

'Sisters doing it for themselves,' Sadie laughed as she slapped palms with Bee.

Christy appeared from the room out back. 'No better woman to talk about struggles against the odds than Bee. Sorry to interrupt you in full flow but we gotta bounce. Maybe see you later, Sadie, for a drink?'

Jabalia, the largest of Gaza's eight refugee camps, was overlooked by an Israeli observation post that towered over everything in the area, a 360-degree treehouse-like structure manned by two soldiers with a machine gun turret. Below it, two Palestinian flags attached to a roof fluttered in the gentle wind.

'Those guys over there, they're Hamas,' Christy said pointing to a group of youths with green bandanas on their foreheads, rifles pointing skywards. 'Very dangerous crew. They've been getting more and more support since the Intifada started. Palestinians feel that the PLO have totally failed them, that after years under Arafat the situation hasn't improved at all. In fact, it's much worse, so people are ready for a new approach. A more militant approach. These guys are way more radical, seriously committed to the Islamic cause. There was a big blow out last October when the Israeli army killed 17 Palestinians who were causing trouble at the Temple Mount. Hamas have now declared every Israeli solider a target and called for a jihad against what they call the Zionist enemy. It's not going to end well.'

'You're right, you know,' Joey said. 'The Arab states have tried and failed to oust Israel, and the PLO got nowhere. Hamas will learn from that; they'll use people's hopelessness to garner support for a more ambitious terrorist campaign.'

On the edge of the camp, Christy parked the car, and they picked their way gingerly through the sloppy mud towards the food distribution centre. The chop-chop roar of an engine drew their attention to the intimidating sight of an incoming Israeli helicopter, which then hovered above them, menacing like a bird of prey. Conversation was drowned out momentarily by the swish swash of whirring blades. Control of the skies had always been at the root of Israel's military success; it was a key reason the 1967 war only lasted six days. From inception, Israel recognised the importance of establishing superior air power in the region and invested heavily in new technology while leveraging American financial support to build up its fleet. Training for those invited onto the prestigious pilot training programme is notoriously demanding, and Israelis considered acceptance into the Airforce to be a badge of honour that only the very best got to wear. With nothing to see, the chopper flew off, spinning scraps of newspaper off the ground in its downdraught.

Christy directed them past a smouldering house in ruins. A tall, thin man with an immense black beard beckoned them inside to meet his wife, who was stirring a bubbling cauldron on a paraffin stove as their daughters ran up the stairs. His family had just moved in after an explosion damaged the building and drove off the previous inhabitants. Loosening his keffiyeh, the man called them closer to look at a photo album. Slowly, it dawned on Christy that instead of showing off his own family, the man was paging through snapshots from the previous residents' lives. Did this hirsute interloper really think, now that he had their home, he would also assume their life? Would he also go on holidays with his wife to Cairo and capture on film their visit to the Pyramids? Would his girls have their starring role in the school play and have it recorded on celluloid for posterity? Christy nodded at the others and as they left, a battered old green Volvo, with both side panels missing and piles of white sacks on its roof rack, beeped hello at Christy. Further on, they came upon a line of people queuing for food handouts off an UNWRA truck tailgate, waiting to have their name ticked off a clipboard list by a bearded man seated at a table alongside.

'Those people are cleared for prepacked food rations, which are typically given to the most needy,' Christy explained. 'They get a plastic bag with a bottle of oil, some rice, and a selection of tin cans – vegetables, beans, definitely corned beef, Joey's favourite when he was a young lad, as I recall.'

'Don't knock it till you've tried it.'

'I have, and it's just fine. Come on, let's go inside.'

As they entered the distribution centre, an elderly woman flashed them a buck-toothed smile, a laden brass tray balanced on her head. It was a huge warehouse with fanlight windows high along one wall and a line of pillars down the middle, between which hessian sacks of rice were piled five high. On the other side of the warehouse, white cardboard boxes stamped with the blue UNRWA logo were stacked on top of each other, reaching up close to the ceiling. Everywhere, people were in motion: an official handed out white bags of flour, which people carried away on their shoulders, or on various forms of wheeled vehicles: a bicycle or a cart or an improvised trolley. Across the room, a bald man with a smoking cigarette dangling from his mouth measured out portions of olive oil and poured them into whatever container people had brought with them. A line of women in traditional embroidered (now mud-caked) dresses shuffled patiently in a line to collect their rations. Three young men, wearing high-vis jackets with UN printed on the back, scooped chickpeas into small plastic bags.

'I like to help out every so often, just to get involved on the ground,' Christy said. 'Here, you two, grab a jacket and get stuck in.'

Christy loved having Joey and Bee around, seeing first-hand the difference his work was making. Once again, his life had meaning; he had something that gave him a sound reason to get up every morning and that drove him forward during the day. From an early age, Christy had wanted a career in law, as it worked for him on several levels: it brought job stability and a clear career path; it provided a moral support system that appealed to his basic sense of fair play (the righteous man fighting the good fight against evil); and a defined set of conventions, rules, and precedents governed the work. For a while, his job in London had ticked those boxes. But after his visit to Joey and Sam in Lebanon, and his balcony discussions with their neighbour Abu Amar, that all changed. When he announced his intention to pack in his safe job in London to go help Palestinian refugees, a parade of disapproving family members — uncles Sean and Barry (both solicitors), brother-in-law Fintan (a Guard), his grandmother Marie (a retired judge) — lined up to vent their dismay but Christy had held firm. For once, he had done just what he wanted to do.

21.

THE YELLOW SUBMARINE MUSIC CLUB in Talpiot, on the outskirts of the New City, was heaving as Joey peered out from behind the stage curtain at the assembling crowd. It was a popular live music venue in Jerusalem, with a growing reputation for launching new local acts like Moshe's band, The Cute Hoors. A roadie called out, 'Hey, Moshe, two minutes,' the cue for Joey and Maud to move out front and get another drink. Moshe adjusted his stool and rolled the snare drum; three guitars joined in, and the crowd pogoed towards the stage in one heaving mass.

Having swallowed two tequila oranges in too-quick succession, Joey had shifted onto plastic-glassed, flat Goldstar. Everyone in the place was buzzed, all amorous eyes, grinding teeth, and constant liquid consumption to tame the chemical madness. In no time at all, the crowd's enthusiastic send-off was drowning out the final bars of The Cute Hoors' encore and the house lights came back on.

'What are they called again, the main act?' Maud roared into Joey's ear as she wiped her sweaty face and gulped the dregs of her beer.

It was confusing, really; here he was perfectly able to rattle out a full band history — they were named after a sign the singer saw in a Hull shop window, which proclaimed that everything was for sale but the mannequin girl — and yet sometimes he worried he'd forget his own name. He never used to be so forgetful, even when he was regularly stoned. Now, he seemed to be forever misplacing his wallet, books, and items of clothing; he'd even lost Maud's car the last time she'd lent it to him, spent ages wandering the car park until he remembered that he'd left it on the street. He'd lost his house key so many times that he didn't bother with one anymore; instead, he scaled the neighbour's back wall and climbed the fire escape to his unlocked window. Fucking medication was seriously messing with his memory.

Alongside him, Maud joined in the collective whooping and hollering for the band to come on. Joey was still trying to come to terms with the revelation that he was a father. There was a weird vibe now every time he met Maud. He wondered whether he should be getting more involved in Kathleen's life, maybe taking more responsibility for her, but how the hell would that work. It was a lot to get his head around and there was no one he felt comfortable talking it over with, and that was a concern too. He'd never kept anything from Christy before; he'd always been the one Joey could share his troubles with. Christy was a born listener, and was also greedy with secrets, liked to keep them all to himself. Ma too of course, she would have had some telling words of wisdom, would have found a way of reassuring him.

Christy showed up with refills just as the house lights went down, and a pair of non-rock stars ambled unnoticed onto the stage and launched into an acoustic number. Joey stood transfixed, staring at the androgynous vocalist in her sack-like white dress, with short cropped black hair and an expressionless face. But oh, the voice! Joey was mesmerised by the singer's melodic voice, warm and alluring, cut with a slice of melancholy. Her melted honey words washed over him as if she'd laid down these lyrics specifically for him. She got his regrets that everything that he thought would last had fallen apart. That there was no way for him to put things back to when they were all right. And yes, how he wanted to shout at someone, anyone! But there was no one to blame. Except maybe himself.

Moshe's after-gig party was in full flow by the time Joey and Christy found the squat in nearby Rivka Street. It was good to get inside as there was a nervous atmosphere walking the eerily deserted streets. For the last few weeks, since the US coalition went to war with Iraq, Saddam Hussein had been firing Scud missiles at Israel in an effort to broaden the Gulf War into a regional conflict. At the request of the US, Yitzhak Shamir had held back from retaliatory strikes in the belief that Israeli military engagement wouldn't in any case reduce the missile threat and because he didn't want a confrontation with his major ally. Although the physical damage from the missiles was limited, the psychological shock to the nation was significant. For the first time in decades, the battlefield had moved to mainland Israel. Hundreds of thousands of Israelis took cover in bomb shelters as they were subjected to nightly missile attacks and the implied threat of a chemical attack. Although downtown Jerusalem was untouched so far, everyone knew there was never any certainty regarding security in this city.

Shoving through the crowd gathered at the doorway, the brothers made their way towards the back room, past a sea of grinning, unfamiliar faces. Joey hugged Moshe and then held him back, hands on his shoulders. 'See, they love you, man.'

'The gig was okay, but you can hear in the solos we missed Gideon. This new guy on guitar, he's not as good.'

'Any news about him?'

Gideon was one of Moshe's more radical friends, an active member of the Yesh Gvul "There's a Limit" movement. A group of Israeli soldiers who refused to serve in Lebanon started the movement in 1982 and it had been growing since as more soldiers selectively refused to perform military service in campaigns they disagreed with. Gideon had been court-martialled after his arrest for writing graffiti on military vehicles and for placing stickers around airbases that read: "Only the worst ones go to the Air Force", inverting the well-known Hebrew phrase by replacing the word "best".

'They gave him three months; I suppose it could have been worse,' Moshe said. 'The maximum penalty is six years.'

'What a fucking country,' Joey said. 'They really—'

'Hey, you seen Maud anywhere?' Christy interjected, scanning the mass of heads in front of them.

'She was around earlier, with that Amy one. Pretty pissed, the pair of them.'

'Nothing new there then.' A pause and a frosty look. 'She's gone very bad; it's like I don't really know her anymore.'

On cue, Maud appeared, arm wrapped around Amy, although it wasn't clear who was supporting whom. Maud's cheeks were flushed, her blue eyeliner smudged below her bloodshot eyes, and her red hair gathered into a high ponytail. Amy's short blonde hair was dyed purple, and she was all bare skin save for a leather skirt that stretched to mid-thigh and a strapless puce top that just made it over the mound of her boobs. Maud's opening line was, 'So wha' you boyz talkin' 'bout?'

Christy struggled to hide his disgust, morphing into anger, as Joey headed off the potential flash-point. 'You girls enjoy the gig then? Wasn't himself great?'

'Yes, my darling Moshe.' Maud mock swooned as she threw her arms around his neck. 'Keith Moon the second, or maybe not, but trying hard all the same.'

'Enough, Maud, that'll do,' Christy said with an icy stare as Moshe shook himself free from her grip.

'Is that bass player hooked up?' Amy said. 'He's cute.' With which she released a heaving guffaw and rocked forward as if overcome by the funniest thing she'd ever heard.

'Waaa haaa, ger up, ya boy ya,' Maud said, kicking off another round of girl screeching.

'Fuck this shit,' Christy said and beckoned the band's singer Avi to come over. The group got bumped around as others joined, and Maud staggered off with Amy, who was looking to score; no one was quite sure what or with whom.

And then it was much later. Taxis had been involved. At some point, they'd grabbed a pizza slice from Richie's, a favourite late night grazing spot off Jaffa Street. Then it was back across town, and a stumble down narrow stairs to throbbing music and a psychedelic light show in a nightclub behind the Old City walls.

Joey was distracted by the blinking smoke alarm on the ceiling, which he was pretty sure had been connected to the pipework and electric wiring to form a gigantic eavesdropping system. Mechanical and electrical objects — clocks, phones, everyone knew they installed cameras inside TVs to monitor you at home — made him suspicious that they were spying on him. It was the same on the rare occasions he ventured out driving. Barely audible voices dictated instructions through the car speakers so that now he only ever drove a random route home, taking a right turn in the direction of his apartment when the last digit on the dashboard clock was an even number and a left turn when the number was odd. Mostly, he preferred to walk.

When he zoned back into the conversation the gang had thinned down to just four after Maud was sent home in a taxi with Amy. Then Avi and his lady split, leaving just Christy and Joey in a booth, eyes popping, noses dribbling, and mouths motoring.

'What do you reckon about Maud then? You can see things are bad, right?' Christy asked, swirling his beer.

Joey hauled himself back in the game, 'How'd you mean, man?'

'I mean, we're not getting on at all. We've become so different, like night and day, like . . . mixing frost and fire. These days, Maud's all talk about where did it all go astray, and do I realise all the dreams she had to let go, so I could follow mine.'

'I dunno, Christy. I do wonder how much control people actually have over their own life choices. You know . . . events just bleed into one another; you randomly move from one thing to the next, not much thought given. And then one day . . .' Joey gulped back the rest of his whiskey, 'suddenly, five, ten years have passed, and you're living a life nothing like you thought it would be. That's all the wisdom I have for you, man,' he ended with a bark of a laugh.

'You're right. This fecking business of life is difficult. I reckon that the amount of people who've got things figured out rounded down to the nearest whole integer and expressed as a percentage is one big fat zero.'

'Wise words, dude. Guru Christy.'

'What about Maud's drinking, though? Don't tell me you haven't noticed. What am I going to do?'

Joey had certainly noticed, couldn't miss it. That last time he'd been out with them, he'd made the mistake of suggesting to Maud that maybe she should cool it on her boozing. She had hissed, shaking with anger, the cheek of it, lectures from Mr-Party-Animal himself, isn't that just the limit now? 'She was just a bit out of it tonight, man, no big deal.'

'That's just it, though, it's not just tonight. It's often . . . most of the time. It's out of hand, Joey.'

'How, you mean serious, serious?' Joey ruffled his crop of floppy, brown curls, vaguely hoping this might help clear his head.

'Yes, shit, very serious. We've seen it before, you know that.' The penny dropped through Joey's fuzzy brain towards buried history: their grandfather Billy, who had died young from liver cirrhosis after years of alcohol abuse.

'Maud's mother's an alco. And before that, her grandfather. Word is her older sister Brigid's got it too,' Christy stated gloomily. 'What's bred in the bones comes out in the blood and, in Maud's case, what's trickling out is an addictive taste for alcohol.'

'Got it? You make it sound like it's some disease you catch, like AIDS.'

'Exactly,' Christy said. 'That's precisely what it's like. It has passed through the generations in her family. Maud's got it now. God knows what's in store for our kids, but right now, all I can focus on is her. And she's losing her grip on reality big time.'

Every time the kids were mentioned, it triggered a mild panic in him. He became fearful of what he might say, or anxious that Christy might already know, or . . . he wasn't sure what. Now he was worrying that he should be doing something to prevent Kathleen becoming an alcoholic. He took a deep breath and tried to think of something helpful to say. 'What about some sort of detox programme, a rehab clinic maybe?'

'That's what I reckon too. Will you help me convince her to go?'

And so, it had come full circle. Joey resisted the impulse to laugh at the irony of it. After years of being the one under instruction to detox, of being cajoled into taking control of his substance abuse, now he was being recruited in support of his brother's attempts to get his wife into a give-up-the-booze programme. About the only solace for his jumbled brain was the certainty that marriage was one track he would never be heading down, ever.

22.

A HYSTERICAL WAILING MARCHED ITS WAY down the corridor, a high-pitched scream in close single file behind it, and assaulted Maud's ears as she scraped the mess off Charlie's one-year-old bottom. She rubbed on a wad of Sudocrem and attempted to tag the nappy's Velcro straps in between the baby's lurching kicks. Envisaging the skirmish in progress in the sitting room, a wave of exhaustion rolled over her body, and she battled an overwhelming desire to just lie down for a moment. She shoved a soother into Charlie's mouth and chanced a peek out the door, from where she roared, 'Kathleen. Kathleen dear. Can you please see what's going on with the twins? Mummy's just trying to change Charlie's nappy,' *for the fourth time this morning,* she restrained herself from adding.

Although she had only just turned seven, Kathleen relished any opportunity to act grown up, and Maud could do with all the help she could get. Her life had become progressively more fraught with each new baby. She'd been lulled into a false sense of security with Kathleen; from birth, everyone said what a pleasant, well-behaved child she was, and Maud had naturally assumed that it was all down to her expert parenting skills. Now she realised that she had merely copped a lucky break with her first; that 'I'm a natural as a mother' bubble had been popped ever since the warring Aisling and Áine double-act had arrived. Sometimes Maud worried that she had inundated Kathleen with whatever motherly love she had in her so that by the time the twins started demanding her attention, let alone Charlie, her baby love-well had been drained and now only sediment remained. Maud brushed away her tears and scooped Charlie up, head resting on her shoulder, so she didn't have to see his face, which was the spit of Christy, same round face and piggy eyes. Guiltily, she pushed aside the thought that if she was going to be rearing a boy, then she really wanted one that looked like Joey. That picture, of how things might have been, remained vivid in her mind, lit by the torch she still bore for him.

Kathleen had managed to restrict the twins' combat zone to the sitting room although the blitzkrieg that greeted Maud's arrival resembled something that Sam might have photographed in one of his warzones. The toy box was upended, and its contents scattered across the room, then cloaked in a layer of talcum powder as if part of some scorched earth manoeuvre. Both the twins' faces were streaked with a patchy white mask. The current hostility involved a tug-of-war over a naked Barbie doll and, just before Maud could clear her way through the debris to drop Charlie in his crib (having first tossed out of it a pile of books and Lego bricks) and struggle to her feet again (having twisted her ankle on a spiky-backed, rubber dinosaur) and lunge toward the fighting twins, Aisling slapped Áine and gave a solid pull to amputate the arm from the doll's already legless torso.

A sudden metallic taste in Maud's mouth alerted her to stop biting her lip. In despair, she crossed the room and threw herself down on the sofa next to Kathleen, who had stuck her fingers in her ears and was humming while staring at the TV with the volume close to max. From the crib in the corner, Charlie bawled with venom, demanding his next feed because, for fuck's sake, Mummy, I'm hungry. Well, you can forget about getting onto my boob, sonny boy! My lumpy, bruised tit is swollen with flaming mastitis. It's going to be bottles all the way for you now, laddie. I've had it with these constant demands for the best of mother's milk.

Maud mimicked Kathleen's tactic of fingers plugging ears, and she shut her eyes so she didn't have to look at the sprawl of felt markers that covered the walls or the festering damp patch that seemed to spew out a little more of the wall's innards every day. Naturally, Christy never had no time to fix anything around the house; if he wasn't too busy at work, then he was off messing around with that waste-of-space gang he played football with.

'Come on, Mummy, it's time. We need to go to school,' Kathleen said.

'I know, pet. Sorry. Mummy's very tired today.' Suddenly, she was overcome by the colossal effort required to get the twins ready to accompany her and Kathleen to school. It would require a logistical operation with significant odds of failure and near-certain likelihood of further collateral damage. 'Maybe we'll just stay at home today, sweetie. Sounds like Charlie's nodded off, and if we move him now, he'll just wake up all over again.'

This was what her days had become: an endless cycle of feeding and pooh-cleaning and washing and shouting to behave and on and on. Maud cuddled up to Kathleen and rested her head on her shoulder. Better not to think too much about her sad, frantic life, a quick inventory of which revealed: thirty years old today, twenty-four hours a day mothering, tiny circle of friends, no social life, no fun. She really missed the hairdressing, way more than she ever thought she would; even an occasional opportunity to cut someone's hair at home would be some kind of pleasure. She felt so fat and couldn't see how she was ever going to shed the pounds that had accumulated one pregnancy after the other, not helped by all the cakes and biscuits she could never seem to resist. These days, she burst into tears at the slightest provocation, so that it was a toss-up who cried the most between her and Charlie. Even the things she used to enjoy – like cooking, going to the cinema, reading, even walking – all seemed like so much effort beforehand and then such a disappointment afterwards that she rarely bothered anymore.

How had she ever thought she was cut out for this domestic goddess scene? At best, she could muster a television version of a mother, mouthing the scripted lines and playing the expected roles, but behind the façade, she was a hollow shell. And to think that at one point, she was planning, just like her own mother, to have six children! She couldn't wait for the trip home next month to the green, green grass of the farm in Limerick. All the clan was assembling to meet her new baby; it was over two years since any of them had seen the twins. Her eldest siblings, Sinead and Brigid, who had both left home after school for banking jobs in Dublin, were coming down at the weekend with their kids. She made herself a promise to try to show off all her children, and not just Kathleen, a failing which even Mam had commented on the last time.

Taking advantage of the lull in hostilities – the twins had joined Kathleen on the sofa, and all three were engrossed in the babbling Pingu, and Charlie had miraculously cried himself to sleep – Maud slipped into the kitchen for a quick glug from the bottle on the shelf behind the fridge. She took another and, with a trembling hand, returned it to the shelf. Mummy's little helper. She knew she shouldn't be drinking. Of course she did. She's seen the damage alcohol can do. And Kathleen was no fool, she was clued in like her father. But in a life where nothing much else made her feel good, that feel-good buzz was hard to give up. Her shoulders drooped, and her legs wobbled as she stumbled back into the sitting room and flopped into the armchair, just in time to see the penguin's mother tantruming at the mess Pingu had created in the bathroom, which the three girls on the sofa found hysterically funny.

23.

MAUD ARRIVED EARLY AT THE BIRMAN BAR and found a quiet corner towards the back. She'd chosen this out-of-the-way venue in the New City, just in case they ran into someone she knew, as if that was likely to happen, given the small number of people she knew in Jerusalem and how infrequently she went out to a bar or restaurant.

Spending time back on the family farm in Limerick had been good for the soul, and Maud felt rejuvenated. Restful, lazy days pottering about the kitchen with her four sisters, helping Mam when she'd allow them, in between endless cups of tea and easy chats. Her mother was all over Charlie, of course, her thirteenth grandchild, and it had been lovely seeing all the young cousins playing together like they'd never been apart. On her last day, they all helped to prepare the scones and sandwiches and barmbrack and cakes for the hay-making workers in the fields up above. The sisters hauled the feast through the fields, past the paddock where Maud used to keep her herd of miniature goats (Bramble, Lavender, Nettle, and her favourite Hazelnut, white all over except for the brown tuft on his head). All around them, a chorus of chattering birdsong drifted on the light breeze, the warmth of the sun on their faces a welcome relief after weeks of summer rain. Up towards the horizon, Maud watched the tractor, Daddy driving, and alongside her two brothers, Paudie and Declan, tossing bales onto the trailer. She felt a fleeting dagger of envy for Paudie and the simplicity of his life; he helped Daddy run the farm, which, as the eldest son, he would inherit in the fullness of time, and so the cycle would continue. Just as quickly, the covetous thought passed, replaced with an unfamiliar contentedness and a clarity of purpose that she couldn't place at first. Strolling up the hill between her two sisters, Maud's heart leapt at the new course she would set her life on, a course she should have followed a long time ago. If she didn't at least try, she would be forever tormented by the neglected action, by the never knowing what might have happened.

Her reverie was interrupted when Joey slouched in and beamed a warm smile that showed off his recently whitened teeth. The seventies sideburns were gone, in their place a tidy goatee. At the bar, he ordered them both a drink and made his way over. Leaning down, he brush-kissed her. 'Belated happy birthday, Miss thirty years old.' July the third was not a date he forgot, although she knew it was the anniversary of Jim Morrison's death rather than Maud's birthday, which provided the reminder.

'Oh, Joey, you shouldn't have bothered,' Maud said, blushing as she unwrapped his present of two paperbacks, *Persuasion* and *Presumed Innocent*.

'Not a bother, it's just a token,' Joey said. 'You're looking well. The hair looks great bushed out like that around your shoulders.'

'Ah, shur, got to make a bit of an effort if I'm meeting a young lad like you, still one year off the big three O,' Maud said, her green eyes sparkling like diamonds.

'Of course, you know I'd love you however you look, don't you?'

Maud twisted the wedding ring on her finger and licked the vodka orange off her lips. 'Love Joey, that's a big word for four letters. I think we probably mean different things by it.'

'How's Christy? Haven't seen him in a while.'

'He's grand, busy as ever. He's at another conference this weekend, up in Caesarea.'

The waitress arrived with their drinks, and Maud stroked Joey's arm in thanks as he passed her glass. 'Are you seeing anyone these days?' she asked.

'Nobody special, keeping a low profile, working on the Lebanon book. Looks like I've got a publisher for it.' His face was fresh and unblemished, chestnut irises in a sea of white. The picture of medicated happiness, she thought ruefully. Once this schizophrenia gets its claws into you, it never lets go. Either you take the meds and have some sort of normal life, or you live without the meds, and then everything goes to shit. They're your only two options.

'Well done you,' she said, touching their glasses together and crossing her leg so that her right foot rested against Joey's leg.

The chat moved on to Kathleen and how she was getting on at school. Maud managed to hold it together for another three drinks, an attentive expression pasted on her face until the misery slipped its moorings and flooded out in deep, wretched sobs. 'Everyone else has something meaningful to do, something . . . interesting. Look at you Joey, yes you . . . you're getting your life sorted, writing for the Jerusalem Post, soon to be a published author no less. You've had all those amazing experiences in Lebanon. My life is so empty, so pointless; I never seem to have any fun.' She paused and accepted the proffered napkin. 'Ah, finally, my knight in shining armour shows up.'

After a few moments, Maud continued, 'Christy's gone all week and often at the weekend, and then he's too exhausted to do anything when he is around. Dear God, I hate the drudgery and routine of our life together. I've tried to be supportive of his career . . . I've tried to display some interest in the petty office gossip. And then when he comes home, I *really* try to make my week sound not too miserable for him, but you know . . . mostly, I just try very hard not to drink alone during the day. Or at least I try to wait until the kids are in bed before having the first one. There, I've said it now.'

Panic was too mild a word for what Joey felt. As he battered the shut doors of his mind searching for the right words, he arranged his face into a sympathetic demeanour, then went with a strong hug into which Maud yielded willingly. She sniffled and laughed through her ebbing tears. 'The only time you ever get Joey

Hogan stumped for a line is when the conversation moves towards anything remotely intimate.'

Joey chuckled with relief; counselling alcoholics really wasn't his game.

'Oh, Joey, I'm sorry. It's so good to be out with you. I just want to have a normal adult time tonight.' She took his hand in hers and stroked his palm in circles. 'Things are bad with me and Christy, you know . . . we're not connecting on any level unless it's arrangements about the children or the house.'

'I'm sorry to hear that, Maud, really,' Joey said, confusion etched on his forehead.

'You know, we haven't had sex in nearly a year now.'

Maud sat back after she'd dropped that grenade and watched the disbelief spread across Joey's face as he struggled to imagine the concept of a year without sex. He reached an arm behind and hugged her close to him. 'Maybe we need a change of scene. Are you hungry? Let's get something to eat.'

Half an hour later, Joey was feeding Maud roasted red peppers rolled in grilled aubergine in the Sea Dolphin restaurant. 'Ooh, it's so gooey.' Maud giggled. 'Try some of my vine leaves,' as she fed the tube of wrapped rice and lamb into Joey's eager mouth.

'Great choice of venue, by the way,' Joey said. 'This place has only reopened recently; it used to be in the Old City until it got blown up. It's got a great reputation for seafood, which is bizarre considering how far Jerusalem is from the sea.'

'There ya go, I'm a pure genius.'

'Do you like the Arak? It's got quite an aniseed taste.'

'It's lovely. Let's get another.' As his hand reached out to wipe the pepper juice dripping from her mouth, Maud exhaled as if blowing out a candle. She wondered if he realised that underneath their spoken words, a whole different conversation was taking place.

'Do you ever feel old? Like life is passing you by, and you better grab your chances when they come along?'

'I'm not sure,' she said, taking another aniseed sip while she considered the question. 'I usen't to think that way. But I do more and more now, yes. Do you?'

Joey tugged at his beard and then beamed at her. 'I think I've always thought that. Maybe that's why I end up in so much trouble. I'm too impulsive, too much living in the moment.'

Under the table, Maud pinioned Joey's closed legs between hers. They had arrived at the cards-on-the-table moment, where she unwrapped everything that had been concealed. There would be no more secrets, and she would rely on the truth to absolve them of any guilt. 'Speaking of living in the moment, I've got the babysitter to stay the night,' she whispered, aflame, a lustful hummingbird banging against her chest. 'I told her I was at a friend's party and was going to stay there for the night. So . . . we could go back to your place.'

'What?' Joey reeled back in his chair. 'You're joking; hang on a minute. What's all this?'

'I thought you wanted to also, Joey.'

'Wanted to? Wanted to what? Fuck my brother's wife? Why would I want to do that?'

'I don't know,' Maud said, avoiding his eye. *Because we love each other* was her hoped-for answer. *Because all this time I've been with Christy, I've hidden this mad desire for you,* she had planned to say but was suddenly wary.

'I know we used to before, Maud, but that was a long time ago, before Christy. You're married now. You've got kids. And I—'

'One of your kids, actually.'

'Don't tell me you're going to use that against me. I really couldn't handle a serious relationship again. For me, Lena was the love of my life; she can't be replaced.'

'But there's still something between us; I can feel it,' Maud said. That fucking Lena woman was always there in the background; why did she get to have all of his love?

'Maud, you mustn't read more into my words than I put into them. And what about Christy? I couldn't do that to Christy.'

'Shur, Christy has no more interest in me than the man in the moon.'

'I never meant to . . . to . . . lead you on? To tempt you with the possibility of some no-strings-attached action? I dunno why you would think any of this. It's just not a runner, Maud. I'm sorry.'

'Is it because I'm so fat? Is that why you want to ditch me?' Maud said, with almost a smirk.

'I don't want to ditch you, hell I'm not even with you in the first place. It's just . . . we need to stop this, Maud. Christy needs you. The girls and Charlie need you.'

Maud's face slumped, and she placed her hands over her eyes. 'Oh, dear God, I've made such a complete fool of myself. I'm so sorry. I'm going to go now.' She gathered up her sequined clutch purse and her new blue suede jacket and pushed past Joey.

'Wait, Maud, I'll come with you. Let me pay for this first.'

'No, you stay. I want to be by myself,' she called back, her eyes fixed on the door and her route out of the restaurant.

Head bowed and tears flooding down her face, Maud bustled along the footpath towards the taxi that would take her home instead of to Joey's. As she passed a bar, the thought came to her that she wasn't expected back yet, so she may as well get a little bottle of vodka and head to the park. It'd be a shame to waste the lovely evening weather, especially now that everything else had been wasted.

SHINE ON YOU CRAZY DIAMOND

Pink Floyd

ISRAEL

December 1991 to July 1993

24.

WHEN THEY COLLECTED JOEY ON CHRISTMAS MORNING, Maud knew immediately that he was off his medication. Who knew what the trigger was this time? Failing to find a publisher for his Lebanon book? The stream of rejection letters certainly hadn't helped; one went as far as to say the writing was "naïve and amateurish". Or maybe the anniversary of Ma's death? He'd gone on a week-long binge in honour of that. She'd heard there was trouble at work again, problems with his lax time keeping. So many ways for Joey's life to get knocked off course. But here they were, with a carful of boisterous kids, excited about seeing the birthplace of Jesus, so it was too late to turn back. Wasn't this supposed to be one of the advantages of living in this country, that you could retrace Jesus' footsteps and visit all these iconic places that had formed the backdrop to their religious upbringing? And what better way to celebrate Christmas than mass in the Bethlehem church where Jesus was born? Hopefully some of the goodwill from the joyous occasion would rub off on Joey. The day had already started badly with Kathleen throwing a tantrum after she ripped open her main present from Santa, the Monopoly board game, only to discover that instead of Park Lane and Old Kent Road, she would be buying houses and hotels to put on Ben Yehuda Street and the Mount of Olives. Let her search high and low in every Israeli toyshop for the England version and see if she fares any better!

The road out of Jerusalem was treacherous after the overnight snowfall. Maud still couldn't get her head around the idea of snow in this part of the world but because it was quite hilly, Jerusalem could get very cold in the winter. As they arrived into Bethlehem, they passed under Palestinian flag bunting that straddled buildings either side of the road. Large posters advertising a now-defunct boycott event were partly ripped off the wall. Alongside, two Israeli soldiers, weapons slung over their shoulders, were frisking an Arab guy who had his hands up against the wall and legs spread apart. By now, the Intifada had mostly fizzled out, but the peace still felt fragile.

Christy parked the UN VW minibus on Manger Square, and they all piled out as the local imam's call to prayer blared out over loudspeakers. Everywhere in Israel, there were constant reminders that three major religions jostled for eminence in the Holy Land. Stooped on his haunches, a man called them over to look at his wicker basket of tourist trinkets: religious icons carved from olivewood, earrings fashioned from faded Ottoman coins, brooches with replicas of saints' faces. Joey waved goofily and called out, 'Ah, Yuletide, that happy time of year when consumerism grabs us by the ankles, spins us upside down, and shakes out every last penny for a final gluttonous bash.'

Outside the Church of the Nativity, Israeli soldiers were lined behind metal barriers, young, suspicious, and armed. The Hogans entered the basilica through a low opening in the wall that forced the adults to bend under a lintel. Inside, the air in the stone antechamber was cold and slightly damp. Two lines of columns ran down the length of the church, and their footsteps echoed as they approached the altar towards the back. Pictures of Mary holding baby Jesus in the manger and of the three wise men adorned the walls as they went down the stairs to the holy spot. Joey slipped on the final few steps and let out a roar, causing the priest to halt his chant. The low-ceilinged grotto was hot with body heat. Incense smoke stung Maud's eyes, and myriad candles flickered, providing the only light. Everyone nudged towards a rectangular recess in the wall, framed by parted red velvet curtains. The kids milled around Maud's legs to get a better view of the pointed star embedded in the marble floor, marking the exact spot where Jesus was born. As far as anyone could tell. Maud had read somewhere that the star wasn't installed until AD1717, so there had to be some question about whether they'd got its positioning accurate. But, as she explained when Kathleen quizzed her, it didn't really matter; Jesus was born somewhere around here.

The priest had finished his service and was moving off, his entourage in tow, when Maud caught sight of Joey to her right, forcing his way through the worshippers. He crouched down on all fours to lean in and touch the star as she had seen other good pilgrims do, but Joey went further. He twisted his body around and sat on the star, lotus pose, facing the crowd. In a loud voice, he began his rendition of the Sermon on the Mount. Cue mayhem. The crowd hissed and shouted, 'Blasphemer', 'Heathen', several moved to grab Joey and tried to drag him out, but he shook them off. Maud called out as Christy pushed forward, flashing a badge (nothing more official than his UNWRA identity card) and shouting with great authority. After some persuasion, Joey ended his sermon and crawled out. The crowd was in a high degree of agitation, many calling for the police. Christy pushed hard on Joey from behind, frog-marched him up the stairs, out of the church and back to the minibus. Maud bustled the kids along behind them, Kathleen full of questions as to why Uncle Joey was acting so strange. It was the first time she'd seen him like this, and God knows what she made of it. Maud had really had her fill of Joey's never-ending dramas, and now he was dragging her family into it too. Was there no end to this?

A week later, they gathered for the traditional New Year's Eve Ball in Government House, the centrepiece of the UN peacekeepers' social calendar. Government House had served as the seat of the High Commissioner for Palestine until the British left in 1948, and shortly afterwards, it became the UN Truce Supervision Organisation headquarters. The building and gardens, surrounded by pines and cypresses, occupied a sixteen-acre hilltop in south Jerusalem with clear views back towards the Old City. Maud had only been a few times, but it was very familiar to Christy and Joey from their childhood when Pops had worked there. Access to Government House was restricted to UNTSO personnel and their families, but Christy called in some favours and got special dispensation for his UNWRA pass just for that night.

Snow still lay on the ground and glistened in the light reflecting off the façade of the white stone building. Out front, the three of them passed a sunken garden, went through the main entrance, and down the long corridor, which echoed with the click-clacking of stiletto heels. Above them, baubles dangled from wide sweeping arches, and along the walls, colourful streamers straddled photos of the former UN Secretary Generals, leading them to the heartbeat of this extravaganza: the bar area. After quaffing two G&Ts and mingling with Christy's colleagues, the gong sounded, and they were led into a huge ballroom; the dividing doors between the two rooms had been swung open to accommodate the large crowd for tonight's festivities. Tens of tables filled the floor space, laden with place settings, gold table runners, and silver napkins. There were party poppers, toy trumpets, and black plastic glasses with "Hello 1992" across the eyepieces. "Happy New Year" banners and bunting adorned the walls and attached to the ceiling, a wide net held a multitude of colourful balloons primed for their midnight release.

All through dinner, Maud kept a watchful eye on Joey, and he seemed on top form, chatting to beat the band with all around him. When the tables were cleared, and the James Last Orchestra tribute act struck up, Joey grabbed hold of Maud's hand and took her waltzing across the floor, but she lost track of him when she went to the toilet. Next thing she knew, there was a kerfuffle with people shouting out the back window. As she made her way over, she saw Christy racing across the ballroom towards the exit. Through the window, she could see Joey in the snowy gardens out back, splashing around in a large fountain, totally naked and singing at the top of his voice about a crazy diamond. When Christy got to him, Joey resisted his entreaties, first trying to drag him in and then kicking water to drive him away. With the help of two security guards, he was persuaded out of the fountain and into two UN blue towels, lifted from the nearby tennis courts. That was the end of their night in Government House, and all the way back to Joey's apartment in Shuafat, Christy ranted about what a liability Joey was, that they couldn't take him anywhere, not even Bethlehem, and now he'd embarrassed them in front of all his colleagues, and he'd put Christy's security clearance in jeopardy so that it was likely he'd be PNGed and never let back into Government House, and that he never wanted to see Joey again, until he'd sorted himself out and was taking his medication every single fecking day without fail.

There had been no contact since the New Year's Eve debacle until Christy called around to Joey's apartment with a bottle of bubbly to belatedly see in 1992. He banged on the door twice and was just about to leave when he heard a tremulous, 'Who is it?'

'Joey, how's it going? It's me. Christy.'

After a long pause, Joey's flat voice came back, 'Christy, man. What do you want?'

'Come on, Joey, open up. I've got some champers. Happy New Year!'

The door opened a crack, and Joey's dead eyes looked out. His hair was a straggly mess, and his body, naked except for Y-fronts, was bony and pallid. 'I'm not doing so good. My head feels like it's going to explode. Can heads spontaneously combust?'

Christy pushed on the door and forced his way in. 'Jaysus, this place is a fecking tip. Is this how you live?' Detritus covered the floor: items of clothing, ripped newspapers, takeaway cartons, and overflowing ashtrays. Shoved into the centre of the room, the TV was wrapped entirely in tin foil. 'What's with all the water?' Rows of plastic bottles, three deep, ran along the length of the sitting room wall.

'Can't trust the water in this city. They say it's loaded with chemicals before it reaches our taps.' Saliva streamed from the corner of Joey's mouth.

'Yeah, it gets cleaned along the way, that's the point.'

'I got used to managing my water in Beirut. I know what I'm doing.'

Joey needed to be careful. This friendly visit could mess up his plans. Or was it even friendly? Of course, they had their own opinions. His brain was on fire. Whoever came up with the term "chorus of voices" must have had a screw loose; there was nothing melodic or harmonious about the swarm of voices in his head: *Christy can't be trusted; he may give the game away. If he's happy to cheat on his wife, he'll think nothing of shopping you in. Why is he here anyhow? You need to get rid of him before it's time.*

'Joey, what the hell is going on here? And what's that smell?' Christy followed his nose to the bathroom, Joey shuffling behind like a scolded child. There, he discovered a plastic bucket of rotting food scraps swinging from a rope outside the open window.

'Oh, yeah, that's for the birds to feed on.' Joey scooped the bread crusts scattered on the windowsill into a pile. A grubby tea towel had been shoved into the extractor fan, which continued to make a low, growling sound after Christy pulled the cord to turn it off.

Christy's attention was distracted by a trail of nut shells and fruit peels on the carpet leading into the rooms off the corridor. 'What's with all this mess?'

'That's in case I get lost,' Joey said as Christy followed the nut trail to the bedroom. A beam of sunlight lasered through a hole in the black plastic covering the window and spotlighted dancing dust particles. All the furniture was stacked in one corner, blocking the wardrobe. In the other corner, there was a mattress covered with a soiled sheet and a stained pillow. As Christy moved to switch the light on, he stumbled over a rucksack overflowing with electronic gear: speakers, a radio, keyboards, and cables. In

Joey's eyes, Christy's face seemed to be melting, leaving only the outline of his skull and a film of sweat glistening on his stretched skin. His pale blue eyes throbbed, forcing Joey to look away. The executioner's face may be well hidden, but he was still out there. Head like a dozen beehives, Joey was overloading. The voices were back and insistent: *Don't let him check out your gear. If he looks in there, the mission will be compromised.*

Christy's hostile eyes scanned the room. Every inch of wall space was covered with newspaper cuttings and scraps of paper, interconnected with pinned lengths of string. Photos of war scenes papered one entire wall: camels walking on desert sand below a huge smoke cloud, the horizon flaming yellow and orange; a soldier standing on a tank, a string of oil wells flaring behind him; and rows of burnt-out tanks strewn on the desert floor.

'They're some of Sammy's photos from the Gulf War,' Joey said.

Ignoring him, Christy strode over to the bedside locker and pulled open the drawer to reveal boxes of unopened Thorazine. 'Why haven't you been taking your meds, Joey?'

In Joey's head, a disconnected jumble of fears avalanched as he rustled in the rucksack and pulled out a cap covered in tin foil, which he put on his head. Then he grabbed a walkie-talkie and handed it to Christy. 'Just listen to this for a while, then you'll understand. I'm acting under orders. The bombs are due to explode sometime today, and then the CIA boys will come for me and sweep up all the evidence. You better go, Christy; there's a manhole on the street. Lift that up and hide in there. I'll join you when I'm done here.' Joey grabbed a pair of army fatigues from the pile of clothes on the floor and started dressing as Christy stood watching, his face white and his mouth hanging open.

It was difficult for Christy; he couldn't understand. How could he be expected to? Even in Joey's dreams, the voices came to him. That morning, he'd woken from the now-familiar nightmare, which starts with him arriving at a chained, rusting metal gate covered with Arabic signage, except for the English words, *Stay away! Lunatic asylum* right at the bottom. Then he notices a group of five or six people, clad in once-white hospital tunics, staggering around the roof of a bombed building, like bees fleeing the hive under a smoke attack. The group grows hysterical when they spot him. One woman, on her knees and close to the flat roof's unwalled edge, beseeches Joey, her arms stretching towards him, then pulling back towards her chest. There's no sign of any hospital staff anywhere. And then the old man limps towards the edge of the roof beside the wailing woman and locks onto Joey with an icy gaze, crying out for help with a silent scream. The man's unkempt salt and pepper beard bounces like an automaton as he mutters an indistinct phrase, possibly in French. Then his voice smug and challenging: *I'm not afraid of dying, why should I be? We all have to go some time.*

A week later, Joey shifted the Porsche into fifth gear and swerved into the outside lane. The Jordan TV newsreader, that Ola Hussein, had been emphatic: the Galilean tilapia, what the locals called "St. Peter's fish", a fish that had swum in the Sea of Galilee for thousands of years, were under attack by a mystery disease and Joey's help was needed. So, it was Tiberias next stop, his mission to save these precious national treasures. The Porsche's soft top was down, the wind was in his hair, and the dog in the passenger seat was barking happily. Time for some fun!

All was dark and quiet when he got to the lake, but he drove with his lights off just in case. He parked up, peeled his clothes off, and raced down to the water's edge. With only a moment's hesitation, he jumped into the murky water, oblivious to the chill January wind. At first, the dog was unsure, but after much cajoling, he was persuaded to join Joey for a dip. Everything was going fine, the pair of them splashing about as Joey called out to the half-moon, when a couple of police cars showed up. In the end, the cold forced Joey out and into the welcome embrace of a wool blanket. The unfriendly policeman, the one with the greasy moustache, handed over his clothes and asked, 'What you are doing here?'

Joey pulled on his clothes, teeth chattering and limbs shaking. 'I was trying to do the walking on water thing. If Jesus can do it on the Sea of Galilee, then why can't I?'

'Bah, he's crazy this one.' The moustached cop.

'What you want? Why you do this?' The cop with the hectoring voice.

'We could try fishing, maybe,' Joey persisted, his frantic eyes unblinking. 'Do you have a boat? I could do the miracle catch of fish, you know, when Jesus revealed himself to the disciples around here. After the resurrection, they're struggling with the fishing, and Jesus appears out of nowhere and goes, "Cast out your net on the right side of the boat," and lo and behold, the disciples haul in loads of fucking fish.'

The policemen looked at each other, moustachioed made a twirly forefinger motion by his temple, and annoying voice said, 'You must come with us sir, to the police station,'

'Okay. I just need to get my wallet.' Joey hopped into his car, rummaged in the glove box, then he turned the ignition and sped off, laughing at the startled cops in his rear-view mirror. The Porsche was too fast for them, and Joey was soon back on the highway, heading south at one-twenty an hour.

Before long, flashing blue lights appeared behind him, and Joey slowed down to seventy, concerned they might pull him for speeding. Suddenly, there was another cop car alongside, a policeman hanging out the window and gesticulating for Joey to pull over. Fat chance! But then there was a third cop car in front, red brake lights blinding him. Boxed in on three sides, he took the only option and pulled onto the hard shoulder. Before the cops had a chance to get out, Joey leapt from his car and raced back, looking for a break in the crash barrier that he could slip through. He outpaced them for a while, but one cop, and soon another, caught up and tackled him to the ground. In the end, it took four of them to pin him down and handcuff him. Ola Hussein was going to be very disappointed.

The call came through around ten o'clock that night as Maud was settling down with a cup of tea for her fix of Dynasty. 'Hello, Mrs Hogan, this is Superintendent Ehud Levy from Tiberias Police Station. Do you know a Joey Hogan?'

Maud was always the one they called. How had she ended up as Joey's major-domo? She certainly didn't remember volunteering for it. Where were all the Hogans when you needed them? Miles away and with no clue how to deal with a schizophrenic even if they were here. Christy had tried to help but he didn't have the patience. Typical man, he was no good with things he couldn't understand or readily fix, and just ended up getting angry. His reluctance to get involved was also tinged with embarrassment that Joey was letting the Hogan side down. God love him, there was nobody else but her.

Levy explained that Joey had been arrested near the Sea of Galilee but had since been committed to hospital as he clearly had mental problems. He had become convinced that some Arabic TV newsreader was talking directly to him and had instructed him to make his way to Galilee so he could save some diseased fish.

'But where did he get the car?' Maud said. 'Joey doesn't have money for a Porsche.'

'The car belongs to a Moshe Cohen. I gather he's a friend of Mr Hogan's? They were driving this afternoon in Tel Aviv, and when Mr Cohen stopped to buy cigarettes, Mr Hogan drove off in his car. Mr Cohen's dog was also in the car at the time. Mr Cohen is happy to have his dog and car back undamaged and does not intend to press charges. But I must tell you, this is a very serious offence, Mrs Hogan. If he were not mentally ill, Mr Hogan would be spending some time in prison.'

After nearly three hospital-free years, Joey was again committed to a psychiatric hospital, classified as a danger to himself and others. Why did he always stop taking his pills? When Maud challenged him on it, he would rake over the familiar argument that the doctors were overreacting to his unusual lifestyle: 'It's just I see the world differently to other people, always have, Maud, you know that' — and he therefore didn't need to take his medication — 'What are the tablets made of? Is it organic or plant material? It probably contains human parts.' As far as Maud was now concerned, hospital was the best place for Joey.

The doctors started Joey on Haloperidol, but that gave him constipation and a permanently dry mouth. His belly and shoulders broke out in a nasty rash, which resisted all of Maud's creams. The medical team experimented with alternative drugs, trying to find one that rewired his short-circuited mind with acceptable side effects. Months of inveigling and enforcement followed, a period when Joey's commitment to his medication was no less fragile than it was unpredictable. He remained contumacious and would stop swallowing his meds as soon as he started feeling well again. For a while, the pills were ground up and dissolved in water, and a nurse watched as he drank the mixture. The doctors moved him onto Risperidone, which was administered by injection so that it gradually dispersed into his bloodstream over a period of days. Risperidone provided certainty that he was receiving his treatment but had to be stopped when, again, the side effects became too extreme.

This hospitalisation was different from the last time in the Hadassah because now everyone knew what the problem was. Especially Joey, who now understood that he was no longer master of his own destiny; he had become a slave to the rhythm of the daily medication cycle, every single day, for the rest of his life. Each recovery from a schizophrenic episode helped him realise that the course of his life had narrowed to a simple fork: mind control with the meds or out of his mind without them. If he didn't take the pills, his thoughts ran wild, and he ended up doing bad things and on a one-way track back to hospital. If he took the anti-psychotic drugs, his brain's biochemistry stayed in balance, and with the voices and visions chained up, he could function effectively outside of a hospital. However, his medicated life and its enforced lucid thinking were miles from the freedom he enjoyed before this illness developed. Try as he might, Joey couldn't bear the thought that his damaged mind was the one thing that he couldn't run away from.

Late one stormy October night, the cold steel rain hammering the ground, Maud was home alone, with the kids in bed, when the doorbell sounded for the third time in as many seconds.

'Hello?' she called through the locked door.

'Let me in.' A growling, threatening command.

'Who is this? Please go to the police if you need help.'

'Maud, come on, let me in.'

A long silence. 'Joey? Joey, is that you?'

Throughout the year, Joey had been running away from hospital at every opportunity. Like a Colditz prisoner, escaping, even if only temporarily, gave Joey a sense of liberation, a feeling that he had some small command over where his life was heading. Christy and Maud had visited him in a slew of facilities for the mentally ill, each one apparently more secure than the last but still unable to contain him. Private psychiatric hospitals in Israel were basically nursing homes; they provided shelter and social interactions, but there were relatively few medical or rehabilitative services. It only took a few minutes of inattention by a nurse, an unguarded door, a key left in a lock for a moment, or an open window, and he was gone, smashing through flimsy locks, scaling fences, or shimmying down drainpipes. One time, he walked all the way to Jericho, shedding clothes along the route until he was pulled over by the police, nearly naked, on the city outskirts. Another time, he caused a major security alert by trying to scale the gates of the Knesset while on the hunt for a fountain. He had become obsessed with cold water and jumping into it — rivers, pools, fountains, the sea — he was forever in pursuit of the chilling embrace of water and the thrilling struggle for breath under its surface.

When Maud opened the door, she reeled back, hands sucked up to her mouth in a horrified gasp. Strands of greasy hair dripped from under a wide Panama hat that shadowed Joey's wan face. A filthy once-blue raincoat hung limply on his bony shoulders and his big toes poked out of ripped black Converse boots. His beard was crusty and split in two like a forked tongue.

'My God, Joey, you look awful. What's happened?'

'Have you locked the door?' Maud nodded, but Joey wasn't convinced. 'Are you sure? Is it bolted?' His eyes lasered around the house, assessing the security status of each entrance point. He walked into the front room, tripping over toys, and looked out through a gap in the curtains. Bouncing from foot to foot, he turned to face Maud, eyes darting like a twitching gazelle sneaking a drink at an exposed waterhole.

'Yes, it's all secure, calm down. Who's chasing you? Why are they after you?'

'You tell me.' Vacant, dark pools stared out from where his lovely laughing eyes used to be. 'These days, you're basically my jailer. It's you the cops ring whenever I run away from hospital, and it's you that has me recommitted each time.'

Shock of a different kind now registered on Maud's face. And hurt, a heart-spearing hurt, the kind that flares with rejection. 'That's very unfair, Joey. I'm only trying to look out for you.'

Frightened eyes looked back at her. 'I know. Sorry. I don't know what I'm saying.' Then, with a hollow laugh, 'Oh Maud, I'm so glad to see you.' He rubbed her cheek with a scratchy kiss and ran her auburn hair through his grimy fingers. She threw her arms around him and hugged his wiry frame, but he pulled back from the embrace. 'You . . . eh . . . you got anything to drink?' A frenzied hand, clumsily bandaged with what looked like a strip of bedsheet, raked the hair back off his forehead.

'Let's get you into a shower first. Looks like you haven't had one in a while. Smells like it, too.'

After he had washed, and Maud had trimmed his beard, and spooned half a bowl of warm soup into him, she manoeuvred him into the spare bed. He was asleep before she turned the light out.

Then, in early December, Joey was found by an elderly couple standing naked in their snow-covered front garden, roaring that everyone needed to evacuate immediately; all the houses on their street had been rigged with explosives and were about to blow up. In the end, the couple persuaded him to come inside and seated him in front of the paraffin fire, feet covered with hot blankets, unaware of the dangers of warming frozen feet too quickly. By the time Maud made it to the hospital, Joey was strapped into a bed grimacing with pain, his body hooked into a network of beeping monitors and drip bags, and his frostbitten feet covered in plastic bags that ballooned as tepid air blew over them.

And so, 1992 ended as it had started, with Joey confined in a psychiatric hospital, having been picked up by the police in some unfamiliar part of the country, naked and deranged. Exasperated with the continuous escaping, the doctors placed him in a high-security forensic ward for the criminally insane, where he was kept under one-to-one observation by a nurse who noted down his smallest action and every word he spoke. The intensity of his entrapment shocked Joey into playing ball the system's way, and the escape attempts stopped. No longer believing that he would ever get out of hospital, he took to saying, 'The checking out is easy, Christy, but leaving? That's a no-no.'

25.

SEXUAL FRUSTRATION CAN LEAD A MAN to do awful strange things. Years of not getting enough, of occasional rides that were over prematurely, was what had driven Christy onto this number 47 bus for his fortnightly rendezvous with Naomi. At least that was the name on the card. He'd been too embarrassed to make the call right there and then; like, who else are you going to be calling from a phone box wallpapered with scantily clad ladies beseeching you to call them for a good time? He'd ripped the least vulgar-looking card off the wall and pocketed it to call later.

Once the door was opened to regular illicit sex, Christy had swiftly converted from a man who was squeamish about vaginas — the word had always conjured up an anatomical device whose true purpose was to squeeze out slimy new-borns — to a man whose favourite shape was a triangle. It had started over a year ago when a gang of them had gone out for a meal. After eating, Maud had been tired and disinterested so she went home, and he'd ended up going to a nightclub in the New City with a bunch of the lads. Slouched on a sofa, a bit worse for wear, Christy was about to leave when Roxanne appeared before him as if a vision: her sensuous body snaked to the pumping techno music, and her arms rolled, fingers spread and palms downwards. Positioned directly in front of him, nipples poking through her leotard-like sofa buttons, she rotated her hips and then bent forward, revealing boobs the size of mangoes. Roxanne had liked the colour of Christy's money and invited him to a private show in a room out back. Although he could recall few details the following morning, he'd had a taste for it and wanted more.

Strap-hanging beside him in the bus aisle, the grey-suited girl caught his eye and smiled. A redhead, he certainly didn't need another one of them in his life. More than the act itself, it annoyed him that Maud had been the first to go offside. He was certain she was screwing someone else; there were too many changes for her not to be. Occasionally when she got pissed, she rambled on about her handsome lover. At one point, he'd straight out asked whether she'd ever consider having an affair, and she'd replied haughtily that she'd never put the children through such an ordeal. Did you ever hear such rubbish in your whole life? Methinks she does protest way too much. For months, he'd fumed, but since he finally started to get some of his own satisfaction, he was hoping she'd stick with whoever it was she'd found. He'd had enough of being a foolish loser.

The bus was emptying out, and he flopped into the seat beside a fat Arab woman. Although frequent sex hadn't exactly killed off his prurient curiosity about the boobs on the girls at work, it had at least subdued his fantasies somewhat. There were some days when he barely thought about the mounds bulging inside their blouses or wondered what colour bra such and such had on, or was it edged with lace, and whether she had flattened nipples or pointy-outs. The titillation came from the not being able to see properly, from the fleeting glimpse and the partial reveal. After all, he could see tits and more in one of those magazines, or even in the flesh on a holiday beach, topless girls prancing about or lying spread-eagled on the sand. On some beaches, you could get full nudity if you wanted, which mostly he didn't as those places seemed only to attract fat, ugly people.

With the affliction of hindsight, he could see there were several fateful decisions that he might now make differently. He and Maud had never really explored other options, married before he'd even finished university. Where had the time gone since? Life had evolved into an endless litany of domestic chores and childcare arrangements, snatched grown-up moments, and constant bickering. Like just yesterday, Maud giving him grief about smoking around the children, and why would he not smoke outside like everyone else? Besides Joey, of course, you'd never hear her asking him to smoke outside. It struck him as ironic that you start out as a teenager sneaking fags behind the garden shed, hiding from your parents, and then, after a brief period of liberation in your twenties when you can smoke wherever you want, you end up a parent yourself, back smoking behind the shed where the kids can't see you. They should call it the always-hiding-from-someone addiction rather than a smoking addiction.

In the seat opposite, the sporty guy got off, and an older African woman took his place. Blondes were his hair colour of choice these days. That Esther last month had been a real goer, ended up back at hers, some high-rise flat in Mea She'arim. The 3am cab ride home had cost a fortune, but the taste of her had been worth it. A thin film of sweat glistened on his forehead as Christy checked to see if any of those tiny little bus windows (no more than vent holes really) were open. Hard to imagine people smoking on buses, how airless and smoggy it must have been, and yet that was only a few years ago. Were he and Maud happy three years ago? It was difficult to remember; feelings of marital bliss seemed confined to the age of the carrier pigeon.

Nothing marks off the flight of the years as remorselessly as the annual cycle of kids' birthdays: Charlie in February, Kathleen in March, and the twins September. Shit, he'd forgotten to pick up Kathleen's birthday present this morning. That photo had been a real shocker. In her latest letter, Maud's mum had sent over some old snapshots of a summer holiday in Ballybunion. In amongst all the usual rubbish was a photograph of him and Joey on the beach; they would have been around eight. And there was Joey beaming out at him, happy as Larry and a dead ringer for Kathleen, with the same brown curly hair, same heart face, and same dark brown eyes. That photo got at an itch that had been niggling him for a while and gave it a good scratch.

Christy was a victim of Maud's love for Joey; that was how he looked at it. She couldn't seem to resist Joey, never could, and her obsession had now developed into one of her projects: she was on a mission to somehow rescue Joey from his shambles of a life. As if anyone was ever going to have any influence over what Joey did. Everyone knew Joey as this great guy, but far as Christy was concerned, he was a total do-badder; stuff just seemed to go wrong for him, and anyone close by got dragged into the mess with him. Never was there born a man so easily found by trouble and so deft at off-loading it onto his friends.

At the bus stop, an Orthodox Jewish man boarded, trailing behind him a procession of six small boys, each with a yarmulke on their heads and with their hands on the shoulder of the boy in front. Christy gave up his seat for them. No biggie, he was getting off at the next stop. Time to start working through the sequence of positions he wanted Naomi's session to follow. Start with a blow-job — that was a given with all of them; he had a lot of BJ-less time to make up — then he was thinking maybe move onto the missionary position, for old time's sake, the old reliable go-to position with Maud, in fact pretty much the only position she liked.

As he got off the bus, he noticed an impressive display on the pavement outside the florists. On his way back, he'd get Maud a bunch of red roses. That would help colour over the black and white of his sin.

26.

CHRISTY WAS HAPPY TO LET MOSHE DRIVE, but he was a little on edge about what they'd find to talk about for the two-hour car journey. Moshe was really Joey's friend, and Christy had only ever talked to him when they were out at night, fuelled by alcohol. A gentle breeze blew through the car windows, taming the stifling July heat, as they drove west out of Jerusalem, making good progress until the traffic ground to a sudden standstill. Word from the car up ahead was there'd been a suicide bombing in the bus station near the Hebrew University, and all vehicles were being diverted onto a narrow side road. As they approached the turn, they passed a line of Israeli soldiers hitchhiking. It was a common sight and in a country with compulsory military service for everyone — three years for men and two for women — it was an unspoken code that you gave them a lift. Moshe looked at him with a questioning smile but Christy half-laughed and said, 'Absolutely no fecking way!'

Once they had looped back onto Highway 1, the traffic became fluid again, and Christy settled into the drive. 'Joey was telling me that you grew up on a kibbutz yourself.'

'Yes, I was born on Ein Gev kibbutz, further north beside the Sea of Galilee. In fact, it is close to where Joey had that incident with the police last year.'

'Jaysus, don't remind me. Dark days, indeed. Hopefully, he's in a better place these days.'

'We shall see very soon, my friend. This is a happy day, a day where we see Joey in his new life. Don't worry.'

An awkward silence ensued until Moshe said, 'My parents were one of the original settlers in Ein Gev when they immigrated from Czechoslovakia after the war. The kibbutz was beside the Syrian border, and I remember as a child, there were many shooting incidents and shellings across the border. You know, violence has always been a part of kibbutz life. Many kibbutzim were set up in vulnerable, remote areas, often along the borders of the state, so they have always played a prominent military role. Every kibbutz has a weapons armoury, and kibbutz members have regular shooting practice.' He snorted, 'Some say they live with shovels and rifles in their hands.'

'I don't know much about kibbutz except that it's basically some version of a hippy commune, but the Israeli version seems to work better.' Christy lit a cigarette and offered one to Moshe.

'Toda raba, yes, can you light it for me, please?' Moshe said. 'The kibbutzniks were never pie-in-the-sky idealists; they were doers, focussed on getting the job done. They were on a mission to revive this barren land, swamp by swamp, field by field, and make it fertile again.'

'Moses' land of milk and honey.'

'Nowadays, it is more a land of lush crops and mineral salts, as you will see when we get there. To make the desert bloom, they needed to grow crops in hostile areas with hard ground, so obviously, irrigation was the major issue and led to a lot of innovation. More recently, they have diversified away from just agriculture; many now have industrial plants and high-tech enterprises.'

'When did they start allowing foreigners to do the work?'

'For the founders of the kibbutz movement, the idea was to redeem the Jewish nation through manual labour but only so many Israelis wanted that sort of labour-intensive life. From the 1960s, during harvest time, labourers were sought outside, and it has grown from there.'

Fair play to Moshe; he got Joey into the kibbutz after he was released from hospital, made a few calls, pulled a few strings, and next thing Joey was off to somewhere he hopefully couldn't do any damage: Kibbutz Kalia at the northernmost point of the Dead Sea. Living a whole new life with three hundred others, picking fruit, cooking meals, working in the laundry, and generally helping with whatever needed doing. In return, the volunteers were provided with food, board, and a little pocket money that they could spend in the kibbutz shop. Standing prominent in the arid, rocky land, Kalia suddenly appeared in front of them, an oasis of green leafy trees and palm groves. A chain-link fence, razor wire along the top, ran around the perimeter, inside of which were neatly trimmed grass lawns criss-crossed with footpaths leading to rows of concrete bungalows.

Joey appeared from one of these, looking fresh and relaxed, wearing a ball cap and shades. 'Welcome, my friends,' he said, arms spread wide as he grasped them both in a hug. 'Let me show you around. We've no cars around the kibbutz itself, but we do have a horse, or you can use a bike, or you can just use the two strong legs the good Lord gave you.'

'So how are you settling in? All good?' Christy asked as they walked along, the soles of his feet burning through his flip-flops.

'Never better, man. Forever in your debt, Moshe, thanks for setting this up.'

They high-fived, and Joey continued, 'There we have the chicken coops, and behind that is the milking parlour. I'm on duty this week, up milking at the crack of dawn. Can you believe it, Christy? Just like we used to back home on Uncle Tommy's farm. And over here is the swimming pool, five lanes, no less! I tell you, jumping in at the end of the day after a long shift labouring, that's the dog's bollocks.'

'Joey the milkman, feck me.'

'Hey, what's with the no glasses?'

'Yeah, it's cool, eh? I had the operation. Finally, I've got twenty-twenty vision.'

'Rock and roll. Looks kinda weird seeing you without them, but in a good way. And look at this,' Joey said, clasping his hands around Christy's waist. 'The new slimline version, good on you.'

'Yeah, I've lost nearly ten kilos on this new diet.'

'It's certainly working. Hey, the tour—' Joey bounded ahead, pointing. 'These are the dorms, mind you, not huge dorms like in school, Christy. We share a room with two, maybe three others. Bathrooms are communal, and we all eat in a big dining hall.'

Christy smiled to himself as he adapted to this new Joey, who had clearly swallowed large volumes of the kibbutz Kool-Aid. The good news was that it looked like he was also swallowing his prescribed medication; Christy hadn't seen him in such good form for years.

'Let me show you the beach, lads. Very cool. Actually very hot at the moment! Our big claim to fame is that Kalia is the lowest kibbutz in the world. We have the lowest synagogue in the world, transmitting all the way up to whoever your God is on high. And here,' Joey said as they emerged from an olive grove and the concrete path turned to sand, 'is our very own private beach. Right here on the Dead Sea.'

Ahead of them, rows of blue umbrellas and white plastic sun loungers lined the beach. Crowds of people bobbed in the sea, in classic Dead Sea pose, supine on the surface, buoyed by the dense, saline water. By the shoreline, a young couple rolled in the mud, then stood up waving, covered head to toe in green-black mud, with only two slitty eyes and pink lips visible.

'Let's grab a beer, I'm fecking parched,' Christy said.

They sat on stools at the bar, and Joey ordered three Goldstars. 'L'chaim gentlemen, you now have the honour of drinking in the lowest bar in the world, four hundred and twenty metres below sea level. And dropping all the time if they continue diverting the Jordan River and siphoning off the lake water.'

'Be Jaysus, Joey.' Christy chuckled. 'It's very strange hearing you with all this talk of the lowest this and the lowest that. I'm used to you banging on about getting the highest.'

'That's all in the past, my man. History.'

Moshe and Christy exchanged a sceptical look as Joey continued, 'It's not called the Dead Sea for nothing. Nothing lives in it.'

'It's nice to get that breeze,' Christy said, wiping his face with a napkin.

'Yeah, isn't it? There's usually a breeze blowing off the lake during the day, then weirdly at night, it reverses direction and blows towards the centre of the lake.'

'That fecking rotten egg smell, I always hated it. Used to make me gag.'

Moshe pointed at a couple of large concrete buildings with windows on a ridge behind the beach bar. One was painted red overlaid with ghoulish, man-sized cartoon characters in black and white; the other had a yellow background with leaping human shapes silhouetted in blue. 'What are those over there?'

'They were abandoned and left empty for ages, but last year, a pile of artists moved in and turned them into workshops. I did that painting,' Joey said, pointing at the gable wall, which had a mural of the Doors band members' heads, arranged in a diamond shape, like Queen did for the *Bohemian Rhapsody* video.

'Very Joey,' Moshe laughed. 'Have you been converting the kibbutzniks to your music?'

'See that guy on the shore there,' Christy said, munching on a pretzel. 'Is that a big slab of salt that he's standing on? It's big as a fecking rock. Remember that UN kid who died from swallowing too much of the Dead Sea water?'

'God, yeah. Everyone stopped coming after that. Not that we really came to the Dead Sea that much, in fairness.'

Christy drained his beer. 'That drive home was always a nightmare, all five of us crushed together in the back of the Merc, with dry, salty skin, desperate to get home and shower off. Any cut you had would sting like mad. I see you've lots of showers here now.'

'We do indeed. OK, lads, let's grab some lunch.'

The dining hall was busy as they queued for the tray and rail buffet. It was only when they sat down, and Joey took his cap off that Christy realised his head was shorn to just a spiky brown stubble. His eyes were clear, and his skin tanned.

'Man, the food in this place is topping,' Joey was off again, all evangelical. 'Everything's grown right here on the kibbutz. Lots of veg and fruit, we have one of the largest date groves in the country. I don't eat meat anymore, just an occasional bit of fish, though obviously not from the Dead Sea!'

'What's the story at night? Is there much partying?' Christy asked.

'That's not really what this life is about here. Of course, there's boozing, but no major sessions. No major drugs either, a bit of puff, that's all.'

'Really? So, what do you do all night?

'Reading. Board games. Maybe play some volleyball, toss a frisbee, sit around the campfire playing guitar and toasting marshmallows, maybe blow off a J. Living the dream, man.'

'Yours brother, not mine.'

'Ah, come on! Fridays we have discotheque. Put on your dancing shoes, dude.'

'Yeah, right. Tonight's not the night, my friend.'

'I thought you'd dig this communal, big family vibe, Christy. You've always been a closet hippy. You know, there's virtually no crime here, no point because everyone has the same as everyone else.'

'Which is pretty much nothing, of course.'

'What a sceptic. Hey man, what's up? Be happy for me. I am!' Joey said and proceeded to gobble down the lentil bake.

'No, I get it, Joey.' Christy leaned in and put an arm on his shoulder. 'It's great you're happy. Delighted for you. Just maybe dial down the holy roller enthusiasm for the kibbutz cult, or you'll have me worrying.'

Moshe grinned and said, 'It used to be that on a kibbutz, everyone got paid the same amount no matter what they did, and the money was put into the communal pot and shared by everyone. That has changed now, of course; whatever you earn, you keep for yourself.'

'What about all the layabouts? Don't tell me there's none of them?' Christy asked.

'Sure, there's a few that don't pull their weight, but the court of public opinion sorts out any freeloaders. Parasites, we call them.' Joey spat the words out.

'You know, when I lived on a kibbutz, gender equality was a big thing.' Moshe refilled their glasses from the water jug. 'Women went back to work after they had children rather than being tied to domestic duties. In some very conservative kibbutzim, they would not even use the traditional Hebrew word for husband because it can also mean "master" or "owner". All of us children lived in communal houses; we played there, had school lessons, we even slept there instead of with our parents; nurses and teachers looked after us, and parents would only spend time with their children after work and before dinner.'

'Jaysus, that's another way of doing things, a bit like boarding school when you think about it. How did you feel about that?' Christy asked.

'I didn't know any different. The theory was that relationships between the children and their parents would be better because, when the parents weren't the sole disciplinarians, they would form closer bonds with their children. I have to say that has not been my experience. I am not particularly close to my parents, but that might be for other reasons.'

'His folks were pissed off when Moshe joined Peace Now, said it was a sell-out,' Joey explained.

Turned out that Moshe had become a big fish in Peace Now, an activist group formed in 1978 when hundreds of Israeli soldiers published an open letter to Menachem Begin urging him not to mess up the historic opportunity for peace with Egypt. At the time, many young Jews were disillusioned and had come to believe that, despite Israel's superior military strength, a lasting peace between Israel and its neighbours would only come from a negotiated agreement. In the end, the peace talks led to Israel's withdrawal from Sinai and Egypt's recognition of Israel in the Camp David Accords.

'My parents had many issues with me, not just because I joined Peace Now, but certainly that was a big problem for them. For me, it's important that the world sees another side to the modern Israel and that people understand not all Israelis toe the party line. Some of us are very unhappy with the constant fighting and the oppression of the Palestinians. You know, after the Sabra and Shatila refugee camp massacres in Beirut, people were disgusted with what had happened there in our name. Nearly ten percent of the population attended a Peace Now protest in Tel Aviv to pressurise the government into investigating the camp massacres and to get rid of Ariel Sharon for his role in letting it happen.'

'I've seen photos of that Hands Around Jerusalem event.'

'Yes, we had over twenty-five thousand Israelis and Palestinians linking hands in a chain of peace all the way around the walls of the Old City of Jerusalem.

'The problem with the Israeli-Palestinian conflict,' Joey announced, in the voice of one announcing a significant insight, 'is that it's not a Wild West movie. It's not your typical struggle between good and evil, between right and wrong. Really, it's a clash between right and right, where both sides have rightful claims to this land. The Palestinians want the land they call Palestine, their only homeland, given back to them; they've tried to live in other Arab countries, but everywhere, they've been rejected, sometimes even humiliated, and persecuted by the so-called Arab family. Sam and I saw it very up close in Lebanon. But the Israelis want exactly the same land for exactly the same reasons; there is no other country in the world that the Jews, as a people, as a nation, could ever call home. Both have powerful, very different, yet convincing claims on the territory.

'Paradoxically . . .' Christy paused, as if unsure whether to say, '. . . in a strange way, the Jewish people and the Palestinian people have had a parallel historical experience. The Jews were kicked out of their homes in Europe during the Holocaust and forced to flee, and they came here and kicked the Palestinians out of Palestine, scattering them homeless across the Middle East.'

Moshe was nodding feverishly. 'When my father was a teenager in Czechoslovakia, the walls were covered with graffiti, "Jews, go back to Palestine." When he revisited Europe fifty years later, the walls were covered with new graffiti, "Jews, get out of Palestine."'

'Enough of all this politics,' Joey interrupted. 'This is what happens when you put two journalists and an UNWRA worker together at a table in a kibbutz.' They all laughed. 'What were we talking about before all that?'

'The parents, their relationship with the children in kibbutz,' Moshe said. 'Ah yes, this egalitarian society ideal. I recall one time my aunt visited and brought me a box of chocolates. I was allowed to have a few of the chocolates myself, and then I had to give the rest of the box to the other children.'

'Tell me,' Christy leaned forward, his voice dropped to a stage whisper. 'Were you all shagging like mad when you were teenagers?'

'The honest and surprising answer is no, very little. Even though we were not segregated at night, people were quite prudish. Of course, there was some action, but less than with teenagers elsewhere. Some people researched this, and they found the marriage rate among communally-raised children was very low. They call it the Westermarck effect, when unrelated children if raised together from an early age, tend to reject each other as potential partners because they regard them more like brothers and sisters.'

'That's a bit like the UN kids,' Christy mused. 'Although there were flings when we were teenagers, none of them developed into anything serious. It's strange now that I think about it, no UN kid ever got married to another. You would have thought we'd be very compatible because of the similar childhoods.'

'Thankfully, we have lots of pretty girls here, and none of them is my sister, so you need have no concerns on that front,' Joey laughed. 'I better crack on and leave you to your own devices for the afternoon. We can catch up for a beer later, down on the beach. Magniv?'

'Ha Joey, now with all the Hebrew? Yes, all cool.'

'Good one. I'm thinking, tomorrow's Saturday, Shabbat obviously, so I'm off all day, the holy day of obligation to relax, so let's head out and see a bit of the area.'

Next day, they went on a whistlestop tour of local tourist hotspots, Joey as their guide: 'Up there is the Qumran Cave where the Dead Sea Scrolls were found by Bedouin shepherds. They kept them hanging on a tent pole for ages until someone suggested they might be important and thus valuable . . . And over there is the fortress of Masada, where a long time ago, there was a two-year siege that ended in the mass suicide of its Jewish Zealot defenders. A kind of early Jim Jones event.' They drove up the dusty hill towards Masada and stopped at a tourist shop where Joey bought a pot and saucer with a Bible Land Tourist Bureau authentication certificate, supposedly dating the object from 1200BC and claiming, "This is a guaranteed genuine juglet and plate of the Iron Age period". Christy wasn't convinced, but Joey was chuffed with his precious relic from the past.

Then it was off down the road past the 'world-famous Dead

Sea Works' — Joey was in full flow — 'This is where they mine the lake for all sorts of salts: bath salt, table salt, and loads of chemical products,' and all the way down to Eilat where they went scuba diving, 'for the most mind-blowing colour extravaganza you'll ever experience.' They saw coral reefs of every hue and shape, poked at countless playful small fish (like 'the perennial favourite clown fish', ducking in and out between its protector anemone's tentacles) and swam alongside the more threatening stingrays, moray eels, and barracuda, while off in the deeper water, grey reef sharks whizzed by.

All kinds of wonderful things and Joey all cock-a-hoop, walking on the moon, apparently euphoric with his new kibbutz life. Christy really wished he could lose the feeling that it all seemed a bit too good to be true.

LIKE A BIRD ON A WIRE

Leonard Cohen

ISRAEL & DUBLIN

June 1995 to March 1996

27.

SAM PADDED ALONGSIDE THE BAREFOOTED JOEY, taking measured steps to dampen the echo of his boots in the long, windowless corridor. Footwear was no longer something that Joey bothered with, as the sound of soles slapping against the floor got him thinking the shoes were talking to him. For Sam, hardened, calloused feet were among the easier-to-accept changes in the brother he hadn't seen in two years. When they came to the locked door, Sam pressed on the buzzer. The nurse asked if they'd had a nice walk as she led them into the bile-green reception area.

'Yes, thanks,' Sam puffed, sweat leaking down his face. 'It's very hot for June, isn't it?' He wasn't used to all this walking, but if Joey didn't get his walk in, it would go one of two ways. Caged Joey, who'd pace his room like some zoo animal, chain-smoking, noisy and agitated, or catatonic Joey, immotile face, languid body, and dead voice, if he spoke at all. Walks had become the centrepiece of Sam's visits. Joey limped ahead down another long stretch of corridor. His was the last room on the right, just before the corridor curved in a U around the back of the building. Whoever had come up with the hospital's colour scheme certainly had a grá for the green palette; the mouldy moss green of the corridor walls bled into the mint green of Joey's bedroom, and the bed was covered with a grubby, bottle-green blanket.

Since arriving from Sri Lanka three weeks ago, Sam had gleaned from Maud and Christy the patchy tale of tortured descent that led to Joey's latest hospitalisation. It started one night on the kibbutz when Joey, after hearing rumours of nearby terrorist activity, had taken it upon himself to go on patrol duty with a rifle he'd lifted from the kibbutz's armoury. When he saw what he thought were terrorists on the move around the perimeter (turned out they were two kibbutzniks out for a romantic stroll under the stars), he called out for them to stop. They thought he was clowning around ('just being Joey' was how the guy put it when asked later) and ignored him. Joey panicked, and by the time the shooting had stopped, he'd hit them both, although mercifully they had only superficial wounds. Neither wanted to press charges, but nonetheless, Joey was booted out the following day, bringing an ignominious end to his healthy, clean kibbutz life.

One of the few known facts about Joey's past since then was that on Rosh Hashanah, he fell in front of a bus at Jerusalem Central Bus Station. The police were unclear whether he had stumbled, jumped, or been pushed; there had been a convincing witness to each event. His body was relatively unscathed, with only some grazes down his left leg and three broken ribs; his fragile mind was another matter. Aside from any bus-related damage, seventeen years of almost continuous intoxication, plus the traumas of his experiences in Lebanon, subsequent hospitalisations, and the steady spiral into depravity since leaving the kibbutz, had all taken their toll on his eggshell brain mass. The police had located Maud from a list of phone numbers scribbled on the inside of his journal. By the time she had finally tracked Sam down, Joey had been through numerous hospitals before ending up here at the Abarbanel Mental Health Center on the outskirts of Tel Aviv.

Despite some changes over the years, the reputation of the Abarbanel as the harshest psychiatric institution in the country was unchallenged. Leaked photographs had recently documented its physical neglect and shoddy infrastructure. In addition to staff shortages, overcrowding was the major issue: across the country, most of the patients released from psychiatric hospitals ended up readmitted within thirty days due to a lack of supportive care or residential settings in the community. As in many other countries, Israel first studied the issue of mental health within a military context to help soldiers deal with post-war anxiety, depression, and shell shock. Uniquely, it also had to deal with the mental damage among the civilian population arising out of the country's perpetually unstable security situation, with people on both sides regularly exposed to shootings, bombings, and other acts of terrorism. Although considerable resources had been devoted to treating trauma-related mental distress in its citizens, the system was overwhelmed, quality of care was a lottery, and Abarbanel was not a winning ticket.

While they'd been out walking, lunch had been served, and Joey tucked into the rice and bean curry mountained on the metal plate in front of him. 'I've got used to people looking at me in a funny way,' he said, mouth full of food. 'It's not the food, by the way, causing this weight gain, it's a side effect of the fucking medication.' When Joey spoke, his querulous voice put the hooks into Sam. 'As is the constipation and the belly rash. Still, it's better than the last pills they had me on, which gave me the squits.'

'No, carry on man. I'm not even looking at you,' Sam replied and stared out the window. The ghost of a moon hovered in a blue sky spotted with clouds, like an impressionist painting.

'Yeah, got used to it on the streets, people avoiding me when they saw me coming, like I was a leper with a bell.'

'Do you want to hear some good news?'

'News, man, can't watch it anymore.' Joey grabbed a clump of hair and twirled it as if boring a hole into his skull. 'Those newsreaders get inside my head, start telling me to do things.'

'Not that sort of news, I mean news about me. I'm . . . I'm going to pack it all in. Sri Lanka's my last gig, no more wars for me.'

'No way, Sammy. How come?'

'It's wrecking my head, man, been at it too long. Nightmares, flashbacks, the sweats, the whole fucking nine yards.' Sam flicked the strips of tissue he'd been twisting into the rubbish bin.

'Dude, keep that under cover. You don't want to end up in the nut house with me.'

'Ha, that's for sure.'

Occasionally, Sam caught a glimmer of the sharp and witty brother he once knew, which made dealing with this demented shell before him all the more painful. Conversations never went anywhere now, as Joey flitted from one subject to the next like a bee hunting pollen. It was hard to see much progress in his condition since those dark days in the AUB. He wanted the old, fun Joey back, the carefree, lucid soul who had been his partner in so many crimes.

'Anyhow, that's amazing. No more wars. Delighted for you.'

'Another thing, before I head back, I'm going to one of those UN kids' reunions with some of the gang we grew up with.'

'Why bother? I don't see the point of those get-togethers, rehashing old memories, do-you-remember-whens. Where do you reckon you'll retire to?'

'Oh, nothing's fixed, not even sure it's retirement. Just looking to move to some quiet corner of the world if I can find it.' He laughed, revealing his gold tooth. 'Somewhere I can live in my own bubble, shut off from all the everyday stresses.'

'Still trying to be free, eh?'

Through the window, an argument had broken out in the euphemistically named garden where patients gathered to suck on cigarettes like turbo-powered hoovers. Magpies squabbled in the eucalyptus tree, staking their territorial claim and machine-gun chattering to warn off intruders. Joey started chanting snatches of songs and banged on the upturned metal bin, ten lacerated fingers skittering in time to some tune in his head. Around his fingernails, the skin was shredded from constant chewing, and both thumbs were inflamed where a strip had been gouged out.

The racket stopped suddenly, and Joey said, 'You'll never guess the latest with Pops.'

'How do you mean?'

'Bee called Christy the other day in a right panic. He'd gone missing again. The last time, about six months ago, he turned up in Malahide.' Joey was relishing the opportunity to dwell on someone else's tale of mental health drama for a change. 'He'd gotten a bus from the city centre and was wandering along the beach, looking confused, when this young couple came across him. Couldn't tell them a thing, where he lived, who his family were, nothing. Then, totally random, out of nowhere, Declan comes jogging along the shoreline; you know Maud's brother. He lives out that way, apparently. I mean, what are the chances?'

'Unbelievable. I never heard about that. That's the dementia getting worse, I guess. Horrific illness.'

Joey leaned forward in his chair and started rocking, hands clasping his thighs, humming quietly. 'Well, it gets worse. This time, they'd been looking for him for a day, been in touch with the Gardaí and all. Damien had got a bunch of the lads searching for him and —'

'Jesus, you're joking. I didn't realise it had got that bad.'

'No, neither did I. This time, he turned up in Dromahair, having got the train to Sligo and then a bus, retracing the footsteps of his youth. He's clearly well able to tour around the country off his own bat.' Joey stopped rocking and stared out the window. 'But no getting away from it, shit is going down fast, man. Gives everyone something different to worry about, I guess' — he was back to the rocking — 'something besides poor ole Joey.'

A blue bottle buzzed aggressively against the windowpane. Joey sprung from his seat, a rolled magazine in his hand, and flailed uselessly. 'Die, motherfucker, die.'

Sam opened the window to let the fly out and was just thinking about making his own escape when Maud and Christy showed up.

Now that Maud had seen Joey in the flesh, she told herself to stop all this worrying and cop herself on. She could feel her lungs swell as if surfacing from a free dive. The upheaval in her stomach subsided, and with it, the fear that he would have run away again. Every time she entered the hospital, she heard afresh in her head the policeman's reassuringly official voice informing her that Joey had been arrested in Nazareth for abducting a little girl. She'd known right away — as soon as she heard the girl's age and hair colouring — that Joey must have confused her with Kathleen and thought he was rescuing his own daughter from some imagined, impending disaster. The police were lovely once they understood Joey's history of mental problems and escorted him themselves back to the hospital. There had been no more escapes since then, four months now and counting.

'How's she cutting, cuz?' Christy asked, rubbing a hand through his thinning hair.

'Fucking fly messing with my head,' Joey said by way of greeting.

'I brought you some of that pie you like,' Maud said. 'Sit down, and we'll all have some.'

In the armchair beside her, Joey munched the pie slice and slumped forward, a rictus pasted to his face. He gawped at his three visitors, vapid milky-brown eyes rolling in puffed-up sockets, oblivious to the worry creasing their faces. At least he had started washing again. He still refused to wear underpants or socks and had taken to wearing collarless grandfather shirts and grubby corduroy trousers with nothing on his feet.

'That shake of yours is getting fierce bad,' Maud said. 'If you're not careful, you'll end up with Parkinson's when you're older.'

'It's another fucking side effect, nothing they can do about it, I'm told.'

'Oh my God, Joey was just telling me about the latest with Pops, gone awol in Leitrim.'

Maud shut down that conversation with a silencing look and a dismissive, 'Ah, it's all fine. Bee just overreacted.'

Sam arched his eyebrows and said, 'I can't remember Bee ever overreacting to *anything*; I don't think I've ever seen her getting emotionally carried away or even—'

'Enough, Sam, all right?' Maud cut in, palm raised.

'How much longer do you have, Sam?' Christy asked.

'This is my last week. I fly back next Wednesday.'

'The dogs of war are calling to him,' Joey said with a hacking cough, and then he added apropos nothing, 'They banged Syd Barrett up for years in a place like this. I'll probably still be here next time you're back Sammy. Signing my heart out in the midnight choir.'

'Not at all, Joey,' Maud said. 'Shur didn't Dr Dayan say the last time what great progress you're making and that you'd be out by November at the latest.' By now, even Maud had accepted that the story wasn't going to have a simple, happy ending and that the best they could hope for was that the story would at least continue.

'Take Pink Floyd' — Joey was off on one of his tangents, a word salad of loosely associated thoughts — 'they're a cracking example of a fork-in-the-road band. Look how things changed when they axed Syd. He formed the band in the first place; Syd was their inspiration, and you couldn't imagine Floyd without him. Which one's Pink? Ha! They make their first album with him; it's all going along fine, but then Syd dips himself in the acid bath a few too many times. Now, the fork: do they continue as is or ditch him? They ditch him, and then the new line-up releases *Dark Side*, followed by *Wish You Were Here*. Would those albums ever have happened with Syd on board? Or if Syd had hung around, where would he have taken them? Would they have made even more amazing albums than those?'

Maud wondered where the boy she fell in love with had gone to. In her struggle to understand what was happening to him, she liked to visualise how Joey's brain was working. The shifting searchlight of his brain picking out ideas as they coruscated across his mind. His random vocalised thoughts scattering in the air as if slammed by a pinball flipper, spinning from bumper to bumper until they rolled aimlessly away. Joey himself rationalised his condition as some kind of mystical awakening, a spiritual enlightenment that allowed him to experience life differently to everyone else. Maud got his reasoning: if there was another explanation for why his mind had started working strangely, then he wasn't ill, and there was no need to take any tablets. Agreeing to take the prescribed drugs meant admitting that he was mentally ill, and that the hallucinations and voices were nothing more than a fantasy needing treatment.

It was clear that the medication had robbed him of his brio; he was withdrawing from the real world that he once embraced so enthusiastically. His facial expressions were lifeless, and his whole body conveyed lethargy and disinterest; even his voice was now monotone and dull. Conversations had become tortuous as the gears in Joey's mind ground to a crawl, and he was unable to follow even the simplest train of thought. Most days he spent in bed, rising only for a smoke or a pee, overcome with a profound despair that this was how he would spend the rest of his life. Occasionally, he would surprise them. From nowhere, he could have a totally rational conversation and spend an amusing couple of hours sorting out some major political problem; just last week, he had big ideas on how to deal with the IRA in the aftermath of the new ceasefire.

Suddenly, Joey cackled like a hyena and rubbed his hands together as he sang, 'Poor mad Joey has lost his mind and doesn't know where to find it. Leave him alone; he's stuck in a home, popping his pills each morning.'

Christy was trying to talk sense with Joey, but shur there's no point when he's like this; you have to let him at it. Now that he was taking the pills regularly, he was easier to deal with, although Maud was praying that Joey's accommodating behaviour — he was even going to group therapy sessions, claiming he wanted to strengthen his coping skills — was proof that he was managing his illness rather than a ruse to convince the doctors to let him out. All going well, they expected to move him into a step-down facility within weeks and to discharge him a few months later.

'Gimme a line from your favourite song. Go on, each of you,' Joey said, rubbing the side of his face as he yawned noisily.

And what then? The three of them had spent several nights discussing where Joey would go when he was discharged, but the issue remained unresolved and hung heavy on Maud's mind now that Sam's own departure loomed. Idea upon idea had been tossed around: visit Sam in Sri Lanka (another bloody war, that didn't sound like a good idea); go home to Dublin and let Bee look after him (there was something about that woman; she didn't care for Joey like a brother, and she clearly had enough on her plate keeping tabs on Pops); move in with them (Christy had made it crystal clear that wasn't going to happen). There was no point trying to explore these options with Joey; all their ideas passed in one ear and out the other without ever being subjected to any proper consideration or examination of the consequences. The one scenario to which there was no question mark attached was that of Joey living by himself. If that were allowed to happen, as sure as God made apples, he'd be back in hospital in no time at all.

'Memories get embedded into songs, you know. You hear a song, and you're right back in the moment you first heard it. That's why the same song can mean different things to different people.'

Maud laughed to herself. He had that right. Whenever she thought back to that time she'd come across Joey begging outside Hamleys in London, not long after they'd all left Dublin ('experiencing what the homeless life is like', as he described it) *Love is all around* was playing in her head; she'd heard it pumping out of a coffee shop just before she saw him, a lunatic gleam in his eyes. It had taken weeks of coaxing, but he eventually agreed to leave behind his life on the streets and came to live with them for a bit. In the end, she'd persuaded him to visit Auntie Cissie in Paris, which led him to Lebanon and Lena and life in a warzone and all that happened after that. She tried not to blame herself for interfering and sending him down that track, as if she could have changed the course of events, could have in any way prevented

Joey's descent into madness.

Joey was still on his favourite music thread. 'That's how you know when it's a great album, when your favourite track keeps changing, as you find a new gem of a song you'd missed before.'

'For me, it's—' Sam started.

'Guys, guys, has he shown you his photos from Afghanistan yet?' Joey drilled both his middle fingers into his temples. 'A-fucking-mazing, I tell you. I always knew Sammy boy was a real talent.'

'Too kind, Joey, too kind,' Sam said, pursing his lips.

Joey smiled and said in a long, slow drawl, 'They say it's the warmest colour. Love.'

Sam was already uncomfortable enough without having the spotlight directed at him. Whenever Christy and Maud showed up, the dynamic shifted. Joey became agitated and eager to please. A simmering tension crackled between them and regularly erupted into an argument over some trivial nonsense. Drunk and maudlin late the other night, Christy had confided some dark insights into the state of his marriage and his discontent with family life. No one ever really knows what goes on behind closed curtains. And now that there was talk of upping sticks again and returning to Dublin, they both seemed directionless and trapped in an unwanted life.

Luckily Maud had no interest in his photos — 'You must show us Sam, before you fly off again' — which suited him just fine. Instead, she ratcheted up the tension with, 'Now, Joey, I'd like to bring Kathleen in to see you; she's been asking for ages. Would that be alright?'

'I don't think that's a good idea,' Christy said, looking at Sam for support. 'Joey doesn't want Kathleen seeing him in this place, does he?'

Maud rolled her eyes. 'Shur, why wouldn't he? There's nothing wrong with him now.'

'Okay, folks, let's not have a domestic. I'm just over here,' Joey said, bringing the shutters down on that tricky topic. 'Let's leave off with the Kathleen visit for now.'

Sam caught the dagger look Maud threw at Christy and her silently mouthed, 'Fuck you'. Then all pleasant again, she said, 'Here, Joey, let me give you a little shoulder rub to ease those tense muscles.' She bananaed around Sam, a boozy whiff on her breath, and Christy left to get coffee after a brief, sibilant conversation with his wife.

Finally, they all left, scattering back to their complicated lives. Joey closed his eyes, exhausted from the emotional rollercoaster of their visit. Their enthusiasm and the fake optimism, the bickering, and the nervous tension, it was all because of him. After years in constant crisis mode, he and his three closest friends had drifted far apart and now they were only tethered by tenuous familial bonds. Ever since his illness emerged, he had dragged them from one Joey disaster to the next, with occasional high points when, for a moment, it seemed like things might work out after all. But they never did, and now his life was awash with so much broken cork he wondered how he would ever manage to strain it all out. Lebanon started out great but fell apart after Lena's death, and then he'd gone all Colonel Kurtz. Israel was fine for a while, but that trouble in the kibbutz was the final nail. Joey was down to zero. With a revelatory clarity, he could see that this had all gone on much too long, the constant in-out of hospital, the on-off pills metronome. It was time to end this: he needed to be a good boy, take his meds, and stay out of hospital for good. He had taken his first step on the long road from understanding to forbearance, secure in the knowledge of where his journey would terminate.

28.

SAM RECLINED IN THE PLANE SEAT, his mind abuzz as he replayed the weekend and tried to figure out what the hell had happened to him. He was a man transformed, having fallen madly in love with Greta Newport at the UN kids' reunion. That was the only way of describing it: for the first time in his life, Sam was in love, high in the sky over Spain, on cloud nine, in seventh heaven, on this aircraft back to London, and then onto Sri Lanka.

You couldn't make it up! Sam was four years older and had known Greta all his life, but growing up, she'd always been Bee's friend, another of the kids whose father once worked as a Guard with Pops in Dublin. Micky Newport used to call his only girl "Princess"; well, now she had found her prince charming. The music in Sam's headphones, David Kitt's moody love songs, was blowing his mind; he'd always enjoyed the melodies, but the lyrics never had any relevance for him. They were so detached from his own experiences. Now, the words sparkled with meaning. They danced across his mind, twirling with significance, speaking of things that he didn't think could ever happen to him. Suddenly, his life was laden with dangerous maybes: maybe he should get Greta to come to Sri Lanka with him, maybe he shouldn't be leaving her at all, maybe he should marry this girl. Bound to Greta, he felt truly free, newly liberated from the loneliness he'd never realised was tying him down.

Flying into Alicante four days earlier, Sam's expectations from the reunion couldn't have been lower. Since leaving Joey in the awful Abarbanel hospital and deciding to finally leave the warzones behind, he'd been making up for lost time. Just like the dude singing on that Eagles song, Sam had seven women on his mind, and this weekend, he had thought he might add an eighth; innocent flings, no-strings-attached arrangements, that was all he was after. Over the years, there had been several of these so-called "UN kids" reunions; in the wider UN family, there must have been nearly one hundred children of UN peacekeepers who became friends when they crossed paths as their parents moved between missions in the Middle East. Sam and Greta had been to a few reunions, but never at the same time. The Alicante gathering was a small one, eleven people meeting up to relive the many fun times and some of the freaky ones they had enjoyed growing up. Other UN children were the only people on the planet who knew what their migrant life was really like, who could draw on a similar bank of experiences, and who knew the many strange ways that unique upbringing had influenced their lives since.

Sam was drinking in the hotel bar with Rory and Jim when Greta showed up. Big smiling face, Sinatra blue eyes, and long, dark brown hair pulled up into a whale spout. He was mesmerised by the sight of her after so many years, although his opening, 'Delighted you could make it Greta, great to see you after all these years,' sounded terribly banal. While waiting for the others to arrive, the three lads headed to the beach, and Greta went to the shops for supplies. By the time Greta returned with a black cap for Sam (one that matched his instruction to 'get one with no logos, just a plain cap'), and Lays crisps and juicy oranges for the beach layabouts, and had rubbed suncream onto Sam's back, he was full-scale smitten.

There had been some previous between Greta and Sam, a blast of summer loving when the UN mission-posting lottery threw both their families together in Nahariya, a seaside town in northern Israel; Greta was seventeen and Sam twenty-one. Their first night out, after a party in the UN field office, they headed to the beach, and without any preliminaries, Sam popped the question: 'Do you want to do it?' When Greta was done horrified-laughing at this most rookie of amorous approaches, she reassured

Sam that whatever slim chance he may have had before dropping that line was now truly gone. Any further discussion was halted when an Israeli army patrol jeep showed up, spotlight blazing and megaphone blaring at them to get off the beach immediately. The following days were spent swimming and smooching and flirting, with Greta's mum complaining that they were 'making a holy show of yourselves.' By night, they partied in bars and clubs around town with a few other UN kids and some Irish army lads on R&R from Naqoura, just up the road in Southern Lebanon. In the early hours, they usually ended up in the Newports' apartment, nightcapping and snogging until her mum kicked him out with, 'Sam Hogan, you're like a bad penny, rolling back every night. Have you no home to go to?' They never did do it in Nahariya, but at the end of the summer — Greta on her way back to university and Sam en route to Beirut — they rendezvoused for a weekend in London where the relationship was finally consummated. In the thirteen years since, they had had no contact whatsoever until this meeting in Alicante.

Over dinner the first night, Sam listened engrossed as Greta filled the group in on how her life had been going, noting particularly the fact that she had ditched her boyfriend of three years and was enjoying being footloose and fancy-free. Later, as the crowd drifted away from the bar, Sam tried it on, but she wasn't going to 'fall for those rubbish chat-up lines of yours.' Although it didn't escape Sam's notice that Greta refused to go to bed until Katie went too, lest his eye should wander in that direction during her absence. By dinner the second night, they were seated together, legs pressed close, hands touching arms as they laughed along with the group's banter. Afterwards, dancing in the nightclub, they were all over each other and as soon as they got back to the hotel they tumbled into bed for a night of wild, passionate lovemaking, the like of which Sam had never had before, wasn't sure he'd even heard of sex like that. The following morning, Greta was flying back home a day earlier than the rest of them. She was gone about a half-hour when there was a knock on Sam's door.

Greta was standing there, looking flustered. 'I've screwed up the departure time. I've missed my flight. It left early this morning.'

Sam beamed and said, 'Oh dear, does that mean you'll have to stay another night?'

That night, pillow-talking sweet nothings, Sam told her he didn't know where or when, but someday he was going to marry Greta. She was all, 'Fine, we'll see, let's not rush into anything,' but she insisted that before he did anything, Sam had to make seven phone calls and let all those other girls know that he had now found the big romance he didn't know he'd been waiting for.

A huge smile lit up his face as he looked out the plane window at the sea of clouds below the bright blue sky. His abiding image from the weekend was from the angle of someone standing in front of them: Sam seated on a white plastic chair, dark shades and the logoless cap on his head, Greta's hourglass body standing behind him, faraway eyes smiling behind a curtain of brown hair, her hand in his, resting on his chest. They had let go of each other once before, and it wasn't happening again. There was too much to lose now.

29.

'JESUS, MARY AND SAINT JOSEPH, this is never the place, is it?' Maud said as they walked past two brand new 95D Mercedes, the pebbled driveway crackling underfoot, towards the imposing three-storey-over-basement red brick house.

'Middle of Aylesbury Road, your average modest little pile for this address,' Christy said as they mounted the flight of granite steps to the front door.

Cast-iron railings bordered the lush front garden, which burst into life under the blazing security spotlight triggered by their movement. A cedar tree stood majestic on the lawn, and its wide tabular crown, flat spindle-leaved branches layered below it, cast an eerie shadow on the face of the house.

'A little bit of Lebanon in his front garden. How ironic,' Joey said as he pushed the doorbell, wondering why he had ever agreed to tag along on this scouting trip. After nearly a decade in Israel, Maud had started obsessing about returning to Ireland ('There's bags of opportunities back home, now that things are picking up again, just look at Damien.') and Christy wasn't totally against it as things had now gone to shit in Israel since the assassination of Prime Minister Yitzhak Rabin.

For Israelis, the shooting proved as traumatic as JFK's assassination was for Americans. It was a sobering reminder of the personal cost of peace-making in Israel. Rabin's assassin, Yigal Amir, was a right-wing extremist opposed to the signing of the Oslo Accords, which planned for gradual self-government by the Palestinians in the West Bank and Gaza Strip. As a result, Bill

Clinton witnessed the hugely symbolic handshake on the White House lawn between Rabin and PLO leader Yasser Arafat after both sides had agreed to recognise each other for the first time ever. Later that year, Jordan became the second Arab country that Israel made peace with when Rabin signed a peace treaty with King Hussein. Finally, it seemed that Israel was on the road to peace with its neighbours, but Rabin's assassination called into question the real appetite for that outcome and the ability of Israeli society to settle its internal differences democratically.

Of late, there had been much discussion in the Hogan Jerusalem household about whether they should pack it all in now that things were so uncertain and that a backlash against the Palestinians was increasingly likely. They'd decided to come back to Dublin for a fortnight in late January to check out their options, with Joey in tow for moral support. Since getting out of Abarbanel hospital, Joey no longer liked the company of crowds and found all the noise overwhelming; too many ways for things to go wrong. But Damien had been most insistent. 'It's only a dinner party; you'll get to meet Clara. You've got to make the effort, for old time's sake. Please.'

Damien greeted them at the door all lord-of-the-manor and directed them into the commodious parlour, which Joey calculated was about the same size as the Hogans' entire living space in Beit Hanina. A huge chandelier hung in the middle of the high-ceilinged room, and three enormous paintings of Connemara landscapes filled the burgundy wall space. Neil Diamond crooned from the four speakers set high in each corner of the room. Despite the outward trappings of success, whatever was going on in Damien's life had taken its toll on his body; he looked a decade older than his thirty-six years, with stress lines cut through the skin on his wizened face, and fleshy, black sacks under his watery eyes. Whereas Joey remembered Damien striding with long steps and chest thrust forward, now he lumbered along with a slight stoop.

Clara, the girlfriend who owned this house, came forward to 'mwaaah, mwaaah' each of them an air kiss, her long neck choked by a chain of pearls. She pulled her rouged lips open to smile two perfect rows of teeth as her piercing Bette Davis eyes beamed between mascara-laden lashes. The self-appointed master of the universe made the introductions: 'Joey, Christy, Maud, this is Richard, and Rupert, his wife Imelda, Chloe, Bruce and Eric, Rebecca and Walter and . . .' (Joey lost track after that).

Next, Damien insisted on giving 'the visitors' a tour of the mansion. Joey was glad of the delay in having to converse with this pretentious D4 group, unsure how to answer the predictable opening question, 'And what do you do, Joey?' *Spend most of my time making sure I don't end up back in the hospital I just got out of three months ago*, wouldn't make for very stimulating discussion. By the time they returned downstairs, everyone was seated at the long dining table and engaged in boisterous conversation. Joey took his place, as directed by Clara, between Bruce and Rebecca and braced himself for a long night.

'Were you over in Ascot during the summer, Bruce?' Imelda, or was she Chloe, called from across the table, her mottled, pasty face smothered with layers of make-up.

'Yes, that was a while ago, but it was fabulous. A gang of us went over on the Wednesday, and we ended up staying until the Sunday. Eric had a big win on the Gold Cup, which kept us in Bolly for the weekend.'

'This wine is sensational,' Eric said. 'Is this the one that Philippe put you onto?'

'No, this is from a new contact. It's a 1985 vintage Pomerol, limited edition,' Damien said. He was smoking again after giving up for three years; Joey got that, he understood how a need could resurface.

'Lovely legs, and so smooth, quite a chocolatey taste.' Walter closed his eyes and tipped his head back as he swirled a mouthful of wine.

'Did you hear about that girl who's been thrown out of Alex because her mother couldn't pay the school fees?' Rebecca was aghast. A strand of hair dangled over her left eye, tickling her pearl drop earring like a finger. 'It seems the headmistress hauled the girl up in front of the entire school at assembly to announce that she was being expelled.'

'The thing is,' Richard said, 'you shouldn't be sending your child to private school if you can't afford it.'

A rippling chorus of agreement that started out as a cautious 'I guess' and 'You're right', quickly escalated to near-unanimous condemnation of the mother's behaviour (the disgrace she had brought on her daughter; she would now be ostracised from all decent company for the rest of her life), when the poor woman was only trying to do the best for her child. It was depressing listening to them talking about their own children. Everybody had an Einstein in the family; many had a budding movie star or a musical virtuoso; all their kids were prodigious readers or excelled at sports: these children were universally brilliant and made their parents so proud. What planet were these people from?

Joey drifted off, distracted by the crooning singer who was caught between two shores precisely as he was. Israel was fine in many ways – he had a job, he liked the weather, he lived alone – but it just didn't feel like home. Dublin was sort-of home, as much as anywhere was, but this new version was alien and unappealing and certainly not sufficient reward for all the risks of moving back. He'd always hated the question, 'Where are you from?' No disputing that he was born in Ireland and held an Irish passport, but did that make him "from Ireland"? He'd spent most of his childhood overseas, then went to an Irish boarding school, but during holidays, for "normal living" he was back in the Middle East; the only time he'd properly lived in Ireland was the three years at university, and he'd lived in Lebanon and Israel since. He didn't really feel he was "from" anywhere; he didn't belong to any one place, so whatever answer he gave to the question invariably felt unsatisfactory.

Of course, the Portuguese taxi driver they'd got from Dublin Airport (who had clearly never even *seen* a map of Dublin; none of the London taxi drivers' "The Knowledge" necessary here) was only being friendly when he dropped them off at Pops' house and called out, 'Enjoy your holiday,' but it was totally depressing to be treated like some simpleton tourist in your own country. It hadn't helped when the driver ignored his directions, saying he knew a shortcut, and then proceeded to get lost. He was as happy as the next man about all the good things that were happening in Celtic Tiger Ireland, but the thing that really got his goat was the feeling of alienation he got on returning home these days.

Bruce turned out to be more interesting than Joey first expected, perhaps because the list of problems he was dealing with couldn't but make you feel good about your own lot in life. A bit like Maud's logic for religiously tuning into EastEnders three evenings a week so she could wallow in the difficulties of the Mitchell brothers and the Beals and all the rest at Albert Square: by comparison to their miserable lives, hers was a jubilant festival. Bruce was one of those people who could tick pretty much every available box on those application forms for jobs or visas or mortgages. Under marital status, Bruce ticked yes to: divorced (Kiera, thirteen years ago), widowed (Becky, who died from a dodgy blood transfusion in Cambodia where she was an aid worker), and married (to Eric, who was gay; that ticked another box of course). Under dependents, he could enter one child (Jonathan, adopted, with Eric) or possibly two (Oliver, for whom he was currently fighting custody with Becky's sister). Regarding domicile, it depended on which family context they were asking about, but at that point, he could veraciously tick homeowner (apartment in New York) or tenant (Mayfair pied-à-terre with Eric) or temporary accommodation (hotel room in Dubai, where he lived every second six weeks). Employment he was all of: self-employed (a part-time portrait painting business), employed (with a large IT company, but only when he was in Dubai), and unemployed (his official status in Ireland).

As the talk around the table wore on, Joey felt himself detaching from this ostentatious group to escape his role of awestruck outsider. From the exasperated look on Christy's face, he wasn't faring much better, stuck between the inseparable Rebecca and Walter. Maud was pissed, boring whoever would listen with tales from her troubled life in Jerusalem and loudly proclaiming how desperate she was to set up home in Dublin.

'Ooh, that's fabulous news, Clara, hooray,' Rebecca screeched, shortly accompanied, in similar ear-piercing fashion, by the other women.

'What? You're getting married?'

'When's the big day?'

'We haven't set a date yet,' Clara said, beaming up at the beaming Damien, 'we're —'

'My God, you're certainly not hanging about, the pair of you,' Imelda said, the note of surprise cut with a sliver of envy.

'But what about —'

'Tell them where we're thinking of having the reception, darling,' Damien said as he rose to answer the telephone ringing in the hall.

No doubt it would be one of Dublin's society weddings of the year. Of course, the fact that Damien was marrying Clara Humphries certainly helped. Ensconced among the sailing club set in Dalkey, Clara's family was loaded. Naturally, she worked in PR or something to do with party organising; Joey quickly lost interest whenever Clara's whiney voice launched, with exaggerated enthusiasm, into a rundown of all the *amazing* things that she was doing. I mean, how could Damien ever care for someone else when all his love was bottled up and set aside for just himself? Thirty-six years old and riding the pig's back, Damien had been growing what Joey supposed they now had to call his entertainment empire: four nightclubs, a couple of bars, and a steakhouse. Whatever they might think of his ruthless business streak or his enormous money-making ambitions, he was still family.

As the quantity of alcohol permeating Joey's brain increased, he moved from jocose to morose. Towards the end of his hospitalisation, one of Joey's most troubling worries was that he might have passed his illness onto Kathleen. Statistically, he had been informed, she was thirteen times more likely to develop schizophrenia than someone who didn't have a parent suffering from the illness. Surely, a mentally ill daughter wouldn't be the total sum of his legacy to this world.

And from there, he turned bellicose. All the talk of getting married had tipped him over, and it had become one long struggle to quench thoughts of Lena and what their wedding might have been like. Whatever benevolence he had once felt for this moneyed crowd had long since evaporated. Why was it that the more money people accumulated, the more they talked about it, and the more boring they became? He got up for a piss, desperate for a break from this increasingly dreary conversation. Blood rushed to his head, dizzying his brain and turning his legs to jelly. He paused for a moment to let it pass. As he climbed the stairs to the toilet on the landing, something in Damien's hissing whisper stopped him for a spot of furtive eavesdropping. 'Listen Len, we need to bury this . . .' Joey backtracked a few steps, straining to hear.

'Fucking health and safety people. Tell Jim to get rid of . . .' Damien's combative voice dropped to a whisper so that Joey couldn't hear how the instruction to Jim ended.

'Look, I've got people here . . . yes, Rupert also. I can't deal with this now. Offer him 800 and go to a grand maximum. Just sort it,' with which he slammed the phone down and paced off, heading for the stairs. Joey had just found the toilet when Damien appeared behind him. 'Hey buddy, fancy a line?'

As Joey took a piss, Damien tipped a mound of toot onto an ornate, glass-topped bureau and carved out two white snail trails of powder with the Stanley blade. Gone were the manicured nails, now so chewed that his fingertips were red and swollen. He rolled a twenty-punt note and gustily vacuumed up one line. 'Blow and bubbly, these are my poisons nowadays. Have some.'

'Ah, not for me, thanks. I'm trying to keep it under control.'

Satan's evil finger curled around Joey's willpower, trying to choke the life out of his fortitude, hissing in his ear: *What's the harm? You could use a hit, a proper one, to get through this.*

'Go on, you're no craic anymore.'

'My illness, you know? I'm losing my mind.' Joey fidgeted with the toilet flush, avoiding Damien's eyes.

'Oh yeah, how's that going,' Damien said as he snorted up the other line. 'Hey, have you heard anything from Sam?'

'He's doing good. Did you hear he won a Pulitzer Prize for some of his Gulf War photos? He . . . no thanks, I'm sure . . .' Damien was back again with the temptation. 'You should check them out. There were a couple of his shots in the Times last week.' Joey waited for the follow-on question, unsure what he would say when Damien asked about his own job and how he was coping since getting frogmarched out of the kibbutz and locked up in that crazy hospital. But he needn't have worried.

'Duty calls.' Damien checked his look in the mirror, dabbed the powder grains off his nose, and clown grinned at Joey's reflection. 'We better get back to the cheery dinner party below. They're all Clara's mob, complete and utter bores but needs must and all that.'

They ended up staying until the bitter end at Damien's insistence, 'So that we can catch up properly with what's been going on.' Sit and listen to news of his expanding business operation, more like, all doing exceptionally well except for Peckers, which he was quick to point out Leonard was running.

'I fucking love money.'

'Mazel tov.'

'You've come a long way, big bro.'

Erect in front of his opulent fireplace, the pot belly swell sagging over his belt, Damien launched into a long, hubristic monologue justifying the rectitude of his motivations. 'Throughout history, the qualities, the human characteristics valued by the society of the time, have always changed. In the early days, man's ability to hunt was prized above all else. In other eras, it was chivalrous deeds and knight's honour. Other times, kids grew up wanting to be skilled navigators with a passion for discovering new lands. During the age of reason, logical thinkers were held in the highest esteem. In modern times, people became impressed by a strong work ethic and the ability to produce goods and trade commercially. These are the values that have been held uppermost throughout history.'

Joey feigned interest but was distracted by how stupid Damien's shoulder-length hair looked, with the slicked-back fringe split in the centre and drooping like a bird's wings. God, how boring! Is there no end to this rubbish? Joey wondered if these long-held principles Damien was expounding hadn't just been thought up that morning. He had always been the most ambitious of them, the one striving to get on in the world and to ensure that everyone recognised his progress. From the age of one, when the newborn Sam invaded his solitary world, Damien had been engaged in a full-scale battle for his parents' acclaim. All his actions and words were designed to garner their words of praise, approving looks, and appreciative smiles, even as he struggled to meet their ever-inflating expectations. As the eldest, he was always first to push the boundaries, explore, and set a trail the rest of them would follow. He was certainly way out ahead of any of them in the money-making game. Maybe his time really had come.

Swirling his Hennessy in the bulbous glass, Damien continued in his plangent voice, 'We now live in an age where property is valued above all else. In a country like Ireland, where the land available for building is so finite, property is as treasured as water for an African farming parched land. And across all these revolutionary transitions, man's moral code has been based on the simple principle that the end justifies the means. Declare an aspirational goal and set out honourably to achieve it, and once you stay focussed on the prize, those who write history will recognise that the methods you may need to use along the way are fully justified in retrospect. Once the purpose in what I'm doing, the goal that I seek is noble — for instance, I need to support my family, I want to contribute to a productive society, I will work and pay my own way rather than sponging off the system — then people never have any difficulty with the means used to get to that end-point.'

Finally, a pause, Tiger Damien waiting on trumpets to sound for his magnanimous contribution to Dublin's entertainment landscape. Maud rushed in with, 'What about . . . if we moved back to Dublin . . . could you give Joey a job in your business?'

'Jaysus, just a minute.' Joey reared forward. 'Where did that come from?'

'Just to help him get settled back into something with people he knows,' Maud said.

'I don't need you—'

Clara cut Joey off. 'But Damien's not a charity worker, darling.' There was never even a moment when Joey figured Clara as a fan of his; God knows what she'd heard about the time he used to hang around with her soon-to-be-husband, and the dangers of rekindling that friendship.

'I don't think anyone would ever accuse him of that, darling Clara,' Maud said. 'But before you showed up, Joey and Damien were the best of friends.'

'Okay, ladies, calm it down,' Christy said. 'We're just letting Damien know—'

'For the avoidance of doubt' — Joey's deep voice was loud and measured — 'I have no interest whatsoever in moving back to Dublin, let alone working for my good friend and brother Damien. Perish the thought.'

Joey's mind had taken a dark turn. In his early thirties and with no prospect of ever making real money, his life a failure by conventional standards, his inadequacy would be complete should he ever find himself reliant on Damien's generosity. At

Bee's request, he had agreed to stay on in Dublin after Christy and Maud left, maybe until Easter. She was struggling with the demands of caring for Pops by herself. No sign of Damien getting involved, the others were overseas, and Joey was at a loose end, with time to spare.

Living with just Pops, in that huge house, would be strange but he was looking forward to spending quality time with the father that he saw so little of. The Alzheimer's meant he needed a lot of support and Bee had given Joey an extensive task list. First thing every morning he was to give Pops his "Today list"; Bee had an active programme of activities mapped out for him most days. Whenever he went out alone, she sent him off with a hand-drawn map in his pocket, alongside his driver's licence (identification in case he got lost). Joey was also in charge of cooking, following Bee's direction: lots of fruits and veg, only the odd bit of meat, and no sugar or processed food. Senseless, really, as Pops had lost his appetite and often had problems swallowing. Both common side effects from his meds, apparently. Filling the house with photographs was a great idea of Bee's. Just yesterday, the three of them had a lovely time talking about holidays Pops had taken. A photo of him sitting on a blue Vespa triggered a memory of a summer in Paros, when he and Maeve had rented a scooter and beach-hopped their way around the island, the breeze in his helmetless hair, her arms around his waist. Long boozy lunches at seaside tavernas. Lazy afternoons on the beach, dozing and canoodling. Drunken, naked, moonlight dancing on the balcony. Freebirds both.

'Well, that's Joey for you, isn't it?' Damien laughed and drained his brandy. 'What was it you used to call him, Maud? The Breeze, wasn't it?'

'Speaking of which,' Christy said, grasping at the fortuitous exit opportunity that had been lobbed his way. 'We better hit the road. The kids will be awake early in the morning.'

As they walked home, Maud's arms linked through Christy's and Joey's, they concluded that the idea of moving back home was a fantasy. 'What's after happening to the country at all?' Maud exclaimed in despair. Dublin was a place they no longer recognised nor felt any desire to live in. These just weren't their sort of people and observing them up close had definitively confirmed that.

30.

SIX WEEKS LATER, THEY WERE BACK FOR POPS' FUNERAL, in the Leitrim village where he was born sixty-four years ago. Up in the front pew, under the curving embrace of the church's oak frame, sat the Hogan siblings, bewildered and flailing in the huge void left behind. Joey glanced back at the vast congregation that had gathered from across the globe to pay their respects to the Hogan family patriarch, standing room only and overflowing onto the rainy churchyard. Not long ago, you wouldn't get a church funeral if you went and topped yourself, but good ole Pope JP the second ('young people of Ireland, I love you') had done away with that edict.

Maudlin organ music reverberated around the church and rattled Joey's eardrums as a soprano bawled out some lugubrious hymn. Pops had selected his two favourite bible readings and the music he wanted. But *Nearer my God to Thee,* come on. Didn't Pops realise it was too late to petition the lord with prayer? Besides, it wasn't the big boss himself, in the heavens up above, that these people should be concerning themselves with. There were spies closer to Earth who'd obviously read the death notice in the papers and got into the church yesterday to set things up. Joey had clocked the chain of five speakers on the pillars either side of the nave in which they'd hidden the cameras. He wasn't that bothered; surely they could see he was feeling better and didn't need those pills messing with his head. From here on, he was taking control of his own mind, and he was finally going to kill off all those voices before they had a chance to ruin everything.

What started out as just a few close relatives soon became an elongated line of people, nameless and faceless, shuffling towards the altar to shake hands with the mourning family, an endless stream of mouths mumbling, 'Sorry for your trouble,' leaning in to regard him with an earnest dip of the head. Months ago, he'd stopped making eye contact because, with every glance, people could read his mind and inject bad thoughts into his head. Even though it hurt his eyes, this one time he decided to make an exception and commiserate with this community in their hour of loss.

All this rapport with the dead was a load of shite. Catholics banging on about feeling the presence of those who had passed away and them looking out for us from on high. No way was Ma up there in heaven, watching over her family, waiting for Pops to arrive, and saving a seat for the rest of them when their time came. Pops had waited until their last conversation to tell Joey that in his will, he was leaving the pile in Sandymount aka the family home, and the three Ranelagh houses-in-flats, to the other four: 'I'll leave you cash, Joseph, that's all you're ever interested in, I know that. You're too rootless; you'd just sell the houses if I left them to you.' Bemused by the satisfied look on Pops' face, apparently content that this father-son chat had passed off so well, that he understood Joey's motivations so thoroughly, and that he had managed to share his plans for his inheritance in between news stories on the TV, Joey could manage no reply.

Staring at the flower-strewn coffin just a few yards away, Joey was occupying himself with these irritations to suppress the really bad thoughts milling about his mind. Lena's funeral was a blur. No one had ever asked, but they must all have wondered how much of her remains were actually in the urn. What's left after a body is incinerated in a car fire? Dust to dust. To rid his mind of these images, he shook his head sideways as if clearing bathwater from his ear.

Finally, the service was over, and Joey exited the church in pursuit of the coffin, his black jacket flapping over his half-buttoned, Guinness-stained white shirt. A hard rain was falling; the drops edged with an icy bite. Early that morning, it had started as a soft drizzle, then morphed into an Asian monsoon, and it had kept going since. From the west came a rolling thunderclap followed by a renewed burst of rain that machine-gunned into the pavement, the drops rebounding in crowns of water. Joey shuffled over to Sam and Greta to bum a cigarette. 'So sorry for your troubles, Joey. How are you?' Greta asked from under her umbrella. 'Where are your shoes?'

Before Joey could answer, some distant relation came up and repeated the process: comforting words, a brief hug, and a worried downward look at his feet. Then Clara wandered over, a smile slashed across her face, doing her usual so-lovely-to-see-you fake greeting. Prone to burping out strange thoughts at inopportune moments, Joey resorted to his failsafe coping mechanism and started laughing madly. He pulled an orange out of his pocket and tore at it with his teeth, gobbling like a hungry animal, the juice and pieces of fruit smearing his bristly face. At this point of maximum awkwardness, everyone embarrassed by the grieving son's inappropriate funeral behaviour, Christy ambled over and said, 'There's lifts going back to the house for five people if anyone needs transport.' All undertaker-like, the black somehow suited the thinner Christy.

When Joey had woken that morning under the thumb of another black day, it had taken a monumental effort to drag himself out of bed. Nothing about the day so far had persuaded him that that decision had been a good one. An even more excruciating effort was now required to resist the temptation to cross the drenched road and leap the ten feet into the gushing river below. If he ended up in public water again, he'd be back inside. Instead, with his dick burning for a piss, Joey said with a maniacal grin, 'I'll make my own way, see you all there,' and went running off before anyone could intervene.

Later that day, when the bodhráns and fiddles came out and the wake was in full flow, Joey went for a walk with Christy, down to the lake. At the end of the bohereen they leant on the metal gate, arms resting along the top bar. Two cormorants stood near the lakeshore, wings raised to the sun like preachers' hands. The evening sun cast a pewter sheen on the dark brown, undulating water. A squawking, V-shaped flock of Canada geese passed overhead, migrating east at low altitude. 'The wild geese, in flight home,' Joey announced. 'You know, the Irish have been doing that for years. From ports all over this country – Dun Laoghaire, Rosslare, Cobh, Kinsale – heading off into the great unknown, fleeing some hardship at home.'

'Just like we did,' Christy sniggered.

Joey pulled out a pack of Major and lit one for them both. 'Listen, Christy, I've got a confession to make.'

'Jaysus, a funeral and a confession in one day. You're not going all religious on me, are you?'

'Seriously, man. It's about Kathleen.' Joey paused, grasping for courage, not knowing what would emerge on the other side of his words. 'Errmm . . . I want you to know, that thing with Kathleen . . . You know about that, right?

'What? That you're the father, and you never told me? Yeah, I figured that out. From Maud's Mam.'

'What? How does she know?'

'No, she doesn't know herself. She sent us a package to Jerusalem a while ago with some old snapshots from a holiday in Ballybunion. There was one photograph of us two on the beach about seven years old. And you looking the absolute spit of Kathleen at that age. Brown curly hair, face shape, dark eyes, all the same as you.'

When he'd first seen that photo and compared Joey's childish face to Kathleen's, he'd been certain. Over subsequent months, he became less convinced and wondered whether it wasn't just a coincidence. But now, a cold wave of acceptance rolled over him, drowning any lingering doubts. The raw shock of it surprised him, like how news of a terminally ill relation's death still manages to traumatise, despite its inevitability.

'You know it had nothing to do with me? Well, of course, it had something to do with me, in that sense. But what I mean is, at the time, I didn't know Maud was trying to get pregnant. I never would have done it if I'd known, you understand don't you? I've always said kids ain't my thing.'

'You and me both, man. Not the kids thing, I love my kids and wouldn't swap them for the world. But she had us both fooled with that one.'

'And you're okay about Kathleen?'

'Listen, of course I was pissed off at the time. With Maud mostly but also with you. But I love Kathleen. She was a gorgeous baby; those deep brown eyes used to melt me, lying in her cot staring up at me staring down at her. Even if I didn't father her, I'm her dad now. And if it had to be anyone besides me, I suppose it being you is the best I could hope for.'

Joey stood straight and turned to face Christy. 'Man, I don't say this enough; in fact, I'm not sure I've ever said it to you, but I want you to know I love you, Christy, just like a brother. More than, in fact.'

'Right. Well, thanks, I guess. You fuck my wife, but at least you love me.' He was quiet for a moment, and then a titter started, and before long, they were both roaring laughing, heads thrown back and eyes leaking. 'You're some screw-up, you are, Joey. I love you too, man, despite everything.'

'Come here to me,' Joey said as he pulled Christy into a bear hug. Christy resisted the closeness at first, but then he went with it, and they rocked each other left and right in an embrace. As if adding his approval for the love-in, an owl hooted from the copse alongside, then broke cover and flew off, silhouetted against the darkening sky.

31.

SEPARATION, DIVORCE, CUSTODY. Over recent months, this new vocabulary of poisonous, divisive words had come to occupy Christy's thinking. The time to act was upon him. He was long ago done with his whoring and sowing his wild oats; that was just a phase he had to go through to realise what he really wanted. Moving back to Dublin was a total non-runner. Ireland had become an alien nation, one fixated on money and social status. Damien's dinner party was an extreme insight into that mindset, but it was apparent wherever he looked, with his outsider eyes. Maybe he'd been out of it too long, in their Mid-East bubble, but for him, there was no going back to that life. Despite all the difficulties in Israel, he had more to give; his contribution was valuable, and people still depended on him there.

Being back in the Hogan family house, memories of Pops' life everywhere, was just plain surreal. They'd barely settled back into life in Israel when the shocking news came through, and after that, everything happened in a blur. He was dead on the Tuesday and cremated on the following Monday, the funeral delayed until he and Sam could get back home. Year by year, and then suddenly, month to month, the dementia had got worse and worse, and in moments of lucidity, Pops had started saying that he didn't want to live a life where his mind was gone. But Christy never suspected that he was thinking about taking his own life, and with Bee and Joey's help. Them being involved had really pissed him off but for now it was best to let sleeping dogs well enough alone. He had enough on his plate without opening a whole other can of worms. Life was too short, and you only got to go around the block once.

The one good thing to come out of Pops' death was that it had clarified his own priority and spurred him into action: he would make the most of whatever limited time he may have on this earth and wouldn't spend that time doing things he didn't want to do.

The kids had all been bathed and had settled down in bed after a final read through of *The Cat in the Hat*, so that they were well out of the way for the big chat. Desirous of setting the right mood, he'd broken his diet and cooked Maud's favourite for dinner: Delia's baked pork chops and mushrooms in cream and lemon, with peas and fluffy mash. He felt relaxed now that the moment had finally arrived. He had just put a carton of milk on the table when Maud arrived home, flustered after the day's shopping with her girlfriends. Having listened over dinner to the trials of Maud's day and who said what about whom, and having covered the following day's childcare logistical arrangements over pudding, once he had poured Maud's cup of tea, Christy was ready to address the night's main business.

'OK, so that's tomorrow sorted. There is something else that I wanted to talk to you about.'

'Y-e-es . . . that tone of yours is making me nervous.'

Christy paused, as in his head he assembled the words in their oft-rehearsed order. 'Remember we had that chat a while back about how things weren't going so well between us and how maybe we needed to take a break from each other.'

'Yerra, wasn't it me that brought it up?' Maud said, rising to get the sugar bowl.

'Right. Well, I've been thinking about this a lot recently, and I think that maybe with the move to Dublin not happening now . . . I was thinking that . . . maybe this would be . . . it might be a good time for us to split up.'

'Split up, as in take a break for a while, or split up as in break up altogether.' She was doing that really irritating fast-stirring thing, swirling the spoon around her cup long after the sugar had dissolved.

'The latter was what I was thinking.'

'Ha, still the lawyer, even with your break-up speech. That's fine Christy, not a problem with me.'

Arms crossed as if embracing herself and not an eyelid batted, her voice not even a note higher. It wasn't that he'd been expecting a nuclear blowout: they had both fallen out of love some time ago if indeed they'd ever really been in love rather than impulsively corralled into a stereotypical shotgun marriage. But even still, he had been expecting a bit more fight. She seemed almost happy with the decision, which set him worrying that, in some mysterious way, she'd finagled him into initiating the break-up so that he came out as the bad guy, the husband who ran off and abandoned his wife and kids. He stuttered on, 'You can keep the house in London, of course, I . . . I don't want it; it's for you and the kids.'

That came out all wrong, and Maud jumped all over it, her cheeks blazing and eyes flaring. 'Oh, that's very big of you, Christy Hogan, given that it's my inheritance from Auntie Helen that has paid for the house.'

'Hang on a minute' — his voice was rising, but he caught himself and continued in a lower tone — 'I know that helped a lot, but you're forgetting my years and years of slaving away at that shitty job in London, paying off the mortgage every month, and paying for all the other things everyone needed.' Maud may know that money didn't grow on trees, but she had no real understanding of where it might otherwise sprout from. Christy inhaled and took a moment before continuing, 'Anyhow, there's no need to argue on the house, is there? I'm saying you can have it.'

'What's got you so high and mighty, I wonder, Christy boy? You've got some woman, don't you?'

'I do not. Why would you say that?' Typical Maud, damn woman's intuition. He hadn't planned on telling her, not so soon; it would just divert attention from the main topic. 'Thing is, I've spent my whole life trying to do the right thing, always looking out for what's best for others. Didn't I marry you as soon as I discovered you were pregnant, and no questions asked? Well, it's time for some Christy time. For just a little while, I'm going to do things that suit me, the things I really want to do. Mé féin finally.'

'You never told me her name. That's all I want to know. The rest I can imagine — young, skinny, probably your secretary, fucks like a rabbit and services you with regular blow-jobs.'

Christy rubbed his palm across his cheek and ran his hand through his hair, amazed at the accuracy of her pen picture. Looking away, he said, 'Sadie. She's called Sadie.'

'Humph, sexy Sadie, how original,' the hurt creeping into her voice. 'So that's why you were so keen to lose the weight, even though I'd been on to you about it for years.'

'Anyhow, it's not because of Sadie; things haven't been right between us for years. I can't seem to reach you anymore.' Christy got up to put the kettle on again, another cup of tea when he was desperate for something a little stronger, but he'd cleared the house of any trace of booze some time ago.

'You can reach me anytime you want to, shur amn't I just over here?'

'That's just it, though, I can't. It's like there's a wall between us that neither of us can get over. Maybe we're both afraid of what we'll find on the other side.'

She threw her head back and looked at the ceiling. 'I can't bear all these secrets all the time.'

'Secrets Maud? What secrets?' Confidence rising, Christy was ready to force the issue. When no admission of guilt was forthcoming, he looked directly at Maud for the first time that night. 'Well, you're a fine one to talk, carrying on for years behind my back.'

'And what's that supposed to mean?'

'Oh, you know full well what I mean. Go on, tell me, Maud, was he better than me?'

'I have no idea what you're talking about,' but her frenetic blinking and fretful eyes disagreed. There was a long pause, a break in the caterwauling, and a moment to take stock. 'You knew. For how long?'

'Oh yes, I knew. You as good as told me yourself. One night, you were completely plastered, rambling on about your handsome lover . . . it was in the bad days, just before you went into the rehab place.'

'But you never said anything?'

'Well, that would have been telling, wouldn't it? And that's not something we do with each other anymore. Besides, I had my reasons. It's not easy finding out something like that, betrayal by your wife.'

'I'm so sorry, Christy. I never meant you any harm. I couldn't control it. That's why they're called feelings; it's not a rational process. You just feel it in your body, in your emotions.'

Steam billowed from the kettle, and it shook on the worktop as it reached a full boil. Christy brought their teacups over for a refill and looked out the black, steamy window, his back to her. 'Who is he?' he hissed.

'You don't know him. And there is no is. It was nothing, and it's been over for a long time now. Only lasted a few months.'

Turning to face her, sitting at the table with head bent and her face a mask of guilt, he almost felt sorry for her, but just as quickly as it had appeared, her repentant look scuttled off. 'This is all nonsense, pure nonsense. All that stuff is in the past.' Her hands flailed about like fretful birds. 'You're . . . you're the one who's abandoning his family, you're the one with some young wan on the side. This whole thing tonight isn't about me being unfaithful.'

'What an unproductive thing to say.' Christy moved back towards the table, looming over her, raging, 'I'm not abandoning my family as you put it; I intend to remain very much involved, just in a different way.' Now that his tongue was unmoored, his words bubbled out like a spraying geyser. 'And speaking of family and secrets, what about Kathleen? Is there anything you want to tell me about her?'

Maud stood to face him, then went to close the dribbling tap. With her back to him, she said, 'What . . . how . . . What do you mean?'

'Well, like, for starters, who's her father? Is it him?' Christy spat the words out, the edges of his mouth stretched to reveal gritted teeth.

Maud turned to face him, fear plastered over her face. 'I wasn't sure whose she was, swear to God.'

'You let me believe she was mine.'

'You just presumed she was.'

'So it's my fault.'

'I didn't mean to lead you on.'

'When did it happen, you and him?'

'The night before we were together, just before he left Dublin.'

'Our first night.'

'Yes. *Before* our night together, not after,' Maud said as she slunk back to the table from the sink. 'It was only when she started growing up that it became more obvious.'

'And when are we going to tell her? At some point, she's going to have to know who her real father is' – Christy made no attempt to contain the acid words dripping off his tongue – 'this wonderful run-away father of hers, this crazy Uncle Joey who in fact is her dad, this . . . this . . . this kibbutz shooter.'

'Forget about Joey, that's all in the past. This thing with . . . with Sadie. Is it serious?'

He hesitated, aware that once he said it aloud, there would be no taking it back. 'Yes, I'm afraid it is. I'd like a divorce, Maud. I'm sorry, but I don't see any future for us.'

The word lay on the table between them, its smell rising like a rotting fish. Drained of blood, Maud's face had caved in, a startled glare in her bulging eyes.

'I'm so sorry, Maud. I still want to be involved with the kids' lives. I don't expect—'

'Don't be an eejit Christy' — Maud's voice loud again, over his — 'you've no idea what you're talking about.'

They were both silent then, seated opposite each other at the table, avoiding each other's eyes. Gradually, a resigned look came over Maud, her whole body depleted of resistance. When she spoke, her voice was flat and calm, 'I think you should think very carefully about all this, Christy. Don't forget your father has only just died. He's not even cold in the ground, well not the ground but . . . you know, his ashes. Whatever. You're all emotional. This thing with Sadie, I'm sure it will pass.'

Another lengthy pause, as a wave of doubt rolled over Christy, and he went over it all again, the roll call of problems like festering lesions in their fatally wounded marriage. From the street came the sound of two lads walking on the footpath, laughing, their loud voices accentuating the poisoned silence between the married couple. It was time to move onto more practical matters. 'We can discuss it more in the next few days, but in the meantime—'

'Oh, I've had enough of all this.' The anger bubbled over as Maud gathered up her coat and umbrella. 'I'm off out for a while.'

'That's it, head for the pub and a consoling drink soon as there's any trouble to deal with,' Christy called after her and immediately regretted. He closed his ears to her snarled response and the slammed front door, which he hoped didn't wake the kids.

Alone with the sudden sound of silence, Christy settled back to enjoy his moment, the start of his freedom. The next few days would be difficult, but at least the wheels were in motion. They'd have to somehow get through Joey's dinner thing, his big Lebanese feast, all the clan in one place; that would be tricky. Surely, Maud would see that the best plan was for her and the kids to move back to Ireland, what with all the prosperity and the talk of the biggest boom ever coming their way. She could sell the house in London and afford to buy a much better place in Dublin before it got too expensive. Making things happen and moving on with his life that's what he was doing. He kicked off his shoes and called Sadie to tell her the good news.

INTO THE BLACK

DUBLIN

April 1996

32.

DARKENED HOUSES, EMPTY PAVEMENTS, AND DESERTED STREETS. It was well past midnight when Joey hopped in the car for his moonlight drive. He gripped the steering wheel to tame the maelstrom in his head and focus on the first order of business: direction of travel. Like most trips in Dublin, there were numerous options for getting from A to B, so the first move was to run through the route plan in his head. Best avoid the main roads, get to Rathfarnham then weave along the back route towards Ballyboden, and beyond that up to the Dublin Mountains. Nice and slow, he shoved the car into first gear and accelerated out onto the road. The day's rain was expended, leaving a soggy sheen on the tarmac that sparkled in the moon's light.

Everyone was doing better since he'd got them all together to break the bread at his last supper. Naturally, it had kicked off at one point, Damien trying to get his hands all dirty with the money and rope Sam into his grubby scheme. Sammy's wedding news was a bit of a shocker, but he was delighted for him, if anyone deserved a break it was Sam. Dear, confused Christy predictably threw a wobbler when he gave the game away, but he was only trying to keep the nuclear rods cool so that Christy didn't blow his whole life to smithereens by following through on his most stupid decision ever. Poor, kind-hearted Maud, things couldn't have turned out any worse for her, all those broken dreams.

Those final weeks he spent living with Pops had clarified things for him. They'd talked about everything, particularly the big issue of where they were both headed with their illnesses. Pops got his reasoning immediately when Joey said one evening, 'There's only two options, live a semi-normal life with medication or submit to the illness. But both routes you lose control over your life.'

'There is another option. The third option,' Pops had said softly, his gaze intent.

'Yeah, the third option. At least that way you're taking back control of things again.'

They had batted things around for a while, drilled deeper into it, now that their cards were on the table, and then Pops had asked if he'd help Bee with his plan. Joey had known for some time, ever since that day of that tense visit in the Abarbanel, that for him all exits looked the same, and they all led to this endpoint.

Rounding a bend on his way up the mountain, the broad sweep of Dublin Bay twinkled streetlight-orange before it bled into the dark sea beyond. Further on, Joey parked on the side of the road and walked over the wet bogland towards Lough Tay, the Guinness Lake. A couple of sheep, hooves rooted in the soggy bog, followed his progress, glass eyes sparkling in the car headlights. Cresting a small hummock, the egg-shaped lake was revealed in all its lunar glory, ringed by a sandy beach with its dark black water reflecting the moonlight back onto the steep, surrounding slopes. After smoking a joint, he moved on. Just beyond Killakee, the road rose steeply, and the terrain turned increasingly desolate, an empty mountainscape of gorse-bush bogland and trickling streams. All around was the deepest, darkest black. Joey's entire field of vision was delineated by the car's two fish-eye headlights illuminating the narrow thread of road.

At the top, he pulled off the road and turned on the interior light to get his fix sorted. Since his mid-teens, Joey had abused his fair share of drugs and tried them all, bar one. His journey of experimentation, so inimical to sanity, would terminate at heroin. H. Skag. Smack. Now he just needed a little pin prick of that drug for losers. He wasn't trying to ease any pain or get back on his feet. He just wanted to become comfortable. Numb. To think of nothing, especially not himself.

His knowledge of how to inject heroin was scratchy, gleaned from what he'd seen in the movies and from twice watching a junkie he once knew shoot up. Along the dashboard, he lined up the paraphernalia. He ripped the leather belt off his trousers and wrapped it around his arm. With shaking hand, he grabbed the spoon, tipped out the entire dose of heroin, and then added the dissolving liquid. Funny how so weightless a powder could have such cataclysmic consequences. He fired the lighter under the spoon to heat the solution, then suctioned the golden-brown mixture through a cigarette filter into the syringe. Tightening the belt, he smacked his arm to pop a vein and then speared the needle in, easing the plunger part way then retracting. A red mushroom cloud swirled into the syringe barrel before he pushed the liquid all the way in. As the hit circulated, he pulled out the needle and loosened the belt around his arm.

'Hello. Anybody out there?' Joey hollered out the open window into the barren landscape. But, even in Joey-land, there was nobody home. Nausea rose from the pit of his stomach as a mild panic attack gathered. He covered his ears, and the seashore sound comforted him. A wave of milk blood flooded his veins and radiated a thrilling rush along his lower spine to his feet and ankles and up to his shoulders and head.

Falling out of the car, he heaved out a pale puke and then slumped back against the front tyre. He caught a glimpse of the moon before it was wreathed by a grey cloud. A dull toothache throbbed and spread to his jaws and eye sockets, masking the sour taste at the back of his throat. His heart pumped in overdrive, forcing pressurised blood into his arteries and up to his head, which was ready to implode. And then, in the theatre of his mind, the cacophony of voices muted. Bones melted, and limbs flopped lifeless. On his back, the thin layer of sweat chilled. Sinking, what drowning must feel like. Momentary bliss, at one with the hit. Enveloped by an intense euphoric, semi-dream state. Minutes pass like hours, time frozen, but there's no rush. Nearly out of time anyhow. Just before nodding out, Joey mumbled, 'My only friend.'

The suicide note, addressed to Maud, arrived in the post to Pops' house two days later and contained specific instructions on how to mark Joey's passing. And so, on a chilly April night, Joey's three most loved ones took the DART south to Dalkey, picked up a raft at Coliemore Harbour, and rowed out to the island with the ashes in a rucksack on Sam's back. Although isolated from the mainland by only a few hundred metres, the island felt another world away, with its ancient ruins and scatterings of grey rock that jutted out of the barren ground like decaying teeth. Huddled around a driftwood campfire, the friends reminisced with a mellow sadness.

Sam leaned forward and lit a cigarette off a smouldering twig before saying, 'The Joey that came out of Lebanon was a very different Joey to the one that went in. After that, he had no doubt that his life was cursed.'

'He certainly never recovered from losing Lena.'

'It's such a shame none of you saw him like he was in Lebanon. He was so happy despite all the war mayhem. He came so close to grabbing whatever it was he was looking for, a new life with some purpose, one that could have been very happy.'

'I remember that time we met up in Copenhagen, Joey with his mad grey hair. He said then that he wanted to see what having old-man hair would be like, given that he'd never live to see his hair turn grey.'

Sam threw another couple of sticks onto the fire, sending a haze of sparks swirling into the air. 'He always reckoned on burning out early.'

'He was really trying to make things work in Israel. He'd settled down and—'

'Bollocks. He was behaving, but he wasn't ever happy, not like I remember him being before.'

'Shur, wasn't the illness coming on then?'

'I reckon it was Lena dying that brought it on.'

'And Ma. He was so cut up about losing her, couldn't believe it had happened twice.'

Gazing into the receding heart of the fire, Maud imagined how it might have gone if she'd had as much time alone with Joey as Sam had. Instead, all she'd got was a fraught period dealing with the damage to Joey's troubled mind after he showed up in Jerusalem. She stretched out her legs and leaned back against Christy's chest. His hand circled from behind and took hold of hers. Joey's note had rambled all over the place, but his final message was: 'Maud, you gotta love your man. You two belong with each other, and Kathleen needs her proper parents back together.' She certainly couldn't imagine herself back in a dating phase — an endless procession of no-hopers, all with intentions of getting inside her knickers and not much else — and she had long ago decided that the life of a single mom was not for her.

'Remember that time in Galilee, Joey convinced he was some kind of Messiah,' Christy said, glugging from the bottle of Jameson. 'With some crazy fantasy that his voices were directing him on some big mission to save some dying fish.'

'And then he ended up in hospital, or many different hospitals' – a knowing laugh rippled around the huddle – 'until he was finally let go.'

Out of the blue, Dr Shapiro's prophetic words, all those years ago when Joey was admitted to the Hadassah, came back to Maud. *The reality is that you are never cured of schizophrenia, you must learn to cope with it for the rest of your life. Regrettably that is why so many schizophrenics commit suicide, possibly as many as ten per cent.*

'I keep thinking we should have seen what was going on. Certainly, at Pops' funeral, I knew for sure he was off the meds, but I didn't do anything.' Recently, Christy's love for Joey had waned, and he'd pretty much ditched him in his hour of greatest need.

'Ah, the meds, Joey's favourite topic,' Sam sparked up a joint and passed it around.

'Does anyone else wonder about cause or effect? I mean, after he was booted out of Trinity, everything seemed to go to shit.'

'When you think about it, all our lives were completely changed by that decision of his to leave. Maud slept with him for one last time and got pregnant with Kathleen, and then I ended up marrying her, thinking the baby was mine; then we moved to London and onto Israel. Sam's life was wrapped up with Joey as soon as he showed up in Beirut.'

'A lot of things can be traced back to Joey leaving Dublin.'

'This family has sure had a lot of tragedy. It's almost like a curse after we all had such an idyllic childhood. Do you think it's some kind of payback? Some karma?'

An uncomfortable silence followed until Christy said, 'How much of what happened do you reckon was because he had this illness there all the time? Or were his mental problems triggered by all the crazy things he experienced in Lebanon?'

'I often wonder that. His illness may have come on anyhow, but for me, Lena dying was definitely the trigger. I'll never forget the look in his eyes that day in the hospital when we found out how she had died . . . his spirit just evaporated.'

'Shur, you could never tell with Joey. With someone who spends their days high on every sort of drug, 'tis very hard to tell what's causing the fantasies.'

'Those years he spent in and out of psychiatric hospitals, isn't it a frightful irony that we were on at him all the time to take his drugs?'

'And, of course, Joey knew his drugs. He knew what a lifetime sentence to Clozapine would mean. Three tablets a day, every day forevermore, at least until that particular formulation stopped working, and they had to move him onto another. Joey knew better than that: he would control his own exit, thank you very much.'

As the campfire embers cooled, Maud lit the fuse on the firework and stood back as it erupted in a haze of sparks. With a whoosh, the rocket launched into the sky at a sharp angle, stuffed with Joey's ashes in the cone. Six eyes followed the glittering red trail until it reached the apogee and exploded in a palm tree of blues and greens, fizzing like imploding stars. Seconds later, squirming worms of incandescent white light etched the black sky, and then they, too, died out. Rooted to the spot, the four waited for the plop of the spent firework hitting the seawater.

'It's spooky. There are no stars at all. Out here on the perimeter . . .' Christy left it hanging.

Off to the east, a flaming dawn sun bruised the sky crimson purple below the hem of the clouds. Sam turned, and the others followed wordlessly, clambering in single file past a few sleeping goats and on down to the raft at the water's edge. When they were seated, Christy took hold of the oars and pulled against the current, guiding them across the black water to the mainland, the silence broken by the swishing blades, each alone with their thoughts, isolated without their uniting force.

THANKS TO . . .

My early readers, who worked their way through a very different book, but encouraged me to keep going: Patrick McCann, John Bourke, Ronan Daly, and Colm Olwill.

Rachel Evers for talking to me about her time working in Gaza with UNRWA.

The final draft readers, for their insights and suggestions for improving the story: Pamela Marnell, Sean Nolan, Fiona McHugh (sister) and Holly McHugh (daughter).

My darling wife Fiona, who read countless drafts of a novel that started eleven years ago, and has been with me all the way, as the novel evolved through so many iterations (and titles!). Her consistent encouragement and invaluable feedback improved my writing immeasurably.

Printed in Great Britain
by Amazon